A BLOODY CANVAS

A BLOODY CANVAS

ANDREW GALLIMORE

MERCIER PRESS
WHAT YOU NEED TO READ

MERCIER PRESS
Douglas Village, Cork
www.mercierpress.ie

Trade enquiries to Columba Mercier Distribution,
55a Spruce Avenue, Stillorgan Industrial Park, Blackrock, Dublin

© Andrew Gallimore, 2007

978 1 85635 536 0

10 9 8 7 6 5 4 3 2 1

Mercier Press receives financial assistance from
the Arts Council/An Chomhairle Ealaíon

Printed and bound by J.H. Haynes and Co. Ltd, Sparkford

ACKNOWLEDGEMENTS

Lydia, once more, was the essential component in this work. My mum and dad's generosity and kindness were very much appreciated and Nanette, John, Peter, Paul and Te Huruhi Bay provided the perfect setting to complete the work. Bernie's appearance in New York was very timely. A special thank you goes to Joe Breen for his continued willingness to answer telephone calls and emails.

Mike McTigue's story was scattered around libraries, archive houses and private collections across Ireland and the United States but the following establishments deserve a special mention: the New York Public Library, the Newark Free Library, the National Archives and Records Administration in Washington DC, the New York Municipal Archives, the National Library of Ireland and the Pearse Street Library. William Searson's of Baggot Street, Mulligan's on Madison Avenue and Patrick Kavanagh's at 33rd & Third were a constant source of inspiration.

INTRODUCTION

Scandals had always been an intrinsic part of boxing. One of the first American champions had his neck stretched by California vigilantes for a very untidy murder. It was a dirty game that made no claim to respectability and was a recreation for the low-minded and the depraved. The criminal had been in evidence from the beginning but by the 1920s the petty thief had given way to the gangster. It was a time when ex-cons owned the fighters and racket syndicates dominated the manly art.

There was a perceptible change in the relationship between crime and boxing at this time. Prohibition made clever malefactors into millionaires and created racketeers with big profits, minimum risk and an ambition to expand into other profitable lines. The same forces that were behind bootlegging moved into boxing. The customer who bought a drink and a fight ticket were pouring their money into the same pocket. Prohibition was ushered in on 16 January 1920 and the new breed of affluent outlaw created by the Eighteenth Amendment changed the fight game.

It started when Jack Dempsey beat Jess Willard for the heavyweight championship after which the Manassa Mauler became the most famous athlete in the world. During the First World War the American government believed that boxing was a sound way of improving the morale of the troops. Boxing tournaments were encouraged and famous fighters were commissioned to camps as instructors. The Armistice turned out hundreds of thousands of enthusiastic fight fans. This was the dawn of the era of celebrity and sports heroes were among the first to be idolised. Dempsey's victory heralded the arrival of sport as big business in a prosperous post-war United States. Just over 20,000 people had showed up to watch Dempsey win the title on 4 July 1919; less than eight years later, he drew a crowd of 120,000 for his first bout with Gene Tunney; still the largest crowd ever to attend a fight. The big-time racketeers didn't trifle with boxing when purses were small. They limited themselves to liquor and dope. But when boxing became massively popular, they muscled their way in.

These syndicates ran the alcohol trade, the shakedown night-clubs, Brooklyn's laundry racket, the fly-by-night taxi racket and the immensely profitable trade in heroin, cocaine and morphine. Their fighters, regardless of merit, were given important matches and often they'd win. There were stories of old-time fighters who sold 150 per cent of themselves and who went deeper into debt with each fight they took. Other fighters were desperate for matches and weren't getting them. This was the lot of the prizefighter in the Roaring Twenties. This was the lot of Michael Francis McTigue.

Mike was what is known in the fight game as a journeyman; a reliable performer who through a combination of bad breaks and bad management had never got 'his shot'. But in the summer of 1922 a series of unrelated events conspired to produce the most bizarre world championship fight in boxing history and Mike McTigue was a journeyman no more. 'If someone told you he had read a story of a timid old Irish boxer, who never in his life had given his public a thrill and who suddenly at an age where most men have nothing but yellowing clippings to remind them of former glory, began to fight like an 18-year-old and developed a knockout punch that rivalled that of Jack Dempsey, you would put it down as far-fetched fiction,' wrote Paul Gallico. 'But here it is happening beneath our eyes, and it is one of the miracles of the prize ring. Fifty years from now it will be a standout in ring history along with the prowess and strength of John L. Sullivan, the skill of Corbett, the punching power of Fitzsimmons and the defensive skill of Jack Johnson. The mild Irishman, who turned knockout king, will be one of the great stories of the ring. Mark that down.'

This is that story.

ONE

I went into boxing to make a success of it, and the turn of the wheel of fortune has brought me back to my native land.

Mike McTigue

He watched Manhattan's skyline disappear into the summer haze and with it a stinking string of musty fight clubs, blood-stained canvases and sweaty dressing rooms; the grimy gyms, shoddy can houses, ratty flop houses fouled with rank lavatory stench; the speakeasies, mouldy dumps and joints, and the racketeers, the beer runners, the alcohol cookers, the thugs and grafters. Ten years was a long time to keep getting your jaw socked just to cover the rent. The big fights, the championships and the purses were the realm of younger men while the lot of an aging prizefighter was more punishment and less money. So Michael Francis McTigue of Kilnamona, County Clare, was going home.

Kilnamona is a small parish about five miles from the town of Ennis or 'just outside the money' as Mike described it. It is a part of the country that suffered very badly during the famine. Mike's father was a stonemason, whose size and strength won him the local title of 'kippen', or bullyboy – the keeper of the peace. The family leased and worked a strip of land of some thirty acres in a mile-wide valley.

The once-thatched roof cottage where Mike and his eleven brothers and sisters grew up is now a pile of stones. Long stone fences run up the shallow hills. Above the ruins is the hilltop pasture, the size of a football field, where Mike trained. He was a thin, scrawny boy who became a blacksmith's helper at the age of twelve. He was known locally as a good athlete; a sprinter and high jumper and was said to have won the high jump at a championship of the six southern counties.

The McTigues and their cousins, the Rynnes and the Murphys, were well-known Gaelic Athletic Association sportsmen. Mike's childhood coincided with a great awakening of interest in Irish games and the association took a fervently nationalist stance that had a great influence on the cultural and social life of the county. 'They were in any sport that was national,' said Mike's nephew, Joe Breen, to a *Sports Illustrated* reporter, 'national meaning Irish, or any sport not invented by the English.' Mike and his brothers also coursed hares, for which they'd get half a crown and rabbits for which they'd get a sixpence. 'There were lots of hares in those days, but in that rolling country it wasn't easy to get at them,' Breen recalled. 'As soon as you loosed the dogs, the hares would go for the tops of the hills, and once they were there they were gone; the dogs couldn't get to them. Mike didn't care much for the dogs. He liked to hunt, shooting wild ducks and wild geese and fishing in the lakes and up the river.'

But times were hard and the land simmered with anger and resentment. When the people couldn't pay the rent, British troops set up sentry boxes in front of their farms. The local boys harassed the sentries and one day Mike hit one of the soldiers with a rock and had to appear in a Limerick court. He also got into a fight after a soldier shot at a friend of his, Pat Haggerty. It was time to leave, so in 1910 Mike fled to live with relatives in Sheffield. He returned briefly to Ireland two years later but only to set sail on the *SS Baltic* on 13 September 1912 from Cobh, bound for New York. The original ship manifest at Ellis Island lists Michael McTigue, age 21, single male, arriving in New York on 21 September 1912. He gave his nationality as British; but his race or people, as Irish. He paid his own passage but didn't have the recommended $50 in his pocket; he was $25 short. The manifest states that he was going to stay with his brother, Patrick John McTigue, at 335 East 136th Street, New York. Mike confirmed that he wasn't a polygamist, anarchist or a convicted criminal and that he was neither deformed nor crippled.

He settled in the Bronx and earned his three dailies lugging sides of beef at the wholesale provision markets in Harlem and the Bronx operated by Swift & Company. George Gardner, one of the best Irish fighters that ever checked in at Ellis Island, was a neighbour. Gardner was born in Lisdoonvarna, just a few miles from Kilnamona and was world champion for five months in 1903. He won the light heavyweight title in one bout and lost it in the next, beaten by the great Bob Fitzsimmons. George was one of three fighting Gardners, along with his brothers Billy and Jimmy.

It was a tough place. The workers at the plants were poorly paid and overworked in dangerous conditions. Diseased cattle and hogs were strewn across the factories and the stockyards were a pit of poverty and squalor, with rat-infested boarding houses, smouldering garbage dumps and large sewage pits. Corruption was rife in the plants, with bosses demanding 'gifts' of money from workers and grafting off those higher up in the hierarchy. It was a good time and place for a man to discover he could fight. One afternoon a trucker became embroiled in an argument with Mike's boss and the harsh words soon escalated to blows, and the boss was 'knocked for a row of Bronx taxpayers'.

"'Mike,' says I to myself, 'you'll get fired if you don't do something; and you'll get a beating if you do,'" Mike later recalled. 'The firing seemed worse than the beating, so I sailed into the trucker. I was a husky lad, lively on me feet, and while it was a devil of a mix-up, with my face being well bashed, I finally knocked him cold. My boss had been sitting there watching and, when the battle was over, he patted me on the back and said: "Mike, you're too fine a fighter for this business. You ought to be in the ring. I'll back you and be your manager."'

Mike was sent to see an old-time fighter, George 'Elbows' Mc-Fadden, at his gym on New York's East 59th Street, near Madison Square Garden. He paid up front for ten lessons at $2 a piece to learn the finer points of the noble art of self-defence. For his twenty bucks the Irishman was also introduced to the ignoble art of prizefighting.

After he retired from the ring, Elbows was asked: 'What about those elbows, George? Were they just there to use as a shield for your jaw and body?'

McFadden laughed. 'I've never told this before,' he said, 'but I guess it's safe now. Take a look at that elbow and feel it.'

The reporter felt McFadden's elbow. 'The joint looked like an oversized ham,' he wrote, 'and felt like a rock.'

'I used those things for punching,' McFadden said. 'The referees used to think that I was missing a good right cross. Nonsense, I never missed. I'd let the glove go right by the guy's jaw and come back hard with the elbow, see?

'A few of these and the poor fellow was groggy and all cut up. Oh, you couldn't get away with it today. But those were the days. Like I said, I never told this to anybody. What does it matter now? They're all gone, anyway. I flattened a lot of good men with these old elbows.'

Mike was a willing pupil and after a few sessions McFadden told him that he had a natural style that would improve after a few fights.

Elbows sent Mike to Dan Hickey who was a boxing instructor at the New York Athletic Club. Hickey also managed a stable of fighters and he agreed to get the Irishman a four-round fight. 'You better win,' warned Hickey, 'because I don't handle anything but real fighters.' Mike duly obliged and won the bout by knockout.

He could fight, that much was obvious, but the gym-worms thought Mike too old to amount to anything. Boys of fifteen were fighting professionally and the Irishman looked considerably older than that. 'When I mentioned to several people that I intended having a cut in at boxing,' Mike recalled, 'they said I was too old to begin.' He was twenty-eight by the time he donned the gloves for the first time but told all concerned that he was only twenty-two. 'You see, I was twenty-one years of age before I left Ennis,' he told one sports writer, 'but the people who advised me forgot that we Irishmen live a hardy, healthy, open-air life. When I was twenty-two, the age at which I began boxing, I was actually a younger man, physically, than ninety per cent of city-bred chaps of eighteen.' It was a lie that Mike would have to perpetuate throughout his boxing career.

By the time he returned to Europe, Mike had fought at least 111 professional contests, was nearly thirty-nine years old and, had promoters known the truth, would have struggled to get a fight at the bottom of a local club card. But as he and his American-born wife, Cecelia, whose parents came from County Kerry, and their two baby daughters, sat in steerage, they were unaware of events unfolding in Dublin that would leave an indelible mark on the nation and start a sequence of bizarre coincidences that would change their lives completely.

Ireland wasn't a profitable option for a professional boxer looking for work so Mike took his family to stay with relatives in Sheffield where the fight clubs offered him the chance of a living. Just two days after the McTigues landed in England in June 1922, a general election was held to determine the composition of the new Dáil of the Irish Free State. It was essentially a referendum on the Treaty. In the Sinn Féin party, fifty-eight supporters of the Treaty were elected against thirty-six opponents. In addition, thirty-four non-Sinn Féin candidates were elected from parties such as Labour and Farmers who also backed the Treaty. The result cleared the way for the establishment of the Irish Free State later that year.

While Mike McTigue was touting for business in England, assassination, kidnapping and an aging empire dragged a divided people into a bitter and brutal conflict. Shortly after the general election General Sir Henry Wilson, the security advisor for the new state of Northern Ireland, was shot dead by two IRA men outside his home. The British government responded to the killing by demanding action from the Irish government against the anti-Treaty faction, specifically those who had occupied the Four Courts since mid-April.

Michael Collins had supported the Treaty as a means of removing British troops from Ireland, but this attack at the heart of the country's judicial system threatened to prevent them leaving: they would be used to attack the Four Courts, which would inevitably re-ignite the war between Britain and Ireland. Collins was given a way out when, in retaliation for the arrest of one of their officers, the IRA kidnapped the pro-Treaty, popular Assistant Chief of Staff, J. J. 'Ginger' O'Connell on 27 June. This was Collins' mandate to attack the Four Courts: he ordered government troops to take up position and, with no response to an ultimatum to evacuate the building, the artillery opened fire with borrowed British arms at 4.15 am on 28 June 1922. The Civil War had begun.

TWO

Ever since colonialism has existed, the Whites have been paid to bash in the faces of the Blacks. For once, a Black has been paid to do the same thing to a White.

Ho Chi Minh, *La Paria*, 1 December 1922

'I was startled,' wrote George Bernard Shaw, 'by a most amazing apparition. Nothing less than Charles XII, "the Madman of the North", striding along in a Japanese dressing gown as gallantly as if he had not been killed almost exactly two hundred and one years before.' Georges Carpentier had that affect on people. The dashing Frenchman had won the Croix de Guerre in the First World War and when the guns fell silent he combined the twin roles of champion prizefighter and movie idol. Carpentier had a new film to promote in the summer of 1922 and a defence of his world light heavyweight title in front of 60,000 people with the world's press in attendance would ensure that *A Gypsy Cavalier* would get the publicity it badly needed. *The Times*' film critic described the movie as 'rather disappointing' and wrote that as an actor Carpentier, 'has, naturally, his limitations, but he is in a fortunate position, for minor histrionic defects do not seem to matter in the case of a "star" of his magnitude'. But one of the leading actors in Carpentier's promotional extravaganza would ignore the script and as Westbrook Pegler wrote in the *Chicago Tribune*, 'the publicity attending this unexpected turn of events reacted against the motion picture and very few patrons even saw Georges bowing from the waist and dancing with ladies of the royal circle.'

Nobody gave Battling Siki, his opponent, a chance; he was a cumbersome but entertaining fighter from Senegal. However, the match attracted great attention because it was the first time since the end of the Great War that Carpentier would box an important fight on French soil. It was staged at the Buffalo Velodrome on the outskirts of Paris on 23 September 1922 and was billed as a contest for the light heavyweight championship of the world and the heavyweight championship of Europe. The Velodrome was reconstructed and enlarged and a canopy was erected over the ring so that the fight could go ahead whatever the weather. 'It was an event which embraced nearly the whole male population of the country and a not inconsiderable proportion of French women,' reported *The Times*.

Carpentier entered the ring looking unfit but with the air of a man who thought lightly of the task ahead. He started the bout by amusing the crowd and posing for the film cameras. He ended it sprawled under the ropes with his face bleeding profusely, his right eye nearly closed. The referee was as shocked as the audience at the scene in front of him: an unheralded black fighter standing over the prostrate figure of a national hero. It upset the natural order of things, so with Carpentier on the canvas, the referee awarded the fight to the stricken champion and disqualified Battling Siki for tripping his opponent to the floor. The world champion had certainly fallen over the challenger's leg, but he was a bent and broken figure and heading for the canvas with or without the aid of an outstretched Senegalese limb. There was a great deal of confusion and it took a while for Siki's disqualification to become known. But the result did not stand for long and the judges reversed the referee's decision and awarded Siki the fight by knockout. A young Ho Chi Minh, who was living in Paris at the time, commented: 'It so happens that every time Carpentier wins, it is naturally due to his skill and science. But every time he is beaten, it is always because of the brute strength of a Dempsey, or the dirty legwork of a Siki. This is the reason why at the Buffalo match they wished to say – they had even made the statement – that Siki, though having won the match, lost it 'just the same'. But the public, the good public, did not wish to see it in that light. And popular justice was triumphant: Siki was proclaimed champion of the world and of France.'

Siki was hoisted onto his second's shoulders and waved at the disbelieving crowd. 'There were at least sixty thousand of them,' wrote one scribe at ringside, 'and their feelings were deeply stirred, as was natural enough, by the piteous spectacle which Siki had made of their famous idol.'

The seconds did all they could to wipe the blood off Carpentier's face, but what he really needed was a doctor. Carpentier, without even waiting for his dressing gown, crawled under the ropes in a vain attempt to get out of the ring. But he could barely stand and sat slumped on the edge of the ring while a crimson-stained towel was thrown over his shoulders. He was carried back to the dressing rooms and Battling Siki was the first African-born world's boxing champion.

THREE

Two men have founded here. A man-at-arms

Gathered a score of horse and spent his days

In this tumultuous spot,

Where through long wars and sudden night alarms

His dwindling score and he seemed castaways

Forgetting and forgot;

And I, that after me

My bodily heirs may find,

To exalt a lonely mind,

Befitting emblems of adversity.

Meditations in time of Civil War, William Butler Yeats

The match was made with a tremendous thumping of journalistic tom-toms, and the sportsmen of England sat up cheerfully, for this was the fight they really wanted to see. Their heavyweight champion, Joe Beckett, had beaten the American Frank Moran at the Royal Albert Hall and now there were calls for the Englishman to fight Battling Siki. According to *The Times* he could now 'enter the ring against the Senegalese unaffrighted by the fearsome stories and the pictures of [Siki's] massacre of Georges Carpentier'. Until this victory, Beckett's reputation had been fading, but now he was in line for a series of big-money fights. A victory over Siki would undoubtedly lead to a fight against Carpentier, and consequently Europe's leading fighters could keep themselves busy in lucrative fights for many months to come. English boxing promoter Major Arnold Wilson signed Siki and Beckett for a match in London on 7 December 1922 and Carpentier was to meet the winner in January 1923. It was all very neat and the arrangement was sure to make good money for all concerned. But a series of events was beginning to unfold in Paris that would involve the governments and judiciary of both Great Britain and France Nothing less than the survival of both British and French empires was at stake. And all because a black African fighter had the temerity to win a boxing match.

Mike McTigue wasn't part of the plan and he spent Christmas 1922 contemplating life after boxing. He sent a cablegram to his manager in New York, Joe Jacobs, to inform him that he'd given up on getting a match with Joe Beckett and that he planned to sail for the United States in a few weeks. All that detained him in Europe was a fight against Harry Reeve in Liverpool on 17 January, after which he was going to take his wife and children on a long-planned trip to Ireland. Most of the British boxing scribes expected him to lose to Reeve, who had already beaten Battling Siki and Joe Beckett. Reeve was also three stones heavier, but such was the Irishman's desperation for work, he took matches irrespective of how much weight he was conceding to an opponent. To everybody's amazement Mike knocked Reeve out in three rounds. Little did he realise it at the time, but the fight would prove to be one of the most important of his life. Sitting at ringside in Liverpool was Tom Singleton, an Irish racehorse owner who went to see Mike after the fight and offered the boxer a match in Dublin. Mike was only too happy to fight anywhere so the two men arranged to meet up in Ireland the following week.

The McTigues arrived in Dublin on 19 January 1923 and following his victory over Reeve, Mike was the subject of great interest in the Irish press. 'He has the build of an athlete,' reported the *Evening Herald*, 'yet might be taken for an actor.' Every leading newspaper sent a journalist to interview the boxer who was happy to regale them with his life story, his love of Ireland and his dislike of British fighters. Mike said he was tired of offering monetary inducement to the best English boxers for a fight, especially as he had already fought most of the leading American fighters of his weight. 'I was thrown up against all that class when I was new to the game, so you can see I have won my spurs early and am eager for more, only that the spirit and flesh on the other side of Saint George's Channel are weak.'

Mike and Cecilia planned to set off for Kerry the following day to visit his wife's parents who were looking after their two girls, aged three and nine months. They would then travel on to Ennis to visit Mike's mother and father. He planned to return to Dublin for a week or so after his trip west to 'have a look around'. Many years later, John Coughlan of Dublin, who was Mike's driver on the visit to County Clare told a *Sports Illustrated* reporter, 'You'd never think he was a fighter. He was the type of a good businessman, by his looks.'

But as they set off across Ireland, from Dublin to Ennis, the Mc-Tigues were embarking on a journey through a nation torn apart by civil war. Conventional hostilities had ended with Michael Collins' death but the struggle continued with ambush and counter-ambush. The British government had implemented emergency powers, with internment and official and unofficial reprisals that gave rise to the charge that this was a neo-colonial project. The grief and rage at Collins' killing were still strong. The Catholic hierarchy condemned Irregular, i.e. anti-Treaty, resistance to the Provisional Government and its forces. A letter signed by Cardinal Logue and the other bishops stated that a 'section of the community' had 'wrecked Ireland from end to end' and that all those 'who participate in such crimes are guilty of the gravest sins and may not be absolved in Confession, nor admitted to Holy Communion, if they propose to persevere in such evil courses'.

The anti-Treaty forces believed that their excommunication effectively granted a licence to kill to the Provisional Government, a belief reinforced by the execution of seventy-seven Irregular prisoners between November 1922 and May 1923. On 17 November 1922, the Minister for Home Affairs, Kevin O'Higgins, informed the Leinster house assembly that four men had been shot that morning following a secret court martial. The men's relatives were informed by an official form with the wording 'Remains of ... coffined and buried.' The blank was for the name to be inserted. The four young IRA volunteers had been accused of carrying weapons and planning a street ambush.

The first well-known figure to be executed was Erskine Childers who had been an extremely effective chief of propaganda for the Irregulars. Childers was arrested on 11 November and found to be in possession of a gun – a pearl-handled revolver given to him by Michael Collins. It was enough to incur the death penalty and Childers was shot on 14 November.

Following Childers' execution Liam Lynch issued an order that all TDs who had voted for the legislation under which Childers had been executed were to be shot on sight. The warning carried a threat to all the enemies of the IRA of destruction of property and/or death. Its targets included judges, journalists and every member of the Provisional Parliament who had voted for the Emergency Powers measure that set up the military courts. The November executions prompted a new season of atrocities and from then on any captured Republican soldier was in danger of the death penalty.

The Irish Free State came into being on 6 December 1922, with William T. Cosgrave returned unopposed as President of the Executive Council. The state was a dominion of the British Empire – its birth saluted by the volleys of a firing squad. The following day the IRA carried out its threat by shooting two members of the new Free State legislature. Sean Hales and the Leas-Ceann Comhairle of the Dáil, Padraic Ó Máille, were attacked in an open car; Hales died and Ó Máille was seriously wounded. Terror was met with terror. The government responded by selecting four anti-Treaty prisoners – Rory O'Connor, Liam Mellows, Joe McKelvey and Dick Barrett, one from each province – and executed them the following morning, Sunday 8 December.

The death of Rory O'Connor provoked particular outrage. Even though most of the firing squad shot at him, and even set his clothes on fire, O'Connor had to plead with the officer in charge to shoot him with a pistol so that he would not suffer any further. O'Connor had been Kevin O'Higgins' best man at his wedding a year earlier. The execution was carried out on the Feast of the Immaculate Conception and it added to the intensity of an action designed to shock and intimidate. The bitterness caused by these executions festered for years and was the main cause behind the shooting of O'Higgins' father at his home in Stradbally, Queen's County, on 11 February 1923 and of O'Higgins' own death four and a half years later.

It was as bleak a Christmas as Ireland had experienced for many years. And then things got worse. In County Longford 55 per cent of the houses burned down during the entire Civil War were destroyed between January and March 1923, largely in reaction to the increased number of executions. There were thirty-four executions in

January and the guerrilla war had, according to one commentator, all the semblance of a post-colonial dog fight. Into this dog fight went Mike McTigue. He left Dublin on the morning of 20 January 1923 and disappeared.

FOUR

During these seven seconds, as I was kneeling before Carpentier, my mind changed like a flash and I said to myself at the count of six, 'I will fight and make Georges kneel before me'.

Battling Siki, 1922

Battling Siki's real name was Louis Fall. His grandfather was a slave, captured by Moors in the interior of Senegal, who escaped and fled to St-Louis, where he married. A generation later, on 26 September 1897, his grandson, also named Louis, was born. The boxing writers in the United States and Great Britain were agreed that Louis Fall had been born 'in the bush', but it wasn't true. Siki told his own story to Ed Cunningham of *The Ring* magazine and said that he resented statements that he had, 'hopped from the branches of a coconut tree right into the ring and that he is only one generation removed from a prominent family of baboons in Senegal'.

'I was born in St-Louis, the capital of Senegal, which is a big city with streetcars and everything a modern city has,' said Siki. 'My father is an exporter of cigarettes and feathers and monkey fur for hats and dresses. He has money.'

When Louis was seven years old the family moved down the coast to the port of Dakar (now the capital of Senegal) where they met Madame Elaine Grosse, a German dancer, who offered to take the boy back to Germany with her to be educated. The boy's parents agreed and he sailed with Madame Grosse to Marseilles. But the French immigration officer at the port wouldn't let her take the boy back to Germany without his parents' written consent. The consent never came and finally Madame Grosse left Louis on his own in Marseilles with a thousand francs in his pocket. La Société Française de la Bienfaisance, a women's organisation, took pity on the child and put him in a school.

'Every day in school I would have fights,' recalled Siki, 'and at night come home with my shirt in ribbons.' He left school at thirteen and went to work as an elevator operator in a hotel, after which he went to night school to learn 'physical culture and *la savate*'. Then he moved on to Nice where he worked as a kitchen boy in a hotel. The Bienfaisance then sent Louis to Le Somme preparatory school at Amiens where he stayed until he was sixteen and the Great War broke out.

Louis went to Paris, enlisted and was sent to Toulon to meet the colonial troops coming from Senegal. 'I did not mix well with them at first, but got used to it,' Siki recalled. 'I was in the first battle of the Marne and for the next three years I was a corporal in the 18th Territorials.' Siki won the Croix de Guerre, two palms, the Medaille Militaire and seven citations for conspicuous bravery in action. He was wounded three times, the last time badly, and after three months in the hospital he was attached to the heavy artillery at Camp De Mailley in the Marne department, where he worked with American gunners.

The Americans had a YMCA and that's where Louis Fall learned to box. Every Saturday and Sunday he would spar with American soldiers and he learned the lesson that to 'gain favour with white people one merely had to fight'. He was demobilised in 1919 and given twenty-five francs. 'I wrote to my parents for money but they did not send me any,' said Siki. 'They were angry because I never came back.'

So, Louis got a job as a waiter at the Café Royale in Paris before getting better-paid work in a two-franc restaurant in Rue aux Ours as cook. 'It was part of my job to throw out the bad patrons who did not have two francs, and a fight promoter saw me bounce a man through the door one night and offered me twenty francs to fight at a boxing show. I did. When I got into the ring, I shut both my eyes and swung. I knocked my opponent out. How I did it, I do not know.'

His naïve but effective antics made him a good draw and he fought for twenty francs nearly every night in Paris for several months before travelling to Rotterdam, Amsterdam and Berlin where he racked up victories against the champions of Germany and Italy. He then returned to France and scored knockout victories over two leading French fighters, Paul Journée and Marcel Nilles. Siki kept winning until there was only one man left in France for him to fight: Georges Carpentier. It all led to that fateful day at the Buffalo Velodrome on 23 September 1922. The Paris press and public were stunned and the journalists waxed incredulous. 'Carpentier and Des-champs [Carpentier's manager] had only yielded to popular clamour in meeting Siki and underlying the clamour was the confidence which Carpentier and Deschamps shared that Siki was one more example of "vaulting ambition overleaping itself". Great was their disillusionment,' wrote one French reporter.

After the fight Siki issued a challenge to the world heavyweight champion, Jack Dempsey. He told one reporter, 'Better cable to Mr Rickard [Tex Rickard, leading American boxing promoter] tonight that I am willing to fight Dempsey right away.' His manager, Hellers, placed a restraining hand on Siki's shoulder and said, 'This is enough fighting for today.'

Siki celebrated his victory with a champagne banquet in Paris and he swaggered through the streets with a monkey on each shoulder throwing money away. On one night he famously entered a cabaret with a lion on a leash as people ran for the exits. 'I was the idol of the boulevards,' said Siki, 'from Le Plonguer dishwasher – to champion. From the time I was seven until I was champion, I had seen the greatest hotels, the gay parties, and never had been in one. Just night school and day school and elevators and dishes and war. So I became the *bon vivant*, too. But wild? Monsieur, I go wild from *ennui, mais oui.*'

On 26 September, by cable-exclusive dispatch from Paris, the *Los Angeles Times* reported that 'Siki, from available signs threatens to become so omnipotent that one heartily wishes some real American fighter would take his measure.' Siki was a hero and continued to celebrate until his money ran out. It didn't take long. He had received 55,000 francs for the fight but was flat broke after two triumphant nights under the bright lights of Montmartre. His share of the purse had taken the count. 'Happily, French nature refuses to take even an obnoxious jungle man with a white face too seriously so, while the press is still filled with more fight comments than either politics or reparations, it is already in a lighter and sarcastic vein,' commented the *Los Angeles Times*.

The *Petit Journal* of 26 September quoted a letter sent to Siki from a cinema director who addressed the new champion as 'Dear Great Artist' and declared that, having viewed the match, he was convinced Siki was sufficiently photogenic to triumph in the movies 'providing the entire action of the piece takes place in a tunnel'.

There were several more serious offers, however. Tex Rickard cabled Siki with an offer of $100,000 for a title fight with a leading American light heavyweight. He couldn't stage the fight in the United

States but there was no objection to mixed-race fights in Canada and the Montreal Club had declared an interest in staging the fight. A promoter named Augustin at the new boxing stadium in Buenos Aires sent a cable to Siki enquiring about his terms for a match with the winner of a forthcoming fight between the Argentinean Luis Angel Firpo and Australian heavyweight Jim Tracey. The scramble for Siki's services gathered pace when American fight promoter Tom O'Rourke cabled an offer to Paris followed by Major Arnold Wilson, who offered him a fight in London.

Siki's manager, Hellers, told the *Associated Press* that his man's price was 1,100,000 francs, exclusive of income tax, to meet either Harry Grebb or Harry Wills in the United States, or 1,600,000 to fight Jack Dempsey. Hellers added that if he could not get those sums, Siki would remain in Europe.

Unfortunately for Siki, the publicity generated by the Carpentier fight effectively ended his chance of getting a big-money fight in the United States. Newspapers in Europe and America decried the matching of black and white fighters because it stirred up bitter feelings between the races. 'Fighting Carpentier on an equal footing, man for man and pound for pound, and defeating him with ease has set the minds of many thinking men to believe there is much danger in such boxing contests,' wrote De Witt Van Court in the *Los Angeles Times*. 'If our editorial writers are afraid of a war between the white man and the black man, they can easily have their fears removed by having the terrible Siki brought to this country and hook him up with several of our coloured fighters, or quite a few of our white light heavyweights …

'If Siki ever boxes in this country, I am inclined to believe he will never make the showing he has made at any time in Europe. The colour line is too strongly drawn here and he never will be given the freedom of cafés and attention he has been accustomed to receive in France. This is sure to have an effect on the black fellow he will never understand.'

With the United States closed for business Siki's manager was forced to look to England to cash in on his charge's new found status. Bookings were taken for exhibitions in London music halls and there was the much-discussed match with British champion, Joe Beckett. But then Siki's troubles started in earnest.

'Siki's gloves have stirred everything, including even the political sphere,' wrote Ho Chi Minh. 'And M. Luquet, Councillor of the Seine Department, immediately tabled a motion attempting to ban boxing matches. M. Luquet must allow us to tell him respectfully that what he did was an anti-patriotic act. Here is our explanation: from the point of view of international policy, a feather-weight champion makes as much propaganda for our moral influence abroad as an immortal, a glorious man, a song-writer or ten army corps (see the newspapers). From the national viewpoint, boxers are indispensable as an example of, and stimulation to, the physical excellence of the young generation. From the colonial viewpoint, a Carpentier-Siki match is worth more than one hundred gubernatorial speeches to prove to our subjects and protégés that we want to apply to the letter the principle of equality between races.'

On Friday 10 November 1922 *The Times* reported that the Home Office had informed promoter Major Arnold Wilson that it would not allow the proposed match between Siki and Beckett to be staged in Great Britain. Wilson was already committed to the fight and stood to lose a fortune in the event of a cancellation, but the Home Office argued that he must have known there was a risk that the authorities would prohibit the fight when he was trying to arrange it. The British government had stopped another such fight in 1911 between Jack Johnson, the first black world heavyweight champion, and Bombardier Billy Wells, the British heavyweight titleholder at the time. Both Johnson and Wells were bound over at Bow Street to keep the peace, and now the Home Office decided once more that a fight between 'the white man and the Negro' was not in the interests of the empire. The pronouncement was backed by *The Times* which believed the 'fight has been quite properly forbidden by the authorities in this country'. In its leader the newspaper stated:

A WISE DECISION

As we announced this morning, the promoter of the proposed fight between Beckett and the black boxer, Siki, has been informed by the Home Office that the contest will not be allowed. It is to be hoped that this decision, for which there is sound legal precedent, will be accepted without any of the controversial discussion which arose in 1911 out of the similar prohibition between Johnson and Wells. On that occasion public opinion was too strong for those who saw no harm in the fight, and the Home Office, with the same wisdom as it showed yesterday, determined to intervene. It is true that Mr Eugene Corri, the well-known authority on boxing, stated at the time that he had often in England acted as referee in boxing matches between white men and blacks, without incurring any criticism for so doing. But even in those days there were no illusions in distant parts of the Empire as to the danger and inadvisability of the practice. While the Johnson-Wells match was being discussed, the press of South Africa appealed to the Union Government to forbid the importation of films of the contest, if it should take place. The country, said the South African News, cannot afford to invite any expansion of the black peril. The Johnson-Burns fight in Australia and the Johnson-Jeffries fight at Reno both provided proof of the reality of the danger. After the first, it is on record that the difficulties of the white policemen in dealing with the natives, in a colony thousands of miles from the scene of the action, were greatly increased by the result. After the other, our Washington Correspondent telegraphed that the victory of Johnson was the signal for a widespread exhibition of racial prejudice. In the streets of Washington and New York gangs of hooligans collected to maltreat the negroes, and in other parts of the States in one day thirteen persons were killed and hundreds dangerously wounded, the gaols in several cities were crowded with negroes and white men, and the troops had to be called out to put an end to the riots. These are risks which the British Empire in particular, with its vast coloured population in all parts of the world, cannot afford to run. Boxing in itself is a fine and manly sport. But boxing matches between white men and blacks, to be photographed for the delectation of coloured races all over the world, have become a dangerous anachronism. To allow them to take place on English soil would, in these days, be an act of suicidal folly, and the action of the Home Office in this particular case will meet, we are convinced, with the warm approval of the general public.

The Home Office took its decision ignorant of events in a Paris ring a few nights previously. Siki was acting as a second to a friend of his, Balzac, who was knocked out in the contest. The Battler jumped into the ring and according to one report 'the officials had to interfere to prevent him from using violence'. He also tried to assault both

Balzac's opponent, Prunier, and his manager and the audience hollered as the police hauled Siki out of the ring. The French Boxing Federation promptly banned him for nine months but gave him permission to take the Beckett fight because the contract had been signed before the fracas. This act of clemency became irrelevant following the Home Office decision the following day. Major Arnold Wilson told the press that he would test, in the general interest, the government ban of the fight. But he also confirmed that regardless of the decision, Siki had, in his opinion, been guilty of behaviour that week which 'rendered it undesirable that he should meet Beckett in England in December'. Wilson informed Siki that the contest had been cancelled, as had the music hall tour that was to precede it.

The Times published a letter from a Rev JP Parry of Bilsdale, Yorkshire, who claimed to have been 'out East, in a country where there was a vast body of immigrant labour from every country in the Orient' at the time of Jack Johnson's victory over Jim Jeffries. According to the writer, a 'strong and imperceptible wave of exultation passed over the whole community ... That wave undoubtedly fanned the torch of Oriental self-assertion against the West which Japan's victory over Russia had lit. At this moment, when Turkey is the spearhead of the East against the West, the result of the above fight might be most disastrous if it took place.'

'We learn from the same newspapers that the British Home Ministry has banned the expected match between Joe Beckett and Siki in London. This does not surprise us,' wrote Ho Chi Minh. 'As His British Excellency could digest neither Kemal's croissant nor Gandhi's chocolate, he wants to have Battling Siki swallow his purge even though the latter is a Frenchman. Understand?'

Siki was also stripped of his titles after the French Boxing Federation claimed to have proof of his 'unfitness to hold a championship'.

He said he had no complaint against his suspension and that he was glad to be relieved of the championships that exposed him to a 'host of embarrassment and indiscretions'. Carpentier was understood to be in favour of interceding with the Federation on his old adversary's behalf, but on the following Saturday Siki was detained by the Paris police for the alleged illegal wearing of a Senegalese Skirmisher's uniform. A crowd had gathered at about 10 pm at the door of a café to see the boxer in his military regalia. As a policeman approached him he said: 'I am Siki … Siki if you please; not Siki if it doesn't please you.' Back at the police station he said that he had put on his old army uniform to celebrate the Armistice, and that was all. The Federation wasted little time in imposing further and more serious punishment on Siki by revoking his licence to box. All the contracts he had signed – they were worth over four million francs – were rendered null and void. The Federation claimed the decision against Siki was taken 'from motives of public decency to prevent a scandal'.

'We learn from the newspapers that Siki has just been suspended for nine months from all boxing rings in France,' wrote Ho Chi Minh. 'What happened? … We are rather inclined to think this way: Siki, a Black, will never be forgiven for having defeated Carpentier, a White, and if Carpentier bears no grudge, the chauvinism of others does. And this charge is only a pretext … motivated by …'

Siki had long since gone through the winnings from the Carpentier match so he approached an old friend for help, the Senegalese Deputy Blaise Diagne, then a French cabinet minister. The same afternoon as the Federation withdrew his licence, Siki turned up at the chamber of deputies to tell Diagne that the fight with Carpentier, the idol of the boulevards, had been fixed, but that he had double-crossed the fixers. Siki, in front of Deputy Diagne and two witnesses, said that once he was in the ring in front of 50,000 people 'acclaiming him and conscious of his own strength, he had a revulsion of feeling, despite reminders from his corner during his minute's rest after the third round and he had decided to go on and win'. Diagne told an *Associated Press* writer that he had seen proof of Siki's allegations. The scribe wrote that Siki demonstrated how he finished the fight 'for the benefit of deputy Diagne, who looked on with apparent pride at his compatriot. Diagne repeated Siki's story in the chamber of deputies and demanded an official investigation. He claimed that Siki was an uneducated, child-like native who had been preyed upon and swindled and that he was a symbol of the plight of the black people of French Africa. Carpentier's apparent connivance in the fix was an international scandal.

Diagne tabled an amendment that the subsidy given to the French Boxing Federation should be discontinued. The Deputy alleged that the Federation was treating Siki badly out of spite for beating their favourite son. But despite an eloquent speech Diagne lost the vote by 408 to 136.

It was the first time boxing had been the subject of such lengthy debate in French parliamentary annals and it created a huge controversy, especially after Diagne added to his claims of injustice the direct allegation that the match with Carpentier was fake and that Siki had initially been disqualified because the fight was fixed. The council of the French Boxing Federation called on Diagne to prove his allegations and threatened that, if he could not do so within fifteen days, it would ask the Chamber to lift the parliamentary immunity enjoyed by Deputy Diagne so that it could 'investigate whatever legal proceedings it seems fit to obtain redress'. It considered its honour had been injured by the 'calumnious imputations of the Deputy from Senegal'. It sent a copy of the statement to the president of the senate and the chamber of deputies, and to all senators and deputies in protest against the public accusations made in open chamber by Diagne.

Siki was happy enough to expand on the story of the fix to anyone who would listen. In an interview with the American publication, *Boxing Blade*, Siki said he agreed to the frame-up fifteen days before the fight. He was to go down in the first round for a short count and hit the canvas again in the second, take a nine count in the third, come out groggy in the fourth then drop with both arms outstretched and stay down until the referee had tolled ten. Siki said he agreed to the arrangement but 'inside my heart I kept repeating, "I will knock him out if I can."'

'I entered the ring in a bewildered condition and began to do as I agreed, dropping to one knee after two minutes of fighting, when Mr Bernstein, the referee, said sharply, "get up Siki, you are not hurt." I was in a trance in the second round, saying to myself, will I quit or will I fight? Georges hit me on the jaw with two hard rights, but did not hurt me. Going out for the third, I fully decided to take another of the agreed counts. The round went over two minutes before Georges hit me hard enough to give a chance to go down. A right swing then hit me high on the face and I said, "here goes nothing."

'I dropped to one knee, fully resolved to stay there. During these seven seconds, as I was kneeling before Carpentier, my mind changed like a flash, and I said to myself at the count of six, "I will fight and make Georges kneel before me." And at seven I was up and at beautiful Georges. I swung a hard left, landing flush on Carp's jaw. I knew I had him in the fourth.

'I began to feel sorry for him and whispered to him to quit. His blows lacked sting and he was not strong. When I whispered to him he got sore and butted me and hit me low. That settled it. I was now out to knock him out, and I went after him with right and left.

The crowd was cheering me and this further encouraged me. I saw for the first time the light heavyweight championship of the world within my grasp. Georges went down and out and I had won.'

Siki also alleged that he only received 55,000 francs instead of the 200,000 francs promised and he took out a summons against the president of the French Boxing Federation. A cross summons was issued by the President but these legal actions never materialised. Carpentier and Deschamps issued a denial and the fighter pointed to his broken hands as proof of his efforts to hit Siki. The man who was involved in the 'battle of the century' was now in the 'fix of the century'. 'It is an infamous lie,' said Carpentier's manager, François Deschamps, when shown Siki's statement.

'I was sure Carpentier would knock this negro out in the first round. Do you suppose I would let this clumsy fighter stay four rounds with my champion?

'Deputy Diagne is making electoral propaganda out of this stuff. It will go big at the next election with his Senegalese electors, but it may not go so big in the courts when the Deputy is asked to prove his charges. I absolutely defy Diagne to show the slightest atom of proof connecting me with this alleged frame up. You have noticed he was very careful not to mention my name in that connection.

'I believe Deputy Diagne's good faith has been cheated by this negro outside of electoral considerations. Diagne is perhaps acting in good faith, but he is making a big mistake mixing sports with politics. Sports are bad enough without being compared with some of our politics.

'I have never met Siki in my life. He was pointed out to me one evening in a Montmarte bar room, but his condition was such that it convinced me there would be no possible chance of defeating Carpentier. I would have refused to enter any agreement to let him stay four rounds, even if it had been proposed to me.

'The ambition of Carpentier and myself for the close of our pugilistic life was to get this Negro once more in the ring with Georges. It would have been a suicidal policy on our part to work for his disqualification.

'Georges doesn't want any more titles which he does not earn in the ring. Thus, we intend leaving for America next March or April to challenge Harry Greb, who is much more qualified than Siki to wear the title of champion.

'Our defence against these charges will be presented in the ring as well as in the courts. I hope the American and the world public will be satisfied of our innocence. If Carpentier defeats Greb, there will be no further question of ever having asked this second-rater Siki to quit.'

Georges Carpentier proposed another fight with Siki. He sent a letter to the *Journal* in Paris stating that, notwithstanding Siki's disqualification and the risk of his own subsequent suspension, he was ready to meet the Senegalese either publicly or privately, stake or no stake, provided that the winner gave a personal undertaking to pay any proceeds from the fight to charity. Carpentier added that he would beat Siki in three rounds.

The French Boxing Federation decided to proceed with an investigation into the allegations of 'faking' and it set up a Committee of Inquiry that held its first sitting on 9 December 1922. Siki was summoned to attend that day but did not put in an appearance. Instead he submitted a letter in which he protested against the action of the Federation in withdrawing his licence without a hearing and stripping him of the titles.

The following day, Siki announced that he would accept Carpentier's challenge provided his licence was restored and the fight was staged within ten weeks. Carpentier sent a telegram to *Le Matin* newspaper accepting 'in principle' the conditions of the offer of 300,000 francs for the return fight with all the money going to French scientific laboratories. The Federation approved of the rematch on condition that a national charity benefited exclusively and that the fight was staged under its control and under the 'double financial control' of representatives of the charity benefiting and the Federation. Siki was also to present himself before the Committee of Inquiry to justify his allegations. But Siki refused to attend once more, so the Federation ignored his letter accepting Carpentier's challenge until he appeared before them.

On 19 December the Committee of Inquiry viewed the film of the first fight once more, which, according to witnesses, clearly showed Deschamps walking around the ring to speak to Siki's manager, Hellers, during the critical fourth round. But the council of the French Boxing Federation was unconvinced and on delivering its verdict on the evening of 15 January 1923 it announced that the Carpentier-Siki fight was 'not preceded by any improper arrangement, that it was genuinely fought, and that the result was decided in accordance with the rules'.

The committee heard over fifty witnesses and barely anyone supported Siki, not even his own manger who had been sacked by then. Hellers said that the boxer was properly trained and pointed out the mass of contradictions in Siki's statement. Siki's friends told the committee that he had never given them to understand before the fight that the match was a frame-up.

Carpentier energetically denied the charges and declared that he had never in his life made a sham fight in the ring, either for the cinema or to gain money. Carpentier, Deschamps and Hellers were all completely exonerated while Siki was left broke, his world title gone and no prospect of ever being allowed to box again.

FIVE

He is a true child of fortune – for life has been a romance to Siki
so far, I think.

Irish Independent

They blazed away against the sunrise and all over County Dublin the homes of the rich and the powerful crackled, smouldered and burned. It was the night of 30 January 1923 and the blitz began at the house of Michael A. Corrigan, Chief State Solicitor of the Free State, in Leinster Road, Rathmines. Shortly after 9 o'clock a group of armed men arrived and demanded that Mrs Corrigan leave the property in two minutes. Her husband wasn't at home so, with the help of two maids, she got her two small children to a neighbour's house while a landmine was placed in her basement. The building was completely demolished.

As the blast reverberated around the south side of the city a house in Lansdowne Road met a similar fate. And so it went on into the night. Senator Sir Horace Plunkett, the manager of the *Irish Independent* and President Cosgrave's father-in-law, and Senator Lord Mayo all lost homes that night. A third senator, John Bagwell, the manager of the Great Northern Railway of Ireland, was visited at his home on the Hill of Howth by five armed men who carried him off in a motorcar. Marlfield House near Clonmel, another of

Bagwell's properties, had been burned down three weeks previously.

A proclamation issued at midnight by Major General Hogan, Free State Commander of the Dublin district, stated that a conspiracy existed to kidnap members of parliament, army officers, their relatives, and other 'well-disposed persons', and he gave warning that unless Senator Bagwell was released within forty-eight hours, punitive action would be taken against 'several associates in this conspiracy now in custody or otherwise'.

The following morning, one London newspaper claimed to have discovered the identity of another victim of the kidnapping conspiracy, the boxer Mike McTigue. The *Star* reported that McTigue had not been heard of since 17 January, when he had left to visit his wife and children at Caherciveen, County Kerry. Ted Broadribb, who was in charge of the boxer's business affairs, had failed to get any response to repeated wires and letters. Mike had promised relatives in Sheffield, with whom he had been staying since his arrival from America, he would write immediately on his arrival in Ireland. He told them he would be back in seven days but it had already been a fortnight and there had been no word from the boxer.

Within twenty-four hours the whereabouts of both John Bagwell and Mike McTigue became known. The Senator was taken to a farmhouse in County Meath from where he managed to climb through an upstairs window, run across several miles of fields and flag down the Dublin-bound car of a solicitor from Navan. He was covered in mud and in a 'very dishevelled condition', so he went to a barber in a Kildare Street club before meeting with President Cosgrave.

The *Irish Independent*'s Belfast correspondent solved the mystery of the missing boxer. He'd traced Mike back to Sheffield, where the fighter was reported to be alive and well. A man the newspaper described as 'a well-known Dublin sportsman' confirmed the news.

He claimed to have met Mike McTigue in Dublin on the previous Tuesday, and had a further meeting scheduled with the prizefighter in London the following Saturday. The sportsman was racehorse owner Tom Singleton and he and Mike were discussing an audacious attempt to stage a boxing match in the centre of war-torn Dublin within seven weeks. Singleton harboured an ambition to stage a big fight in Ireland and he knew how successful exhibitions by the likes of Jack Johnson and John L. Sullivan had been at the Rotunda, but he wanted to stage a *bona fide* championship match in the Irish capital. Local promoters occasionally staged boxing nights in the city, but these featured lesser-known fighters with the winner lucky to get a few pounds for his labours.

The war was certainly a factor in the dearth of big fights in Ireland, but it was also due to the lack of a building with sufficient seating to permit a championship fight to be staged at 'popular' prices. It was impossible to sell seats for more than a few shillings so an arena seating several thousand people was needed to generate a purse that would attract a champion; unless a champion could be found who was desperate enough to defend his title at well under the market value. And this was Singleton's masterstroke.

Tom Singleton was a friend of English boxing promoter, James H. Harris, who'd recently booked the world light heavyweight champion Battling Siki for a series of exhibition fights in London, Brighton and Liverpool with the possibility of a theatrical tour throughout Britain to follow. However, on 30 January 1923, the *Sporting Chronicle* learned from 'an unusually well informed source' that the Home Secretary, William Clive Bridgeman, was going to invoke the Aliens Act to prohibit Siki from landing in England. Bridgeman dealt with the matter personally and he wasn't required to detail any reason for the boxer's prohibition. The law gave the Home

Secretary wide-ranging powers to exclude anyone whose presence in Great Britain he considered would, in the very wide sense of the word, be 'undesirable'.

It was the second time in as many months that the British Home Office had banned Siki. All the arrangements had been made for the Senegalese to meet Joe Beckett, the British heavyweight champion, at the Albert Hall the previous December. But a few weeks before the fight the Home Secretary informed the promoter, Major Arnold Wilson, that he could not allow the fight to go on. 'We have come to this decision,' said a representative of the Home Office to the *Daily Chronicle*, 'on the general ground that it is inadvisable from all points of view to allow a contest in this country between a man of colour and a white man.' The fact that Siki was black shouldn't have been relevant this time because it was an exhibition tour and he didn't intend to engage in boxing contests in Britain. 'There can be no question of the colour ban,' Harris told one reporter. 'Before I signed the contract with Siki in Paris I went to the British Consul there and asked whether there would be any difficulty raised. I was told that, so far as the British Consul was concerned, no objections would be raised.

'Siki is very anxious to come to London to give British sportsmen an opportunity of seeing he is entitled to the championship which he won. He is anxious to prove that he is a clean sportsman. There is something behind the attitude of the British authorities which I do not quite understand. Siki is the most watched man in Paris today, and he has only to be guilty of the slightest thing to have reports of the most striking nature in circulation concerning his conduct.'

The *Sporting Chronicle* also interviewed Major Wilson, the promoter of the banned Siki-Beckett match. 'Personally I see no objection to a black pugilist giving an exhibition here provided he is a desirable person to enter the country,' said Wilson. 'But so far as black versus white contests are concerned, I am opposed to them on principle. I organised the proposed Beckett-Siki contest, inking for once my principle, with a view to making the white man once again the champion. I have seen Siki fight, and I believed that Beckett could have beaten him. Siki defeated Carpentier, and if Beckett at my promotion had defeated Siki, the way would have been open to Carpentier to have challenged the Britisher again. I am solid on the principle of no black and white fights. The ban placed on the Beckett-Siki fight was, I believe, on the ground of colour. If Siki was banned from coming here to give exhibitions, I think the ban placed on him was not on the grounds of colour, but owing to events subsequent to his contest with Carpentier in Paris.'

The following day the news was confirmed that the Home Secretary, after full consideration of all the circumstances, was not prepared to allow Siki to set foot in Britain. According to the *Sporting Chronicle*, 'his presence in this country, it is thought, would in all probability cause indignation on the part of the British sportsman. After the astounding allegations on the part of Siki with regard to the legitimacy of the fight with the French idol, it is most unlikely that his reception would be that accorded to a best brother.'

Jim Harris had spent a lot of money organising a boxing tour that wasn't going to happen but within days he'd thought of a solution. His friend in Dublin, who wanted to put on a big boxing match in the city, now lived in a 'Free State', beyond the control of the Home Secretary. On the advice of Jim Harris, Tom Singleton went to Paris and found Battling Siki in a café. A meeting was arranged with the boxer's new manager, Brouillet, and both men were said to be delighted at the prospect of coming to Ireland now that England was closed to them. Singleton had found a world champion who was prepared to box in Dublin and who needed money so badly that he was willing to fight for a fraction of the purse demanded by other title-holding prizefighters. What's more, it was St Patrick's Day in a few weeks' time and Singleton knew of the perfect opponent for Battling Siki – an Irishman who was capable of giving the champion a good fight and a boxer who, unlike many of his contemporaries, didn't draw the colour line.

Tom Singleton had been at ringside in Liverpool to see Mike McTigue knock out Harry Reeve in three rounds just a fortnight previously. Mike had challenged the best middleweights and heavy-weights in England, but the Irishman, whose American record was merely respectable, was quietly and effectively side-stepped. After the fight Mike told Singleton that he was out to win the world championship, that he barred no one, white or black, and that he was prepared to fight anywhere; even in a city at war. 'One venue for a fight with a good man is the same as another,' Mike told Singleton.

Unusually for a white fighter of the time Mike had been matched with over thirty black boxers and won every time. He became known as a specialist in 'fighting negroes' especially after he became the first white man to beat Panama Joe Gans, considered to be the coloured light heavyweight champion of the United States. Mike knocked out Gans with a punch to the Adam's apple. 'I thought Gans would turn white,' recalled the Irishman. 'I do not think a coloured man is harder to beat than a white man. I am not one of those who thinks negroes exceptionally tough. They can be knocked out if they are hit right. My experience is that the coloured man cannot stand the body punching that a white man can stand.'

Mike, Brouillet and Singleton met up in London to finalise the details of the match and on 4 February 1923 the *Evening Standard* reported that negotiations for the fight were proceeding well. 'When

McTigue was supposed to be missing in the Free State he was actually discussing the business of the proposed match with Siki, with members of the syndicate formed for the purpose of promoting the contest.'

A special cable dispatch to the *Washington Post* reported that French sporting circles were greatly excited at the prospect of Battling Siki fighting in Dublin. The message claimed that interest in Paris concerned not only the participants, but also that Ireland, 'by planning to receive the Senegalese with open arms, proclaims that it is indeed a free state in view of the ban against Siki in England.' According to the *Washington Post*, 'regret has been expressed that the bout is not possible in France on account of Siki's disqualification by the French Boxing Federation following his knocking out of Carpentier', as well as the 'detestable habit of American managers of counting in dollars and stipulating so many in their contracts that the sight of the figures stupefy the generous French supporters of sport.'

One of the regular correspondents to *Boxing* magazine was 'Jersey City' who in previous letters to the magazine wrote that, 'the great Anglo-Irish-American trouble lay in the fact that Englishmen forget history, Irishmen are unable to forget it, while Americans have never learned it'. On 4 March 1923 he sent the following letter to London:

I see by the sporting news that Mike McTigue fights Siki in Dublin. While I am positively not an admirer of the French coon, I believe that there is going to be a very sore and humiliated Irishman on St Patrick's Day. I saw McTigue fight at the big bowl at Boyle's Thirty Acres, Jersey City. His opponent was a 150-lb negro named Panama Joe Gans, and as McTigue weighed about 158lb, or 160lb, he had quite an advantage over the son of 'Ham' physically. If the negro had been a heavy hitter McTigue would not now have been alive to fight Siki. McTigue is easy to hit, and if Siki can hit him as hard as they say he can, there will be a dead Irishman in Dublin on St Patrick's Day. Warra! Wurra!

If McTigue ever said he licked Greb, or he can lick Greb, he is a confounded lying 'Mick'. Greb is not a heavy hitter, but he can rough-house that Irish clay-pipe clean off of the reservation. Gene Tunney can whip McTigue, as he can Tom Gibbons, Tommy Robson, Loughlin, Floyd Johnson, and others. Tell me where in thunder does Michael McTigue get off at to challenge Jack Dempsey, as I hear are his intentions. Remember my prediction in your issue of February 21. You will be trying to toady to the turbulent Irish by making excuses why McTigue didn't win, as you did with Ted Kid Lewis when he fought Carpentier (you catered to the Jews), and when the Frenchman knocked out Cook you started the old excuse machine going again. The Australian had to be placated. But if an American lost – oh, my, what a difference! No excuses; the Yank was beaten, and you are tickled to death! Why don't Joe Beckett fight Siki? Is your government afraid he will be soundly thrashed? If you want Siki whipped send him to our bruisers.

Tom Singleton returned to Paris and secured Siki's signature on the contract on the night of 5 February. Mike had already signed the document. Siki was reported to be so enthusiastic about the affair that he offered to fight for nothing just to even up the score with the French Boxing Federation, but a few sportsmen present noticed that he cast an enquiring eye over the financial clauses. The purse was £2,000 of which £1,500 went to the winner.

The promoters agreed to place a guarantee in the hands of the French Consul in Dublin on the day of Siki's arrival that, by the terms of the contract, was to be ten days preceding the fight in Ireland. The referee was to be Eugene Corri, the famous British official, or Jack Smith. The job of making the gloves for the fight was given to an Irish company, Messrs Elvery, the printing contract was given to Messrs Manico and the bill-posting to Messrs Allen, both of Dublin. It was announced that early applications for tickets should be made to the Bureau, 24 Suffolk Street, Dublin, which was open from 9 am to 6 pm Cheques (crossed) were to be made payable to Mr T. Singleton.

The venue selected was the La Scala Theatre which, according to the promoters, was chosen because it could accommodate a big crowd as was shown when a tournament for the IRA Dependents Fund was held there a year previously. But there was another reason for the choice of venue. The La Scala stood at the end of Prince's Street, a cul-de-sac running adjacent to the General Post Office on Sackville Street. It could only be reached by one route so it was far easier to protect than any other theatre in a troubled city.

The signing of the contract for the fight sparked worldwide interest in the event. This was the golden age of boxing and the scribes had developed a near obsession with Siki since he took the light heavyweight title from Carpentier the previous September. The Senegalese was the first African to win a world boxing title and as barely anybody outside France had seen him fight, stories of the terrible black man grew to fantastic proportions.

'There is only one drawback to the whole thing,' reported the *Irish Independent*. 'Siki is forbidden by a ruling of the Home Office to land in England. If he wants to reach Dublin he must go directly to Ireland and even then the ban may be extended to the Green Isle.'

At the foot of its report the newspaper added:

> Note: In connection with the last sentence in the above para-
> graph, it may be pointed out that the British Home Office
> has no jurisdiction in Ireland.

A representative of the *Irish Times* asked Kevin O'Higgins, Minister for Home Affairs, whether, following the decision of the Home Secretary in England, he would stop the bout. The minister replied that he had issued no prohibition. There was some dissatisfaction with the high prices fixed for tickets in the Dublin press, however. 'Casual Transport Worker' wrote to the *Irish Independent* claiming that thousands of enthusiasts would be prevented from witnessing it. He suggested holding the contest 'in the even' at Lansdowne Road or at the grounds in Ballsbridge, where he felt sure the promoters would be well rewarded by the crowd they would get.

The sole picture rights for the fight were quickly secured by Messrs Pathé Frères, and although no formal link has ever been established, the day after the big fight was announced in Dublin the company's premises in the city were bombed. Four men, brandishing revolvers, entered the offices on the upper floors of 2 Lower Abbey Street, shortly before 9 o'clock on the morning of 6 February. One of the men asked for a Pathé Gazette, but as one of the four girls in the despatch room was about to go to the film room to get the reel, one of the raiders said he would go himself and took out a revolver. The staff were ushered into the front office while the other three men doused the adjoining rooms with petrol. One of the girls noticed a mine on the floor and begged their captors to allow them to leave. They were told to stay where they were as the raiders set the building on fire and ran off. It was only after the gunmen had made their escape in a waiting car parked on the opposite side of the street that the girls rushed down the stairs and into the road. They had just reached the pavement at the front of the building when there was an explosion on the first floor and the windows were blown out onto the street below. The blast ripped huge holes in the front of the building through which the stock of film could be seen burning furiously with a blue flame. Eight people were injured on the pavement below as they were trapped under the debris.

Within twenty-four hours of contracts being signed, the boxing match had become a part of the Civil War. The Free State government, Battling Siki and Mike McTigue needed each other. Siki needed money, McTigue needed a fight and the politicians needed legitimacy. The stakes were high for the government because the fight provided an opportunity to show the world that it was in control of this new country. The republicans were desperate to prove otherwise.

While the match was a matter of deadly importance to various factions in Ireland it was an irritant and embarrassment for the French. Siki was still banned by the French Boxing Federation yet he had signed up for the most publicised fight of the season. It was time to cut a deal. The Federation conveniently used the occasion of the twentieth anniversary of its foundation to grant an amnesty for all disqualified and suspended boxers and Battling Siki was entitled to box as soon as he applied for a new licence. The deal also involved Siki dropping legal proceedings against the Federation that in turn withdrew its case against Diagne, the Senegalese Deputy.

After his defeat of Carpentier, Siki was 'warned off' by the French Boxing Federation. Pure pique had prompted their action: 'that any coloured man should beat the idol of the Parisians – it was ridiculous to think!' commented one American boxing writer. 'But the absurdity of the situation was too much for the Federation and it went through the solemn farce of reinstating Siki. They gave him as a present, that which he had won by right in the ring. The boxing fraternity looked on and laughed.'

There was no talk of a title being at stake in Dublin at this point. The decision to reinstate Siki did not automatically restore his status as heavyweight champion of France, light heavyweight champion of the world and heavyweight champion of Europe. The *Echo Des Sports* reported that Siki would probably be reinstated in the latter two championships at a forthcoming meeting of the International Boxing Union, but the question of restoring the French title would only be considered when he applied to the French Federation for a new licence. But Siki and his manager, Brouillet, had already achieved what they wanted by signing for the Dublin fight. The French Boxing Federation had been coerced into allowing Siki to box again and the reinstatement of his titles was a mere technicality. Mike wasn't a highly regarded fighter, certainly not as a light heavyweight, so the plan was for Siki to fulfil the Dublin engagement, the win barely a formality, and return to France for a big-money rematch with Carpentier.

Interviewed by *L'Auto* after the Federation's decision to return Siki's licence, Carpentier's manager Deschamps said that a match between his charge and the Senegalese fighter would certainly be arranged. However, the French boxing bosses weren't going to allow the boxers and their managers to embarrass them any further. The Federation addressed a letter to the press stating that it saw no objections, and in fact would be glad, to see Carpentier and Battling Siki fight in a return match for charity purposes. When the fixing scandal had broken out the previous winter, *Le Matin* and *Le Journal* newspapers had proposed to pay all the expenses for a rematch to settle the issue, with the entire proceeds to go to French scientific laboratories. Now, the newspapers, in conjunction with the Federation, maintained their wish to see the contest brought off for the benefit of those institutions and not the two fighters.

At a meeting in Paris on 19 February 1923, the French Boxing Federation ratified its action in pardoning Siki by proclaiming him light heavyweight champion of the world. Over five months after he had beaten Carpentier in the ring, the Federation had finally acknowledged Siki's victory and his right to be called world champion.

The announcement elevated the Dublin match to title-fight status and, after struggling to get a fight of any description in England, Mike McTigue was about to challenge for a world championship. A bizarre sequence of events had conspired to produce the most important international sporting event to be staged in Ireland for a generation. The promoters expected a big influx of English boxing fans. Owing to the ban of exclusion passed on Siki, many English sportsmen were denied the opportunity to see the man who beat Carpentier in dramatic style and they were anxious to seize the chance now afforded. Siki's projected visit to England had been something of a vaudeville tour, not half as attractive as a real fight with a somewhat mysterious opponent.

The syndicate of Irish sportsmen who'd backed the venture couldn't have dreamed of such an outcome, yet Tom Singleton still harboured one big concern over the venture. He'd met with Battling Siki in Paris when the contracts were drawn up and, while he'd managed to secure the boxer's signature, Singleton was far from convinced that the world champion would show up in Dublin.

Siki had gone on a tour through Germany and Czechoslovakia and a short visit to Liège after the arrangements for the match had been completed and as soon as he returned to Paris, Singleton decided to travel to the French capital to chaperone the fighter over to Ireland. On his arrival in Paris Singleton was heartened to learn that Siki had decided to leave for Ireland a few days sooner than was called for in his contract. 'Yes, yes; but I need to be in Ireland soon in order to get accustomed to your climate; your weather is cold,' said Siki. The world champion undertook the formality of writing to the French Boxing Federation asking for the renewal of his licence and within a week, with the bit of card in his pocket, Siki was ready to leave for Ireland. Tom Singleton sent a telegram back to his office from Paris on 27 February reporting that Siki would set off the following day. 'No effort will be spared to make Siki appear a real world's champion in this his first fight since winning the world's title from Carpentier,' claimed the promoter.

The *Irish Independent*'s Ballyhaunis representative interviewed the well-known heavyweight boxer Jim Coffey, popularly known as the Roscommon Giant, and 'gleaned important information about McTigue'. Jim and Mike had become close friends while the men were living in New York and according to Coffey his old partner was the 'cleanest and coolest fighter that ever entered a ring against any opponent, no matter how formidable. Best of all, he has got a punch, which once got in, nothing can endure.' Coffey said that the Siki contest would be the 'greatest fighting event in McTigue's successful career', and while the world champion was bound to be the favourite in the betting, he advised all who could get a long shot, or anything like it, on Mike, to accept it.

Mike had already commenced light training in Sheffield but on 17 February, along with secretary-trainer Charlie Brennan and sparring partner Tom Ireland, he moved his headquarters to the Grosvenor Hotel in Maidenhead. He followed a strict routine that started with a ten-mile run at eight o'clock every morning followed by a bath and rub down. Breakfast was taken at 10.30 a.m. after which he rested and attended to any unanswered correspondence. Lunch was at 2.30 pm and then he'd spend the afternoon chopping down trees and mowing lawns on the estate. After putting the roller and the axe away he dined at 6.30 pm and then read the newspapers until 10.30 pm, which was bedtime. But before retiring for the night, Mike dipped his hands in a secret chemical given to him by an American army doctor. 'It wouldn't hurt my hand if I punched this,' said Mike, pointing to a wall. 'They are always hard as iron. But I shall certainly not attempt to punch the negro's skull. That is not the place to hit a black on.'

The party was swollen by the arrival of amateur boxing champion Eddie Eagan, who was studying at Oxford when he read of Mike's fight with Siki. Eagan had turned to Mike for help to prepare for the Olympic games in 1920 and now he wanted to repay the favour. He had seen Siki beat Carpentier in the Velodrome in Paris so Eagan, in the company of Lord Clydesdale, motored down from Oxford to Maidenhead to offer his help. 'He was strengthening his right by sawing wood,' Eagan recalled. 'I told him about the Siki-Carpentier match and he welcomed my offer to join him in Dublin in a week's time to help him finish training.' The two men boxed every day and Eagan remembered that Mike's relatives 'were everywhere about his quarters'.

Mike eventually set off for Dublin a few days late after business matters had detained him in England. His party consisted of Charlie Brennan, Bartley Madden, a well-known Irish-American heavyweight from New York, Billy Mack, a Liverpool boxer and Philip Welch, a nineteen-year-old middleweight from Bolsover, Derbyshire. Mike had taken Welch under his tutelage, and believed the young fighter would be the English middleweight champion in a few years. Welch was set to take his public bow in the ring at the La Scala and he was being keenly watched as a result of Mike 'talking him up'.

There had been bombings, kidnap threats and clerical denunciations but all these difficulties had seemingly been overcome and Singleton's dream, to stage a big fight in his native country, was about to be realised. He had found a champion no English or American promoter could use and a challenger no English or American promoter wanted to use. The contest between Battling Siki and Mike McTigue for the light heavyweight championship of the world was to take place at the La Scala Theatre, Dublin, on 17 March, St Patrick's Day.

SIX

On Saturday last, McTigue, along with some friends, went out rabbit shooting and the first rabbit seen was a black one. Somebody shouted 'Siki'. 'Bang' went Mike's gun and over went bunny. Mike puts great belief in omens and since that episode he is looking to the result of the contest with optimism.

Irish Independent

The term 'celebrity' was invented in the twenties and sports heroes were among the first to be idolised. This was also the so-called golden age of boxing; the time when it became a sport for the masses. It was also the golden age of boxing writers, and the age might not have seemed so golden if such men had not been around to record the exploits of fighters like Jack Dempsey. The likes of Ring Lardner, Damon Runyon, Gartland Rice, Bill McGeehan and Paul Gallico hadn't wasted the smallest drop of typewriter ink on Mike McTigue prior to his match with Battling Siki, but suddenly the journeyman club fighter had become a contender without throwing a punch. A career confined to the bottom corners of the sports pages was forensically reassessed by scribes who had long since dismissed the Irishman as a broken down never was of a palooka. Mike McTigue was interesting for the first time in his life. Maybe he wasn't a bum after all?

When the challenger was tracked down to the Grosvenor Hotel in Maidenhead the boxing writers found a 'very interesting man, quiet mannered and affable'. He didn't want to talk boxing, but it was the subject at hand. Mike claimed to be thirty-one years of age at this point and the scribes thought it impossible that a man could become world champion at such an age. When asked if his advancing years would be a handicap, Mike replied that it probably would be had he started boxing at seventeen or eighteen years of age, but his career hadn't started until he was twenty-two and so he considered himself to be only twenty-six or seven in a 'fistic sense'.

The self-proclaimed Irish middleweight champion fought regularly around the New York area, winning most but losing some. The fights were mainly ten-round 'no-decision' contests, under the Frawley Law that operated in New York State between 1911 and 1920. Boxing was banned in most states but was allowed in New York because under the 'no-decision' system all the bouts were meant to be exhibitions with no verdict given at the end. The only way a boxer could win was by knockout. The law was designed to foil the fight fixers and 'sure-thing' gamblers who bought decisions from referees and judges. But like every other prohibition there was a way around the problem. If a fight went the full distance, a poll of ringside reporters would produce a 'popular decision' and bets were paid according to this 'newspaper verdict'. Of course it was easier to pay off the scribes than fighters or referees.

After quitting his job at the meat packing plant, Mike had spent his days in the gymnasium of the Polo Athletic Club at 155th Street and Eighth Avenue. From the summer of 1914 he became a regular at the 'blood bucket' fight clubs of New York. His first fight was at the Olympic Club on West 125th Street, which was operated by Eddie and Jess McMahon. He boxed the likes of Rube Howard, Happy

Davis, Paddy Conway, Joe Marino, Mike Greel, Walter McGirr and Jack Emmanon. Even though he was the ideal shape for a boxer: tall, fair and spare, wide-shouldered, narrow-hipped and slim-legged, he didn't look healthy enough to be in the ring. One writer described Mike as 'lank, almost to the point of emaciation, during his younger years, when most fighters are husky, well-fed individuals. During that period old Michael was the type of fighter who couldn't knock out a sick kitten with his Sunday punch.'

John Kelly, one of Mike's best friends during the 'lean days' delighted in telling how the Irishman used to go to his room and indulge in 'strange antics. Bedad, I surely thought he was going batty when he put on such didoes,' Kelly recalled. 'One night he knocked himself out during his exercises. It was like this: Mike was tossing punches at an imaginary opponent when all of a sudden he let go a vicious right uppercut and fell sideways against the brass bedstead, landing on his head. Well, he didn't come to so I had to give him a bath with a pitcher of ice water.'

During that time Mike met up with Jim Coffey, the famous Roscommon Giant, and they became close friends. The two men lived together during the years that Coffey was being groomed as one of the 'great white hopes'. Coffey pressed Mike into service as a sparring partner to prepare for matches against, among others, Al Reich, Carl Morris and Ed 'Gunboat' Smith. But the single most important event in Mike's early ring career was the moment when William J. Breslin walked into the Polo Club.

Breslin was better known as Jack Britton, welterweight champion of the world and one of the most remarkable fighters to have donned a glove. Britton established his training quarters at the club and Mike would sit in the front row when the champion went through his training routine. The Irishman was fascinated by the way

Britton tossed left-hand jabs and hooks at sparring partners without getting a receipt. 'Jack saw that I was raw – very raw – when I was "palling" with him in my novice days – my whole idea then being to get home with my right hand. I might not have had a left for all the good that it was for me; but the left hand is the boxer's trump card,' Mike recalled. 'If you can't make an opening with your left and use it equally as well as your right, you're under a big disadvantage.' Jack designed what Mike called a 'kitbogue', a device to strap the Irishman's right hand to his side and he was made to spar against Britton and other clever fighters using just his left hand. Mike spent long hours in the gym trying to emulate Britton until he finally thought he'd mastered the left hand. 'After a few turns I got it into first-rate order, and it was a most serviceable offensive and defensive weapon.'

It was a hard life. Mike fought for a couple of bucks on the blood-soiled canvases of smoky fight clubs for the pleasure of the six-bit hecklers and the iron-throated mob in the sixty-cent seats. He was hit with knees, elbows and foreheads. His kidneys were swollen, eyes were cut and the rough lacing of dirty old gloves gored a lattice of scratches across his face.

Mike's first lucky break came when Jess McMahon passed over the management of the Olympic Club to his old friend, Paddy Donnelly. Paddy believed Mike to be good enough to top his cards and after two years of flinging fists for florins, the Irishman was a 'main bouter'. Mike was put on a percentage of the gate but he fought mainly to a hall of empty chairs and got just $25 for topping his first bill. He boxed forty times in 1915 and 1916 and won the vast majority of his bouts, either by knockout or by newspaper verdict.

He was always within a week of being fit to fight, but American trainers and promoters wouldn't handle a man unless he kept up to the mark and was prepared to take on a fight at short notice.

'That's one of the reasons we have so few home-trained champions – they don't get enough fighting to encourage them always to be fit,' Mike told an Irish writer. 'A man will never be champion unless he gets practice, practice, practice and again practice – not practice in the gymnasium but practice in the ring. I know of dozens of handy young men around my native place, who with a few years coaching, would make world beaters, but they have no practice.'

Despite his run of victories, promoters found it hard to match the Irishman. Boxers who could go in the ring and beat seemingly better men than Mike, couldn't beat him. You couldn't draw flies to a loser but Mike fought a careful, defensive fight that kept the crowds away. It made him a distinctly unattractive boxer who made an opponent look bad and reduced the gate into the bargain. When he entered the ring, there was only a small dribble of applause and as he danced and weaved through contests the disgruntled roaring and booing grew above which could be heard the occasional throaty-voiced incitement to his opponent to 'kill this sonofabitch'. But Mike never listened to the comments of the crowd, or its razzberries. His watchful, understated style in the ring was an extension of his personality. He was generally described as a temperate, patient and sociable man, invariably polite, quietly spoken and immaculately dressed.

A clever, awkward style wasn't popular with the customers but it ensured the Irishman plenty of work as a sparring partner. He joined Jack Dempsey's training camp at various times over the next three years and also worked with middleweight champion Mike Gibbons. The St Paul Phantom as he was known, was one of the key influences on the Irishman's career. 'Mike Gibbons was my best friend,' Mike wrote. 'Michael J. Gibbons is a "white man". He advised and cheered me, and criticised me, and ended up making a fighter of me.'

Like every other hungry young fighter Mike had to take whatever came on offer, the only difference being that Mike wasn't that young. Boys were fighting professionally at fifteen in New York, yet Mike was still in the lower ranks at the age of twenty-seven. The boxing writers thought him at least five years younger but already dismissed him as too old to be a contender. As Mike entered the ring for a bout at the St Nicholas Rink on 66th Street and Columbus Avenue, Billy Roche, who was refereeing, looked down at a reporter, sitting at ringside, and asked: 'Do you think that old stiff McTigue will ever quit boxing?' The scribe shrugged and Roche called both fighters to the centre of the ring.

But Mike was nothing if not determined and with a few more victories in his ledger he went after bigger game. He got a match against a pretty good fighter called Johnny 'Kid' Alberts of Elizabeth, New Jersey. The fight was attractive enough to fill the house and Mike got $125 for his end. After licking Alberts Mike stepped outside his favourite stomping ground – Harlem – and fought in other clubs throughout New York City. He became a journeyman and beat a string of human shock-absorbers who never created a ripple in the middleweight puddle.

But there was the occasional setback. On 18 June 1917 Mike lost the newspaper verdict to Billy Kramer after six hard rounds in a wind-up fight at the National Athletic Club in Philadelphia, but a sequence of impressive performances against Tommy Robson, Jeff Smith and Augie Ratner in the latter half of the year did much to restore his reputation. These fighters were a big step up in class from his previous opponents but Mike was soon to share a ring with a fighter who was far too good for him. Harry Greb became world middleweight champion in 1923 and the record books credit him with 304 fights, although it's generally believed he boxed a hundred or so more, which ranks him as having the third-highest number of professional contests ever. The sports writers branded him a dirty fighter who resorted to head butts, and jabbing elbows and thumbs into opponents' eyes.

Mike fought Greb three times. The first fight was staged in Cleveland, Ohio. The Irishman was battered in ten rounds although he stayed on his feet to the end. It took Mike several weeks to recover from the beating and it kept him out of the ring for three months. He returned to box Frank 'the Destroyer' Carbone twice in the space of three weeks. The first fight in Red Bank, New Jersey was an eight-round no-decision affair that went the distance. The second at West Hoboken, New Jersey appears in the record books as a fifth-round knockout victory for Carbone. How this fight actually ended is not known. Mike claimed for many years not to have suffered a knockout in his career – he was either lying or the fight was stopped because of an injury or disqualification. But whatever happened at the small club in West Hoboken on 9 July 1918, the hands of 'the Destroyer' caused Mike's retirement.

After losing to Carbone Mike turned to a fellow Clareman for help. John McDermott was a well-known sportsman and he arranged for Mike to become 'Professor' Mike Donovan's assistant boxing instructor at the New York Athletic Club. Donovan had acquired his title because he taught the science of fist-fighting and claimed to have created just about every move in boxing. He had 'won' the job of boxing instructor at the prestigious club by beating Walter Watson in the ring. The New York Athletic Club had a membership roster of politicians, promoters, writers and actors, socialites and financiers and Donovan claimed that pugilistic training helped old men lose weight while simultaneously sustaining or even increasing their willpower, fortitude, and courage. The tap-tap of a jump rope hitting the floorboards and the thud of boxing glove on punch bag constantly echoed through the mahogany-walled club. Professional fighters routinely gave boxing lessons to wealthy clients but there was an established rule at the club that prohibited tutors from hitting back at their pupils. Mike knew that if he punched one of the members with any force the indignant customer would most likely complain to the house committee and have him fired. The boxing instructors at the big clubs learned to protect themselves at all times for it was always considered very smart for an amateur fighter to put one on the jaw of a professional and knock him to the canvas. That's how Mike perfected the defence that served him so well in later years.

Several boxing writers have attested that while at the club Mike became imbued with the idea that all one needed to get by as a professional boxer was the ability to block or avoid a punch and that the experience ruined him as a fighter. 'Forbidden to smack back and required to stand for anything the members might do to him, Michael became a great defensive boxer, which is a terrible thing in the ring,' wrote Westbrook Pegler. 'When you get two defensive boxers into a match it is a great idea to stay home and catch up on your late-fall and early-winter sleep, unless you can sleep in a chair.'

When his contact with the New York Athletic Club expired Mike returned to the prize ring. He wasn't the most attractive fighter before his sabbatical but now the mob was openly hostile. 'The customers learned about Mike and when a promoter would put his name on a card the customers would not speak of seats for the fight but spoke of uppers and lowers, which was a sarcastical crack, but much enjoyed by the peasantry and gentry alike,' commented one writer. But Mike was past the time where he heard or was affected by boos.

He was lured back into the ring with a purse of $150, the biggest of his career to that point, to fight Battling Ortega, a half-Mexican, half-Native-American fighter in Boston. Ortega was a dashing, tear-away scrapper with a victory over world welterweight champion Ted 'Kid' Lewis on his record. The Battler opened up to finish Mike quickly, and the betting swung strongly in Ortega's favour.

Mike remembered little about the early rounds such was the beating he took: 'Honestly it looked ten to one Ortega beating me, and as a matter of fact after four rounds he had given me such a pummelling that my head was stuffed up and I was badly hammered. At the end of the fourth round I was sitting in my corner with my nasal organ almost ceased functioning, until Sam Langford stepped across and gave me a whiff of smelling salts, which cleared my nostrils.' But Ortega could not knock the Irishman out and Mike got the measure of his man in the sixth round. 'McTigue's fighting from the seventh round on was a revelation even to his admirers,' reported the *Chicago Daily Tribune*. 'Both men were toe to toe at the finish and fighting hard.' In the twelfth and final round an exhausted Ortega missed with a wild swing and Mike floored him three times. It was enough to give Mike the verdict. 'I was told that the crowd thought I was so unsuitable an opponent for Ortega, that in the first round a section of them stood up and cried out to stop the fight, but Tom O'Rourke, my manager, said "No. This Irish boy can fight and the harder you hit him, the better he likes it." Let me tell you, it was a great scrap.'

In December 1919 Mike got a return match with Harry Greb at the Ideal Pavillion, Endicott, New York. He'd learned a great deal from his previous lacing and several scribes thought the Irishman was at least the equal of Greb over ten rounds. But despite this performance and subsequent victories over Roddy McDonald, Jackie Clark and 'Sailor' Ed Petroskey, Mike was never written of as a contender and the customers remained unconvinced. So he decided to leave New York for Canada.

Mike arrived in Halifax, Nova Scotia in April 1920 for a match with undefeated Canadian middleweight champion, Eugene Brosseau. At the sounding of the opening bell both men came out of their corners fast. Brosseau extended his hand for the shake but Mike did not accept and hostilities got underway. It only lasted five rounds and Mike won every one, his left jab spearing into Brosseau's face the whole time. After jabbing the Canadian's nose into a different shape, Mike switched to a series of right crosses onto the young champion's jaw. The fifth round was only a minute old when, after a frenetic exchange in the middle of the ring, Mike sent Brosseau to the ropes with another spiteful left jab.

The French-Canadian, 'with a pitiful look in his eyes', knew what was coming. He lowered his gloves and was caught with a vicious, measured right swing that dropped him to the canvas. Amid wild cheering from the crowd referee Tom Foley tolled off the necessary ten seconds. Brosseau tried to get up but collapsed back to the floor with tears streaming from his badly swollen eyes into the cuts that slashed his lips. He tried to crawl back to his corner but fell again. As Brosseau's seconds tried to revive him, Mike was carried back to his changing room on the shoulders of his new admirers.

In the excitement a story swept through the arena that the new champion was a 'ringer', that he was not the original Mike McTigue – the New York middleweight – but a heavyweight sent to Halifax for the sole purpose of dethroning the Canadian title-holder. Mike was forced to meet with the sports editor of the *Halifax Herald* in the company of Alderman WP Buckley who originally came from County Clare and who had known the fighter for many years. The Alderman said:

I knew McTigue would win as he is a gentleman and a clean-living boy and I backed him to the limit. He performs clean, and it will take a great boxer to beat him. While I am also a friend of Brosseau, and sorry for his defeat, I admire him for his gameness and clean boxing, but I must admit that I am happy McTigue won. He is a great boy and has made hundreds of friends in the city. We both come from dear old Ireland, the home of great fighters, and it takes a hard wallop to down an Irishman. Mr McTigue will be my guest for a few days and in me he can count on a staunch friend and backer.

Mike enjoyed being a champion, even if it was a little-valued title, and he stayed in Canada for a year and a half, defending his crown against all-comers. First up was Danny Ferguson at the Armouries in Halifax just a fortnight after beating Brosseau. The bout lasted eight rounds but it was only Ferguson's extraordinary braveness that allowed it to go so far. He was knocked down eleven times before being counted out in the eighth. Ferguson was a few inches shorter than Mike and found it impossible to get close to the Irishman unless he was prepared to take a few punches. He was knocked down in the fourth, and in the seventh he was hit through the ropes and nearly fell off the platform. With a smile on his face, Ferguson made it back at the count of nine and rushed at Mike and caught him with a low blow. It seemed to anger the Irishman who battered his opponent for the remainder of the round.

Jack London was knocked out in two rounds in Montreal a week later after which Mike returned to Halifax for a hard-fought victory over Joe Eagan on a decision at the end of fifteen rounds. Many in the crowd thought the challenger had done enough to get a draw and when referee Tom Foley raised Mike's arm at the final bell, Eagan protested. But this was a title defence and champions were usually given the benefit of any doubt.

Mike stayed on in Halifax for the summer of 1920 and boxed regularly. He knocked out Young O'Grady in five and outpointed Jack McCarron in ten before resuming hostilities with an old adversary, Jeff Smith. Mike wrote of this contest as 'My Hardest Fight' in the June 1925 issue of *The Ring*:

I came into the world with two good fighting hands. They were hard as nails. But five years ago I broke the right mauler in the hardest battle of my career, on Jeff Smith, and since that time I have suffered the tortures of hell. Through some wonderful surgery performed by WG Fralick, I am glad to say that the hand is as strong as it ever was, and from now on I am going to defend my title against all-comers.

That gosson, Jeff! How can I ever forget or forgive him! In the winter of 1920 … Smith and I clashed in a fifteen-rounder at Halifax, Nova Scotia. In the second round I felt a pain in my right hand and notified my manager and my seconds that the mitt had gone back on me.

Had Smith known what had happened he might have tried harder to knock me off. But I knew how to use the left paw, jabbing and hooking him when he threatened to knock the skids from under me. He gave me an awful pasting.

As much as I can remember, he started to work on me beginning the third by shooting left hooks to the body and crossing the right. He seldom missed. As the battle raged I grew weak, but Smith was getting stronger. The fact that I scored a knockdown in the thirteenth didn't make Smith back up a bit. That made him fight back all the harder.

His punches, carrying dynamite in every delivery, started to cut my face. As early as the seventh session he had both of my eyes closed. The referee wanted to stop the slaughter, but I pleaded he allow the bout to continue. 'I feel all right. Please don't stop it," I kept saying to him.

The spectators were howling 'Stop it! Stop it!' but the third man in the ring promised to give me a break, and, although I was on the receiving end, I fought back as hard as I could. My left was in good working order, and the way I rallied got me on the good side of the fans. They rooted hard for me to turn the tide. But I just couldn't make it.

Smith knew he had my number. He threw science to the four winds in the ninth and battered me from pillar to post. First, he tried to knock down my left hand and if that was unsuccessful, he would crowd me to the ropes belting me around the body. The sting of the blows hurt me so that I could almost cry. I couldn't protect myself.

How in the world I ever scored that knockdown I'll never know. Smith got sweet revenge in the fourteenth. I could feel my feet slipping from under me, but I managed to stand up, acting the part of a baseball catcher. Again in the fifteenth and last round Smith let fly a fresh barrage, and before the smoke of battle cleared, I was hanging on the ropes. He missed a right that, had it landed, would have surely put me to sleep. But, thank goodness, it whizzed by my head. The wind almost knocked me down.

He jabbed lightly with the left and then took another gamble with the right. This time the punch found its mark – right on the whiskers. It was a terrific blow. I almost caved in.

Smith got the decision, and he deserved it.

After the fight a doctor rushed in the ring and asked if I needed any assistance.

'Need any help? I sure do, Doc,' was my answer.

A few minutes later he was dressing my wounds. He had to sew up the cuts over my eyes. That required ten stitches. It was over two days before I could get out of bed. I received an unmerciful licking. It wasn't the beating so much I cared about as the broken hand.

Despite his battering at the hands of Smith, Mike held on to the Canadian championship because both fighters were over the middle-weight limit of 160 pounds. But Mike's standing and reputation had taken a blow. He responded with a clear victory over Johnny Alex at the Armouries in Halifax. 'Alex received enough punches on the jaw and head to knock an ordinary man out a dozen times,' reported the *Halifax Herald*, 'but his superhuman gameness won the admiration of the crowd.' Mike returned to Montreal and fought two close ten-round, no-decision contests with future British middleweight champion Jack Bloomfield. He then signed for a series of fights at the Freeport Sporting Club, New York, the most dramatic of which was a defeat to Harry Krohn on 9 May 1921. It was a bitterly fought contest but Mike, thanks to greater aggressiveness and harder hitting, was well ahead on points when in the ninth round he was disqualified for wrestling Krohn to the floor.

Mike returned to Canada in the summer of 1921 for a match with George Robinson in Montreal. It was staged at the city's St Denis theatre and advertised as being for the Canadian middleweight title. The billing upset Jeff Smith, who claimed to be the Canadian champion since beating Mike in Halifax. The weight issue had saved the Irishman's title and the publicity helped boost the gate for the McTigue-Robinson match. Not that it really needed any boosting. Robinson had recently trounced world middleweight champion Johnny Wilson, scoring several knockdowns, and he was the short money favourite to beat Mike. They boxed on a percentage basis and the bout earned about $3,000.

When they met in the centre of the ring Mike towered over the squat Robinson by almost a head. Robinson, as expected, started the fighting, shooting his left hand a dozen times to Mike's half-turned face and the Canadian crowd settled in to see the Irishman slowly picked to pieces. For the first two rounds it was all Robinson, but he inflicted no real damage except for a reddened spot on the right side of his opponent's face. Towards the end of the second Mike sent in a couple of left hooks that bloodied Robinson's lips. He kept his right back until the beginning of the third round when Mike suddenly threw a vicious right into his opponent's stomach. Robinson seemed to take the punch well and continued the attack but as he jumped in to try and land another left jab Mike pitched a right hook in a short arc that crashed flush on his opponent's chin. Robinson fell to his knees, and then, slowly, he slumped face down, his nose on the canvas in a neutral corner.

Referee McBrearty, amid a pandemonium of noise, started to count and failed to hear timekeeper Johnny Smyth sound the bell for the end of the round. Even Robinson's manager, Jim MacDonald, hadn't heard the bell. Meanwhile Robinson was still twitching on the canvas, blood trickling out of his mouth in tiny rivulets and mixing with the dust and resin on his lips. When the referee and Robinson's seconds were made aware that the bell had tolled, the stricken fighter was dragged unconscious to his corner where desperate attempts were made to revive him. They managed to get Robinson to his feet and as the bell sounded for the fourth they pushed him out on unsteady legs to the centre of the ring.

Mike swept in without mercy. Robinson tried to save himself, crouching and forming a barricade of elbows and gloves over his jaw and stomach. But Mike was able to push him about the ring until he finally tore the guard away and smashed a right cross onto Robinson's jaw as he was trapped in his own corner. Robinson's legs appeared to fold up and he was left hanging with his arms twisted in the ropes. McBrearty counted four and Robinson, his dimmed eyes half closed, staggered to his feet. The referee had seen enough and walked over to Mike to raise his arm while Robinson collapsed again in his corner. The *Montreal Daily Star* pronounced it the most spectacular and surprising knockout ever accomplished in a ring in that city. It was Mike's fourth consecutive knockout victory and it led to the biggest fight of his career to date.

Tex Rickard had signed a world middleweight championship match between title-holder Johnny Wilson and challenger Bryan Downey at Boyle's Thirty Acres, Jersey City, on 5 September 1921. Wilson wasn't a highly regarded champion, especially after his beating by George Robinson, and the fight was proving to be a hard sell. There was certainly no great line standing before the box office pushing and pulling to get to the window for choice seats.

The most interesting fighter on the bill was Cyril Quinton Jr, better known as 'Panama' Joe Gans. He was a very gifted boxer but he was black and was ignored for world title fights so had to settle for winning the 'Coloured Middleweight Championship'. Rickard came close to dropping Gans because he was unable to find a suitable opponent who wouldn't draw the colour line but then the promoter heard about Mike's knockout of George Robinson in Montreal and the Irishman was offered the fight. Nobody gave Mike much of a chance but he battered Gans, coming close to scoring a stoppage in the seventh. It was the best performance of his career to date and the most lucrative – he got $4,000 for his end.

After the Gans fight Mike journeyed to the west coast for a return match with Battling Ortega. Ortega withdrew and Sailor Petrosky stepped into the breach, only to take a terrible beating in four one-sided rounds. The victory made Mike middleweight champion of the coast, a title that, according to Jack Farrell of the *New York Daily News*, 'had no more cash value than a cigar coupon at the New Garden box office'. Mike returned to Montreal, where he was to engage veteran light heavyweight Battling Levinsky in a ten-round contest at the Mount Royal Arena. Levinsky carried a twenty-five pound advantage into the ring and Mike couldn't overcome the handicap and lost the newspaper verdict. He then took on English middleweight Gus Platts in New York. Platts later wrote in the *Topical Times* that Mike was the only man to have scared him in the ring. 'He troubled me more than any of my other one hundred and ninety-nine opponents.'

Next up came the Buck Crouse mystery in Montreal. Mike was due to fight Buck Crouse, but not the original Buck Crouse, who lived in Pittsburgh and had already retired by that point. Bobby Saunders, the new Buck Crouse's handler, produced credentials to show that he and his fighter came from Philadelphia. 'We fought under the name of Young Buck Crouse for a number of years, this being the time when the old and original Buck Crouse of Philadelphia was fighting. When he retired, we dropped the Young and went by the name of Buck Crouse under which we have been fighting in Philadelphia and all through the state of Pennsylvania, and claim the middleweight title of that state.' Saunders denied any attempt at misrepresentation, all correspondence having been addressed from Philadelphia, and no claim being made that his fighter was the Pittsburgh Buck Crouse, though he and his fighter had lived in Pittsburgh for a time.

But whether it was the Crouse of Pittsburgh or the Crouse of Philadelphia, Buck came very close to becoming the first man to knock out Mike McTigue. In the second round Crouse caught his opponent with a short right just under the cheekbone that blinded the Irishman in one eye for the remainder of the fight. Mike admitted afterwards that had the punch landed two inches lower he'd have been out for the count. He had never been hit so hard and stumbled back to his corner at the end of the second. But Mike soon recovered and stopped Crouse just a few rounds later.

It had been a vicious, dirty fight and the customers were ready for more. A return was arranged just a few weeks later and it was a real grudge match. 'Crouse doesn't seem to like Michael worth a darn, despite the fact that Mike is a pretty likeable sort of chap,' reported the *Montreal Daily Star*. 'Crouse took a deep dislike to McTigue when they fought at the St Denis. His pride was considerably ruffled by the way the bout was terminated and he claimed he was given a raw deal. He was so peeved about it that he insisted on the return match being somewhere else than the St Denis … McTigue doesn't like Crouse because the Pennsylvania "mystery" came within an ace of knocking Mike for a goal in their first bout. Michael declares that if Crouse survives at all tonight, he'll never look human again.'

The much-discussed return followed an almost identical pattern to the first. In the opening round, as in the previous fight, Crouse rocked Mike with a hard left hook to the head then staggered him again with a right cross. It was a furious opening; they really didn't like each other. Mike hurt his right hand after mistiming a punch to his opponent's head and as the Irishman stepped back, instinctively shaking his hand to relieve the pain, Crouse stepped in with a left smash to the jaw.

This was Crouse's big chance. Mike was rocked back to the ropes as Crouse followed up with a hard right to the body. But the Irishman blocked the rest of the attack and just before the bell sounded he clipped Crouse with a short punch from the damaged right. Crouse's opportunity had gone. Half-way through the third Mike ripped into his opponent with both hands and the sheer volume of punches drove Crouse to his knees for a count of nine; yet, undaunted, he got up and took the offensive. Within a few seconds however, Mike sent in a right uppercut to the solar plexus that lifted Crouse off his feet. The bell sounded as the referee reached three but the damage was done and Crouse was still unsteady on his feet at the start of the fourth. Crouse was floored as the round got underway and took another count of nine. Courageously, he got up again only to be bowled over by a right hook to the body. Referee McKimmie had seen enough.

'"The pitcher that goes to the well too often", "history repeats", and a few other choice epigrams of disaster are probably echoing through the dome of "Buck" Crouse today, together with ringing in the ears and a blurring in the vision that you read about in the patent medicine advertisements,' wrote the *Montreal Daily Star*. 'Crouse just WOULD fight Mike McTigue again, despite the lacing he got from the Irishman at the St Denis two weeks ago, and last night at the Arena discovered that what Mike has done, Mike can do. This time, McTigue hammered Crouse to oblivion in the fourth round, and left no doubt about it.'

Mike's streak of knockout victories ensured he was in constant demand in Canadian fight halls. Jack Stone, a rangy, hard-hitting Jewish fighter with impressive knockout victories on his record, was Mike's third opponent in nine days. After a good deal of trouble Mike battered Stone down in the eighth round. According to the *Montreal*

Daily Star, 'fans go to see him get licked, and the anti-McTigues, who were out in force for the largest fistic crowd of the season, set up a terrific wail from the start last night when they saw it was not to be.' Mike made Stone's knees sag with a right cross in the first but for several rounds thereafter Stone tucked his jaw under a protective shoulder and kept his defence solid. In the third the house cheered after Stone managed to tag Mike with a couple of right hooks, but that was his only success. Stone's defence remained solid and Mike resorted to 'rabbit punching', hooks to the back of the neck, which finally weakened his opponent. In the eighth the Irishman shot through a rare opening to catch Stone on the top of his head. Stone bounced off the ropes, bleeding and unconscious, before hitting the canvas. The referee didn't bother counting.

His seconds held the middle rope down and Mike climbed through onto the apron that ran around the outside of the ring. The crowd was still yelling, but as he started down the short wooden steps the booing rose, dimly echoing around the arena. Mike forced a smile to his lips, opening up the dried cracks as his mouth curved.

One of the main reasons for the crowd's hostility towards Mike was the continuing feud with Jeff Smith and the customers were firmly on Smith's side. Both men claimed to be the middleweight champion of Canada and the row had taken up enough column inches to make the match a lucrative proposition. Smith's manager, Al Lippe, wrote to the papers after the Crouse bout that the fighter Mike had knocked out twice in as many weeks was an impostor by the name of Billy Kramar of Milwaukee, a man Lippe described as blind and decrepit. I don't think Mike McTigue has enough heart to box Jeff Smith again, as he will never forget the lacing he was forced to take in Halifax. In that battle McTigue tried to quit several times during the bout. On one occasion he laid down on the floor and tried to claim a foul when he was hit in the stomach. However, the referee, realizing he was trying to quit, forced him to get up and fight,' said Lippe. He denied that Mike had a cut eye or a damaged hand and said that the trouble was with his heart.

Lippe claimed that Smith had accepted five offers to fight Mike during the previous few months and that the Irishman ran out on every agreement. He also said Mike had sacked four managers because he was scared of Smith. The managers in question supported Lippe's argument and Miles O'Donnell, Tom O'Rourke, Harry Neary and Leo Flynn all claimed to have lost Mike because of the Smith fight. He certainly had a reputation for losing managers.

Mike once joked that he'd had so many managers, he was figuring on getting the boys together at the dinner table some evening to talk over old times. Throughout his career he had been managed, and occasionally mis-managed by Paddy Donnelly, John Kelly, Willie McDonald, Jack Moore, Leo Flynn, Dan Morgan, Tom O'Rourke, Myles O'Donnell, Paddy Mullins, Charley Rose, Ross Layton, Joe Jacobs, Dan Hickey, Paddy Breen, Cliff McCaffery, Doc Bagley and Jimmy Johnston.

Mike finished his Canadian tour of duty in Quebec City by defending his disputed title against Roddy McDonald. He scored his fifth straight knockout within two weeks. McDonald was knocked down for two counts of nine and then took the fatal ten. 'There is no doubt now that McTigue is the Babe Ruth of the boxing game for he is scoring as many knockouts in the boxing game as the great slugger scores in the baseball world,' wrote the *Montreal Daily Star*.

Before he left Canada to return to New York, Mike finally signed articles to fight Jeff Smith at the St Denis in Montreal. No date was stipulated but he was guaranteed $4,000 – the largest promised to a boxer in Montreal at that time. During the previous few months he had become the biggest box-office attraction in the city and his match with Jack Bloomfield attracted the largest gate pulled in Montreal at over $9,000. The fight with Smith was expected to beat that record. But then the biggest boxing promoter in the world wanted Mike's services and he returned to New York.

Mike's previous appearance on a Tex Rickard bill was his Labour Day victory over Panama Joe Gans. Rickard was sufficiently impressed to put Mike on at Madison Square Garden. After boxing in and around the city for seven years Mike would finally get to perform at the Garden. The obvious opponent for the Irishman was his nemesis, Jeff Smith, and Rickard easily outbid the St Denis in Montreal to get the fight.

Mike beat Smith in an uninteresting fifteen-round bout in front of the smallest crowd in the Garden that year, about 5000 spectators. He was given the decision because he was the aggressor throughout a fight in which both boxers missed repeatedly. 'McTigue, an awkward boxer in pose and action, missed miserably on numerous occasions with lusty rights,' wrote one ringside reporter. In every round after the fourth the crowd manifested its dissatisfaction with demonstrations of booing and hissing as the two boxers worked like a pair of novices.

'It went fifteen rounds, and to the best of my recollection, not a blow was struck,' wrote Bob Edgren. 'Side-stepping and back-pedalling were the features of the evening's entertainment and spectators who admired that kind of boxing had a lovely time, although they must have been much annoyed by the ribald remarks of those uncouth souls who wanted action.'

Before starting the eighth round Referee Jack Appel cautioned the boxers to put more zest into their efforts and the crowd cheered his admonition. 'The bout was one of the most unsatisfactory seen at the Garden this season,' reported the *New York Times*. 'Neither boxer exhibited any qualifications which would warrant serious consideration for either as a championship prospect. McTigue won beyond a question of a doubt, but his victory failed to impress.'

Although his long-awaited debut at the Garden ended in victory, it was a real setback for Mike. After years of fighting palookas in small clubs Mike had been given the biggest stage in boxing and had failed to impress. He was soon back in the blood buckets.

He was dealt another blow a few weeks later when he dislocated his left shoulder sparring with Jack Renault at Grupp's gymnasium in Harlem and was forced to cancel matches with Augie Ratner in Montreal and Joe Chip in Scranton. His shoulder hadn't really recovered by the time he fought Young Fisher at Syracuse and Mike lost the bout on points. He fought Fisher again a few weeks later at the Pioneer Athletic Club in New York and avenged his previous defeat by hammering his way to victory. Mike took eleven of the fifteen rounds and floored Fisher four times.

Mike drew with Lou Bogash at the Commonwealth Club in New York and was then matched with a young fighter called Tommy Loughran in Scranton. Loughran was a nineteen-year-old from Philadelphia who had spent thousands of hours in his basement teaching himself to box in front of a mirror. It was a no-decision fight and the newspapermen were split on the outcome but Mike knew who'd won. 'Kid, you licked me tonight, regardless of what the papers say about it. Take care of yourself and some day you will be world champion,' he said in the dressing rooms afterwards. Little did the Irishman realise when he made the prophecy in the dressing room after an eight-round bout in Philadelphia in 1922 that such a thing would eventually come to pass at his expense.

But in the spring of 1922 Mike wasn't thinking about world

championships. Fighters over a decade younger than Mike were now beating him and surely his time had come and gone. Mike was chasing money not titles, and he figured that the novelty of a returning fighter might attract better purses in Europe. He also figured, correctly, that there was easier game on the other side of the trench. A young unknown newspaper reporter once wrote of 'champion' prizefighters who were preliminary boys before they crossed the ocean. 'The only rule seems to be that you must choose to be a champion of some very distant country and then stay away from that country,' wrote Ernest Hemingway for the *Toronto Star Weekly* on 25 March 1922.

So with a respectable record in America and a claim to the Canadian middleweight championship Mike managed to secure three fights in Sheffield in the winter of 1922. The 'youthful' thirty-one year-old (he was actually thirty-nine) made short work of them all: Johnny Basham was knocked out in three rounds, Charlie Penwill in the first and Harry Knight, a much taller and heavier man, suffered a similar fate in the fourth.

Mike pummelled Knight's midsection until the Londoner left his jaw uncovered for the first time and the Irishman promptly smashed his right onto the spot. Knight went down for the count of nine. He arose full of fight and managed to hit Mike before another right sent him down again for a count of nine after which he could barely stand and was easily persuaded to retire. But these were not top-flight opponents and the London promoters ignored Mike's claims for a big fight, just as their counterparts in New York had for the best part of a decade. 'You don't seem to bear many marks of your hard work; on the contrary you look as if you have given up the game,' remarked one reporter.

Mike smiled and said, 'Well, it's like this. I've been busy looking for work since I arrived, and probably if I stay much longer, I'll be counted as good as out of the game. 'My real intention of coming to England was to meet some of the top-notchers: Carpentier, Beckett, Lewis, etc. But they all seemed to steer clear, or demand the impossible. The English public, where boxing is concerned, is all right, but their boxers are nowhere. Their champions are what we call on the other side "cheese champions"; they want to have the fight won before they enter the ring.

'Considering that I am Irish, I hold that I have a better right to challenge the holder of a British championship than any foreigner. Yet, I have been sidestepped at every turn round. Perhaps it is because I have beaten everybody of my weight and heavier in the world – no colour line drawn.'

But British boxing writers regarded him as a foreigner and took issue with his constant criticism of their champions. *Boxing* publicly rebuked him for tainting the sportsmen of England with what it regarded as unsporting methods from across the Atlantic:

This gentleman, with all Sheffield to back him, has already given tongue, and in the unkindest fashion possible he has been hurling defiance at 'the three cheese champions', Joe Beckett, Jack Bloomfield, and Ted 'Kid' Lewis, as he impolitely terms them. Mike has been making defiant and aggressive noises designed to attract the attention of the trio in question for quite a while now, but we are far from sure that he is wise in attempting this American policy here. It goes all right in the States, but is calculated to cut little ice in British circles. The fault, dear Mike, does not lie with the men you have challenged. They would doubtless be quite willing to engage you in combat – Jack Bloomfield especially, were promoters as eager to oblige as you are yourself, but unfortunately the three victories you have won so far, clean-cut though they have been, have yet been insufficient to start a general buzz round your name. Mike must reflect that it is by no means easy even for a British boxer with a fairly decent home record, established some years since, to return bearing American sheaves, to secure a home rating on his Transatlantic record. There is no reason why McTigue should command recognition on his American feats. One can only hope for Mike's own sake that he will escape from the string of annoyances and buffets from Dame Fortune.

SEVEN

In Battling Siki he saw easy game – if he could be inveigled into accepting a bout for the title. The innocent child of the African jungle fell for the proposition.

Boxing

Battling Siki escaped his managers just before the boat train pulled out of Gare Saint-Lazare. The world champion jumped back onto the platform declaring it useless to go to Dublin as he had been badly injured in a taxi accident. He disappeared into the city. But Siki wasn't a difficult man to find and he was soon spotted carousing along the boulevards with friends. The Battler insisted he was badly crippled but his seconds examined him without finding more than 'an insignificant scratch on his left leg'. Siki told friends that he feared he would not be permitted to land at Cobh but would be compelled to continue on to New York from where he would be sent back to France on account of not having the necessary passports.

Brouillet and Singleton tried to get their charge on his way the following morning, 1 March 1923, but by now Siki had convinced himself that once in Ireland he would not be allowed back into France and that the British authorities were going to catch him. Siki was taken from the station to a nearby hotel but fled during the night and was later found at home with his wife. He was corralled and a guard placed at his door. The next day a strong corps of care-takers accompanied him to the station where he was 'plied freely with copious drafts of the cup that cheers'. Siki awoke the following morning to find himself in Cherbourg awaiting the boat to Ireland.

A French newspaper carried a story that the Dublin promoters were so fearful of Siki crying off at the last minute, they'd sent a 'second guardian angel', Jim Harris, to look after the world champion. Harris claimed to harbour no such fear and that a 'misconstruction' had been placed on the presence of Tom Singleton in Paris who was in the city under the terms of the contract that called for the promoters to provide transportation and act as escort for Siki's party all the way to Dublin. There was 'no question of keeping Siki under observation in Paris' he added.

By this time Siki was being guarded by at least four men at all times and was constantly becalmed with alcohol. But by the time the party reached Cherbourg, Siki had found an unlikely accomplice in his efforts to stay in France. The shipping company that owned the vessel on which he was to have taken passage informed Jim Harris that it would only allow the party on board if the British government permitted the Senegalese boxer to disembark on British soil. But Siki was barred from landing in England and the ban also held good on any British ship. The promoters were left with four ways of getting the champion to Ireland: French liner, American liner, by aeroplane or by French fishing boat. The *Weekly Dispatch* sent a correspondent to Cherbourg to check on Siki's progress. The bulletin read:

Today he lunched with the airman, Manyerol, who is at Cherbourg awaiting a favourable opportunity to renew his attempts to create a new glider record.

Siki's entourage are nervous that when tomorrow dawns the Senegalese boxer, who complains bitterly that he has forcibly been dragged away from the company of his three pet dogs, who have been left in a veterinary establishment in Paris, may decline to embark for Ireland. The Senegalese also declares that he does not want to fight anyone else until he has again met Carpentier.

The newspapers in Dublin on Friday 2 March 1923 announced that the fight was off. However, a writer from the *Evening Herald* called at the promoters' Suffolk Street offices to be informed that Siki was still expected on time and that the fight would go ahead. Tom Singleton had been in communication with the Home Office ministry in Dublin and had long since accepted that the English route was out of bounds and that the most likely option was an American boat from Cherbourg sailing directly to a port in Ireland, probably Cobh. The promoters claimed stories of the fight being in difficulty were circulated with mischievous intent because of 'anti-Siki jealousy and other reasons'. If this was the intention, then it worked. There was a dramatic slump in business at the booking office, which had been very brisk up to that point.

But so confident was Tom Singleton that the big fight would go ahead he was already planning to bring the much-talked-about rematch between Siki and Georges Carpentier to Dublin later that summer. *Le Matin* was no longer willing to organise the event because both boxers had reneged on the original agreement to settle the issue in the ring and without profit. Now they wanted a percentage of the gate before they would agree to meet in the ring. On hearing the news the Dublin syndicate announced it was ready to put up £10,000 for the match to be staged in Ireland.

The promoters were also buoyed on hearing the news that Mike, his trainer Charlie Brennan and sparring partners Bartley Madden, Billy Mack and Philip Welch were on the mail boat from Holyhead to Dún Laoghaire on the afternoon of 2 March.

A large crowd assembled on Carlisle Pier and they recognised the fighter as soon as the boat came alongside. Dressed in a chrome leather storm coat and a light felt hat Mike's demeanour, according to one writer, 'suggested very little of the accepted idea of the professional pugilist'. When the gangways were placed from the mail boat to the pier a little dark-eyed girl, dressed in a traditional Irish costume and saffron kilt boarded the steamer. Sheila Clarke-Barry, the daughter of a well-known Dublin musician stepped up to the boxer, bid him welcome and presented him with a box of shamrock.

Mike laughed as he extended his arms and submitted to the body search along with all the other male passengers arriving at Carlisle Pier. He then obliged the large deputation of press photographers before entering a reserved compartment on the train. The party spent the evening at the Standard Hotel in Harcourt Street where Mike entertained a group of Dublin journalists. He was especially keen to contradict a statement attributed to him that he was born in England and claimed to be an Irishman through and through. 'People here, allude to me as an Irish-American,' said Mike. 'Now, in America I have always been called an Irishman, and it's only when I come to my own country that I am spoken of as Irish-American. I was born in Ennis, and my mother and father are both Irish.'

'Is Siki as great a man as they say?' asked one reporter.

'I can't tell,' replied Mike, 'we will find out on the seventeenth of March! I am confident that I will beat Siki. He may have beaten a great many boxers, including French and Englishmen, but when he meets a real Irishman, he will find out he is up against something.'

The following day Mike, Charlie Brennan and Phil Welch spent the afternoon at the Leopardstown races as guests of the press. They were accompanied by the well-known jockey Johnny Dines and Gertrude Gaffney of the *Irish Independent*, who was suitably impressed by the boxer:

McTIGUE RACE-GOER

LEOPARDSTOWN IN MARCH

(from our Lady Correspondent)

The subject and object of general interest at Leopardstown on Saturday, apart from the sport of the day, was Mike McTigue. The young Irish boxer experienced his first Irish race meeting since he was a lad in Clare and 'put on his bit' at Miltown-Malbay. I wager he hasn't seen mud like that he sank in the paddock, outside his own country. It was of a brand peculiar to our land, and fatal to elegant footwear.

McTigue submitted to be interviewed and filmed with good grace. He speaks with just the faintest trace of an American twang, and strikes one as being much more cosmopolitan than either Irish or American, though he has a typically native face. It seems to me that Carpentier's feminine fragility will give way in fashion before our own man's lithe muscularity.

McTigue is six feet or thereabouts of the purest brawn and the handsomest look that any sentimental public could demand. He has an Irish wife, too. At all events, in spite of the mud and the nipping wind, he was enjoying Leopardstown. He said it was 'fine'. And that fine went the whole hog in enthusiasm.

Meanwhile, Siki was battling with life on board the *President Adams*. He was accompanied by his wife, sparring partner Stuber, manager Brouillet and the promoter Tom Singleton. The full, sensational story of the voyage from Cherbourg to Cobh appeared in the *New York Herald* several weeks later after members of the *President Adams'* crew spoke to reporters on their arrival from Ireland in the United States. They confirmed the story that Siki had disappeared four days before the ship was due to sail and also alleged that he assaulted his wife and had to be carried on board.

An even more lurid account appeared in the *Chicago Tribune*. The newspaper claimed that 'six stevedores roped him and dragged him on board, but after he had broken the cabin furniture and needed refreshment and asked for liquor he learned the dreadful news that he was on a dry ship. His spirit broke.' The latter part of the story certainly wasn't true. He asked for wine, which wasn't available, but was offered whiskey, which sustained him for the rest of the voyage. The sailors said Siki left the boat peaceably along with his wife, sparring partner Stuber, manager Brouillet and Tom Singleton.

Mr Gordon Lewis, head operator of the Irish branch of the Pathé Company, left Dublin with his camera and assistant on Sunday evening at 7.30 pm to film the world champion's arrival in Cobh. It was a beautiful moonlit night, the roads were good and all went well until they reached Tipperary. They lost their way not far from Cahir and eventually came to a military post where they were held up and asked from where they came. Believing they had left Cahir behind they spoke of passing through the town en route to Cork.

But Lewis and his assistant had inadvertently found their way back onto the road leading into Cahir from Tipperary and having aroused the suspicion of the troops they were taken before an officer whom they eventually satisfied by 'a long explanation and proof'.

They were allowed back on their way but detours owing to broken bridges had to be made, then they were fired upon by irregulars from the Galtees when nearing Michelstown and crashed over a trench when going at close to 40 mph. According to Lewis, only a set of powerful headlights saved the party from crashing into a deeper trench. Once they got to Fermoy the car was battered by heavy rain and they finally reached Cobh at 8.30 am on Monday morning – just in time to see the *President Adams* docking in the harbour.

The voyage had taken fourteen hours over a rough sea but Siki told awaiting pressmen that he had not been seasick. An enthusiastic crowd greeted the world champion's landing and an admirer presented him with a blackthorn stick. The party spent a few hours walking through Cobh and according to the *Cork Examiner*, 'they were the centre of a good deal of attention by the townspeople. And the National soldiers seemed to be especially interested.'

They left Cobh in two reserved firsts on the morning mail that left for Dublin at 11.25 a.m. For much of the journey Siki took a keen interest in the broken bridges and damaged buildings that dotted the line. Tom Singleton told a pressman that the party was thoroughly tired after the journey. He said that Siki had done some training on the boat and boxed a few rounds with his sparring partner as well as working on a punch ball. Singleton said they'd had a great reception in Cork and at every station on the way up, people crowded around the carriage and gave them 'a real Irish welcome'.

The train was stopped in Charleville where all the passengers were ordered off by National Army soldiers to be searched. The troops left Siki's party alone once their identity was established. But one of the soldiers saw an opportunity and with a 'serious and business-like air', he stepped towards Siki and felt the boxer's biceps on the pretence of searching for 'arms'. Siki flexed his muscles and enjoyed the joke. He cut a striking figure as he readily posed for photographers; when he walked he swayed slightly from the hips up in the characteristic manner of a boxer while the movements of his arms and shoulders further betrayed his calling.

Just a few hours after Siki's train had passed the point between Maryborough and Mountrath on the main Dublin-to-Cork line, a goods train was derailed blocking both up and down lines. This was the third attack on this section of the line. The early trains left both Dublin and Cork on time but passengers were held up for many hours at the point of the break as they were transferred to trains on either side.

After a long and exhausting journey the train arrived on the platform at Kingsbridge Station, Dublin on time at 7.30 pm Siki could be seen through the window as he stood up to don his overcoat and there was a rush to his reserved compartment. The crowd cheered as the world champion paused in the doorway and waved to the mob before stepping onto the platform. He was immediately surrounded by well-wishers who tried to shake his hand, clap him on the back or just catch a glimpse of his face.

Eventually Siki managed to work his way to the waiting cars but then the more enthusiastic members of the crowd climbed onto the footboards and flattened their faces against the windows. Siki seemed to enjoy it greatly and appeared to be in good humour. 'Neither his photographs nor the cinema do him justice for the expression on his good-humoured face is much kindlier and more pleasant than his pictures would lead one to believe,' commented the *Evening Herald*. The *Irish Independent* quoted the opinion of a leading medical authority to the effect that Siki was 'anatomically perfect'.

The party drove to the booking offices at 24 Suffolk Street where a large crowd of curious sightseers had gathered outside and accorded

Siki a genial cheer as he drove off, after about half-an-hour's delay, to the Claremont Hotel, Howth. One wag in the crowd shouted, 'Good luck, sport; may you barely lose.' When asked of his boxer's condition, Siki's manager Brouillet said he was in splendid form. 'He never says much before a fight, but he is always confident. Oh yes, he is confident.' Brouillet offered to bet even money on his man's victory.

Howth was a favourite spot for boxers preparing for a fight and much was made of the benefits of breathing in the ozone-laden air. The steep stretches on the paths around the head were ideal for roadwork and the scenery helped relieve the tedium of training. It also kept Siki away from the war. A room at the Claremont was adapted into a gymnasium complete with punch balls and exercise equipment with a great mirror standing against a wall at one end. At dinner that evening Siki made a speech in which he claimed to be charmed and delighted by the welcome in Ireland.

But not everybody welcomed the boxers and Mike received a death threat on the day after his arrival. It wasn't reported in the Irish press of course but the *New York Times* informed its readers, somewhat speculatively, that 'the Black and Tans overran the country and they flatly told Mike that they'd shoot him if he went through with the match ... the Sinn Féiners told him the same thing.'

When Kevin O'Higgins was asked if the government had any intention of prohibiting the fight he said that he did not feel called upon to interfere and there was no question of stopping the event. Higgins was actually desperate for the fight to go ahead. Newspapers from around the world were sending reporters and it was crucial for his regime's credibility that it could provide the necessary security for such an internationally significant event in Dublin. The way in which the war had developed from the time of Collins' death, with National Army troops defending the towns and cities from a 'lawless countryside', seemed to justify the 'protective' ideas of the pro-Treaty leadership. But by September 1922, the image of a 'fallen society' was more than just a rhetorical device utilised by the Provisional government; the issue was, as Patrick Hogan described, one of anarchy against order.

> Our position now is that the effective Irregular war has definitely taken the form of a war by different sections, different interests, and different individuals, with no common basis except this – that all have a vested interest in chaos, in bringing about a state of affairs where force is substituted for law. Not only is there a variety of interests and motives, but there is a variety of methods. Houses and farms are burned in a wages dispute; men are shot in a similar dispute; haggards are burned in a land dispute, and men are murdered in a similar dispute; trains are attacked; post offices robbed; banks raided; individuals robbed without patriotic pretences or in the name of the Republic, men are murdered for personal reasons or in the name of the Republic and so on.

Siki was also threatened with death, but nobody told him. Troops were stationed at his hotel and no one was permitted to see the boxer without a permit from his manager, Brouillet. 'This precaution is said to have been taken in consequence of certain information which had reached the authorities,' the *New York Times* reported. Several English newspapers printed a story that attempts had been made to pirate the cinema rights to the fight, which were the property of Pathé Frères, and that the Claremont was under the protection of the civic guard to keep prying cameramen away. So under the watchful eye of a small platoon of soldiers, Siki awoke at 7.30 am on his first morning in Ireland and, accompanied by his training partners, went for a forty-minute walk around Howth Head. The heather was in full bloom and the air was clear. After a bath and massage he took a coffee and then rested until the afternoon when he went for a ten-mile run up and down the Hill of Howth. Dan Murphy, the Dublin physical culture expert and trainer, then gave Siki a massage before the champion indulged in gym work under the supervision of Brouillet who was both his manager and trainer. Siki spent a few hours skipping, shadow boxing, exercising and wrestling. He enjoyed his first day in Dublin and expressed himself 'very pleased' with the views of Howth from his window, particularly Ireland's Eye, that he could see across a sunlit sea. 'Siki has an eye for the beautiful, and in many ways is quite an admirable fellow,' commented the *Evening Herald*.

At the exact hour that Siki was enjoying the splendour of Dublin Bay, five National Army troops were lured to their deaths in an elaborate trap that led to a trigger-mine at an arms dump at Knocknagashel, Castleisland, County Kerry. The main target of the operation was Lieutenant Paddy 'Pats' O'Connor, who had a reputation for torturing republican prisoners. That afternoon the following dispatch was issued:

Field General Headquarters,
Kerry Command,
Tralee,
March 6th, 1923

To all Officers of the Kerry Command.
    All officers and men in the Command are notified that, in the event of their encountering any obstacles, such as stone barricades, and also dugouts or dumps, they are not

to interfere with same. The officer or NCO in charge should immediately proceed to the nearest detention barracks and bring with him a sufficient number of Irregular prisoners to remove same.

The tragedy of Knocknagashel must not be repeated, and serious disciplinary action will be taken against any officer who endangers the lives of his men in the removal of such barricades, etc.

Since the Four Courts fight, mines have been used indiscriminately by the Irregulars. The taking out of prisoners is not to be regarded as a reprisal, but as the only alternative left to prevent the wholesale slaughter of our men.

(Signed) P. UA DÁLAIGH,

Major-General,

GOC Kerry Command

The following day nine IRA prisoners, one with a broken arm another with a fractured wrist and one crippled by spinal injuries as a result of being tortured, were taken by lorry to a country wood near Ballyseedy. They were bound with ropes, tied together to a log and blown to pieces by a mine. Body parts were strewn over a wide area and there were stories of birds eating human flesh off the trees. Miraculously one man was blown clear into a ditch and managed to escape to tell the tale. Five other prisoners were killed the same way in Cahirciveen just five days later; only this time they were shot in the legs to prevent any escape. Another bloody cycle of outrage and reprisal was set in motion.

On the stroke of 6 am on Wednesday 7 March a terrific explosion was heard throughout Dublin. A large mine had been detonated outside a block of buildings in front of the ruined Custom House.

A CID officer, PJ Kelly, was on the premises and was killed in the blast. The block included the headquarters of Customs and Excise and part of the Colonial Parcels Office. Armed CID officers stopped and searched all vehicles passing through the area for the remainder of the day. According to a special cable to the *New York Times*, 'a sickening sensation pervaded the city all day. Never had so much military activity been observed, with lorries of soldiers flying in all directions, the occupants armed with rifles, revolvers and machine guns.' A raid on the printers of Poblacht na hÉireann in a house in Fairview later that afternoon uncovered a document the authorities claimed revealed the extent of the threat to the Free State.

> To meet the desperate and barbarous methods being adopted by the enemy to destroy the government, the republican army's general headquarters has decided to amend and in some cases make more drastic, action ordered in recent general orders to commandants.
>
> Some of these orders have been cancelled and the action directed in them embodied in a new order which will come into operation if any further executions by the enemy are carried out in this area after this date.

Included on the list of those liable to be shot on sight were members of the Free State government, army officers of all ranks, legal advisors and the 'proprietors and directors of the hostile press in Ireland and the senior officials employed by the same, such as editors, sub-editors and leader writers, in cases where it is known that those officials are hostile'.

The big fight was a welcome distraction for the city's pressmen. They got their first chance to see Siki in action at an exhibition for their benefit at the Claremont just a few hours after the explosion had rocked the city. He made quite an entrance. Dressed in green tights that ran over his shoulders over which he wore a white loincloth, Siki and his sparring partner, Stuber, moved to the centre of the red carpet and the quiet was broken by the dull thud of leather on flesh. 'He is quick as a cat and as boneless,' wrote Gertrude Gaffney. 'His joints might be made of India rubber for all the indication of their presence they give. He is slippery as an eel. He has no corners or angles. As one man remarked to me, he hasn't even a nose that could stop a blow; there isn't a ghost of a bridge visible.'

After they finished three hard rounds Stuber's hair was drenched while Siki's skin was covered in a gossamer of sweat. But with barely a moment to recover the champion was on the ground, on the flat of his back, the timekeeper counting his exercises rhythmically.

Mike was closeted away in the sanctity of the Spa Hotel in Lucan. The building was part of the Sarsfield Estate and built to commemorate the legendary Irish cavalry commander, Patrick Sarsfield. 'The Clareman has made himself a great favourite with all classes,' reported the *Irish Independent*. 'He has made many friends in high professional circles in Dublin and they are taking the keenest interest in him and his doings.'

Mike told reporters that he planned to do very little roadwork in Dublin because 'too much foot-slugging has often caused a man to leave the fight behind him. I never enter the ring musclebound, over-trained and slack; if one is to win one must feel in anticipation the joy of the battle.' Mike had already been in training for a minor fight in England so he was in condition by the time he arrived in Dublin. During his stay in Lucan he would rise at 7 am and take a short walk before a breakfast that would consist of a little fruit, bacon, eggs and toast. After a short break he'd play a round of golf and by 12.30 pm he was ready for a meal of fish, steak or chops with raw vegetables. He rested until 3 pm when he donned the gloves for bag-punching, shadow-boxing and fifteen rounds of sparring with his partners and any other men they could find. The day's activities ended with some skipping and an exercise regime followed by another light meal in the evening after which Mike would work on his scrapbook, write letters, play music and then go to bed as early as possible.

'I am no faddist in any way; I have nothing special to recommend to anybody,' Mike told reporters. 'I have no secrets to divulge nor tips to give. My advice is to live a healthy, outdoor life, be sparing at the table, take as much exercise as possible, and eat what agrees with you. It has always suited me best to take my principal heavy meal in the middle of the day.'

When it became known that Mike was a gifted runner James Keays of Pallasgreen, County Limerick, challenged to race him from a hundred to two hundred yards for any amount up to £100. Mike claimed to be 'not far from being a champion sprinter', although Keays' challenge was not taken up. 'I will take on anybody, except a professional sprinting champion at a hundred to two hundred and twenty yards. I am pretty useful over these journeys and they flatter my vanity by telling me that, if I had not devoted myself to boxing, I would have made a Sheffield handicap certainly; but maybe they are pulling the wool over my eyes.'

Mike and Battling Siki went to the Dundrum races on the Sunday before the fight. As the fighters were mingling in the paddock, three British Navy ships approached Dublin Bay. The cruiser *Castor* and two destroyers, HMS *Wolfhound* and HMS *Viceroy* came into the Liffey under 'sealed orders'; their ports of departure were not quoted. The ships were carrying over three hundred prisoners who had been rounded up in raids in London, Liverpool, Glasgow, Manchester,

Bootle, Birmingham and St Helens over the weekend. They were kept below decks until 3.00 am on Monday morning when they were transferred by charabang, escorted by armoured cars, to Mountjoy Jail. The prisoners were suspected of gunrunning and various activities directed against the Free State government.

In that morning's *Irish Independent* 'An Irish Catholic' wrote from Manchester to complain that the fight was to be staged on the feast of the Patron Saint of Ireland and 'more a Sunday than Sunday itself! Can Ireland have deteriorated so much that the taboo of Paris and London is received with open arms in Dublin on St Patrick's Day, a day known all over the world better than any other in the calendar?'

A few days later, the *Weekly Dispatch* carried a reply to the religious hostility towards the big fight: 'I do not regard seriously the talk about clerical opposition or the 'desecration of St Patrick's,' wrote 'The Corner Man'. 'You may stop anything in Ireland but a fight, and I know that the promoters consider that they overcame the biggest obstacle when they got Siki to Ireland.'

And the promoters were determined to capitalise on their achievement. They booked the Rotunda and charged the public for the privilege of watching the two fighters prepare for the big event.

MEN IN TRAINING AT THE ROTUNDA
DAILY 3 TO 4 p.m.
Siki shows: Saturday, Monday and Thursday
McTigue shows: Tuesday and Wednesday
Each will give a display of his training methods Boxing,
skipping, physical exercise etc.
Admission 1/-, 2/-, 3/- (including tax)

The advertisement caused great interest because the low admission costs of 1s to 3s allowed Dubliners who could never hope to pay the price of a ticket to the actual fight to see the boxers. Over a thousand turned up to watch Siki's first performance and the world champion outdrew every picture house in the city. His demonstration lasted an hour, starting with a little skipping and shadow boxing and then a few rounds with his sparring partners. Stuber, who was champion of the French army, was up first, followed by the welterweight, Mike Ronan. He finished up with a sharp rally with Dan Voyles, another heavyweight. Siki then put on a wrestling show and an exercise routine to finish. 'Siki's display was very pleasing for the spectators, who did not withhold with merited applause,' commented the *Irish Independent*. 'In perfect good humour throughout, Siki obviously revelled in his work.'

The hardened boxing scribes were not so impressed. 'We know that he ducks, crouches, and performs corybantic evolutions in the ring, and we have the evidence of Carpentier's hands to convince us that he is easier to hit on the top of the head than on the softer sections of the body,' wrote the correspondent from *Boxing*. 'Yet there can be no doubt that he did a lot of execution on Carpentier, reducing that hero to a state of pulp, which Dempsey failed to do. McTigue, for all we have heard, is an upstanding boxer, a man who can shoot in a good straight left and whose right cross is a blow which calls for bated breath in description. But if Siki goes swaying across the ring, sweeping the floor with his front hair and slinging punches from all angles, it is not impossible that Mike may break his knuckles on the negro's head and find his own strength and stamina severely sapped by the negro's body blows. In that case McTigue may meet trouble in the ring and Siki may meet with it later on. In which event it is on the cards that the referee – whoever has taken on the job – may find himself in equally hot water. But then the man who would venture on any prophecy as to Irish events is entitled to medals for recklessness.'

The following day, Tuesday 13 March, news reached Dublin of the executions of two republican prisoners in Mullingar. Henry Keenan of Newcastle, County Down, and Michael Greery of Athenry, had been found guilty of participating in an armed raid on banks in Oldcastle, County Meath and of being in possession of £400. This was quickly followed by an official communiqué from Army Headquarters confirming the execution of James O'Rourke of 1 Upper Gloucester St, Dublin at 8 am that morning. O'Rourke was shot for his part in an attack on National Army members in Jury's Hotel on Dame Street in February and with having in his possession, without proper authority, a Webley .45 revolver and thirteen rounds of ammunition. It signalled the Free State government's return to a policy of uncompromising severity against rebels convicted of bearing arms or participating in acts of violence.

But fear of republican reprisals did little to quell the public's enthusiasm to get its first sight of Mike McTigue in action at the Rotunda that afternoon. Such was the demand for tickets that representations were made by the promoters to allow more people in, but this was refused because of a Corporation By-Law necessitating that the passages and exits of the building had to be kept clear.

One of Mike's sparring partners was Eddie Eagan, a Rhodes Scholar who became the first American to win the British Empire amateur heavyweight title while at Oxford. 'It was my first visit to the land of my father's forbears,' Eagan recalled. 'I liked the brilliant green countryside and its people, though I thought them a race more mournful than merry.'

It was certainly a day for mourning. There had been a feeling among the populace that the executions had ceased so the morning's developments came as a great shock, accentuated hourly as the news arrived in the city of further executions in Cork and Wexford. The shooting of William Healy for his role in the attempted destruction of the house of Michael Collins' sister was the first execution in Cork since the arrival of the feared RIC reserve force, the Black and Tans, who had been hastily drafted in from Britain to bolster the beleaguered police force. James Parle, Patrick Hogan and John Creane were the first men to receive the death sentence in Wexford since the war began. By the time Mike McTigue had finished his exhibition in the Rotunda the death toll from the executions had reached seven. The following day the war and the fight became inextricably linked with a proclamation from the republican government.

Government of the Republic of Ireland Proclamation
(English Translation)

In view of the present national tragedy caused by Britain's threat of war and the yielding thereto of certain Irishmen who have allowed themselves to be used by an alien power in an effort to coerce by arms loyal citizens of the Republic to abandon the Republic, to give allegiance to an alien king and to acquiesce in the partition of our country and the sub-version of its independence.

In view further of the murders of distinguished patriot soldiers taken prisoners in war and the daily violation of the usages of war by the torture and ill-treatment of republican prisoners and their 'execution' in large numbers for the supposed offence of being taken with arms in their hands.

And in consideration for their bereaved families and relatives and for the many thousands of republican prisoners unlawfully imprisoned and for their dependents and the poor generally who are suffering, and in order to direct public attention to these and to the national sorrows and to the many crimes disgraceful to the name of Ireland committed in the interests of the British Crown by deluded Irishman.

It is hereby decreed that until further notice the present be observed as a time of national mourning, that all sports and amusements be suspended, that all theatres, picture houses and other places of amusement and resort be closed, and in particular that all horse racing, hunting, coursing and all outdoor sports be discontinued.

Dated this 14th day of March, 1923

PADRAIG O'RUITLÉIS, Minister for Home Affairs

A bloody night on the streets of Dublin followed. Two National Army soldiers were shot dead, one near Mountjoy Jail and the other at Charlemont Bridge. Private Henry Kavanagh, stationed at Portobello Barracks, was unarmed and returning to barracks after a night in the cinema when he was accosted by two men near Charlemont Street Bridge at 10.45 pm. Kavanagh was found dying on the canal bank by a woman who lived locally. He'd been shot through the mouth. Fifteen minutes later Corporal Donald McGuiness, in charge of the Glengariff Parade near Mountjoy Prison, left his post to search three men loitering in the area. As he approached them, one drew a revolver and shot McGuiness through the heart at point-blank range.

The following morning, after a day of carnage, the authorities decided it was business as usual. The decision was taken at midnight that all places of amusement would remain open on Friday night and that the fight would go ahead as planned on Saturday.

The government forbade the publication of the proclamation and it did not appear in any of the Irish newspapers. Mike got a letter threatening to kidnap him in the morning mail. The Free State authorities sent a guard to Lucan but Mike, 'quite sure he would come to no harm, sent him back again'. But there were journalists from around the world in the city, many of whom managed to get the story back to their newsrooms. One American newspaper reported that, 'from the moment Eamon de Valera, through the republican self-styled Minister of Home Affairs, had decreed an indefinite period of national mourning 'in view of the murder' of prisoners of war and bereavement of the families of men recently executed, Dublin had been at a high pitch of excitement. Theatres and moving picture houses had been closed for a day and then reopened and promoters of one of the greatest matches ever staged in Ireland had announced that they would ignore the rebel ban, which was directed particularly at the fight, and put on the bout.'

In a special cable to the *New York Times*, the newspaper's correspondent wrote that 'theatres and movies in Dublin were closed this evening as a result of the republican proclamation of mourning for yesterday's executions. Free State troops visited all the places later and ordered them to open again. Large crowds watched the operations but no performances were given, except in the Abbey Theatre where the military guard remained during the performance. The O'Mara Opera Company at the Gaiety Theatre did not attend.'

'There is one curious side of de Valera's threat,' commented *Time* magazine: 'Any Irishman should have known that it was manifestly absurd to deprive the nation of their traditional joy on St Patrick's Day, no matter what might be the political or economic exigencies. Again, when framing the 'order,' de Valera must have known that he could not possibly enforce it. The cause of this bravado seems somehow lost in its effect.'

Following the proclamation troops were dispatched to guard

public buildings and patrol the streets where they stopped and searched passing vehicles and examined citizens for weapons. The Free State government ordered all theatres to open and the terrified managers of 'amusement resorts' were bound to comply. The Dublin correspondent of the *Daily Sketch* wrote that 'tonight lights everywhere were blazing, but the audiences were sparse in the theatres, moving-picture houses and other places'. The manager of the La Scala refused to comply with the military command at first because of mysteriously delivered threats to blow up the theatre if it was opened.

Similar threats were made to the fight promoters but they remained determined to hold the contest. The La Scala was closed to the public on the Thursday preceding the fight and CID officers took possession of the building. 'The management refrain from offering any explanation,' reported the *Sporting Chronicle*, 'but pointed out that it was general knowledge that republicans had issued a proclamation closing all places of public amusement and banning all sport forthwith in consequence of the execution of republican prisoners. The premises were to remain guarded until after the fight.'

The promoters received over three hundred applications for press tickets from Great Britain, Europe and the United States. Many had arrived in Dublin a few days before the fight and were clearly amazed at the events unfolding in the city. While the Irish press carried stories about training regimes, fighting styles and the briskness of ticket sales, the boxing writers from overseas were more concerned with death threats, censorship and bombings. According to *Boxing*:

Siki is a brave man. He proved that he was in the war, but we are certain that he has never done and will never engage in a braver or a more reckless enterprise. He must already have had its multifarious dangers impressed upon him by the presence of the armed guard which surrounds his hotel in Dublin. That armed guard gives one to think. If the Free State Authorities are so careful of Siki's safety already, one can but anticipate the establishment of super-precautions next Saturday. Can any more be taken?

Irishmen, we know, experience little difficulty in picking quarrels at any time, but it is difficult to conceive of any quarrel they can have with Siki at the present moment. One would imagine that Free Staters and republicans alike would be so keen on the winning of the world's cruiserweight [light heavyweight] title by an Irishman that neither side would venture on any action which would deprive McTigue of all chance of embarking on the adventure. On the other hand, if Siki happens to win we can well believe that the 'broth of bhoys' might be tempted to display resentment. One wonders whether the Free State government has fully visualised this contingency.

It is a highly possible one. More especially since one of our representatives was informed by a fervid 'patriot' the other day, that he (the said 'patriot') didn't know on which side, or for which cause, he was fighting, but that he was satisfied they were sure to win. Neither Siki, McTigue or anyone else associated with the promotion of this contest may have contemplated the inclusion of this brand of partisanship among the disputes of Ireland, nor may they have allowed for the potential effervescences of men who are not pausing to consider whom they are fighting against or why they are fighting at all, but when such a spirit is abroad it is quite conceivable that some hero may imagine that a bomb thrown at Siki may be a gallant blow struck for the independence of Ould Oireland.

Still, it was business as usual as far as the promoters were concerned. Bookings for the big fight were reported to be very brisk in the case of the cheaper seats, which could have been sold twice over. There was no great rush for the dearer seats. The famous promoter Major Arnold Wilson led a large deputation of sportsmen, including the referee for the contest, Jack Smith, from London on Thursday night. Before departing for Dublin, Wilson told journalists that the event would establish whether Ireland, once supreme in the pugilistic ring, with her production of such giants as John L. Sullivan, Peter Maher and Tom Sharkey, was going to awaken from her long sleep, and again show a world-beater. The English heavyweight champion, Joe Beckett, arrived in Dublin, feeling none too pleased after a restless night crossing the channel and was staying at the Marine Hotel in Dún Laoghaire to recuperate.

Dublin's sportsmen believed Siki had trained better than Mike who was thought to have not extended himself in the workouts. By the eve of the fight the betting was favouring the world champion and a bet of 5,000 to 4,000 francs was laid by one of Siki's supporters.

The *Irish Times* reported that both men had completed their training and would spend the intervening time very quietly. He was invited by the Baldoyle Race Company to watch the Metropolitan Steeplechase but declined for fear of catching a chill. The newspaper assured its readership that the arrangements made for the reception of the public at the La Scala were 'in keeping with the importance of the event' and that special cables had been laid on to provide high power for the taking of pictures. It published the full programme in its advertising columns and announced that a pictorial souvenir had been prepared with a message from Tom Singleton. The promoter wanted to publicise a series of contests he intended to stage during the course of the next three to four months in Dublin between native-born Irishmen at the various weights and 'one or two other bouts that would create worldwide interest'.

Later that day there was a great rush at the booking office and nearly all the seats ranging from twenty-eight shillings to £9 were sold. The promoters were anxious to point out that there was no collection or delivery of letters the following day so prospective spectators were advised to complete their arrangements as early as possible. In spite of the heavy bookings they informed the public that there were still good seats remaining at 500/- and upwards.

The promoters declared themselves to be so happy with the level of support in Dublin that they had decided to press ahead with a scheme to put on a series of fights to establish an Irish champion at each of the weight divisions. They invited any claimant or aspirant to a title to submit his name and record and to undertake, if approved, to engage in a series of elimination bouts. A substantial prize was to be offered for each championship, the amount to be so divided so that, besides the winner, others who had performed well would get a good return for their services and thus be encouraged to continue boxing. The winner of each championship was to receive a belt.

The Free State authorities had little trouble in limiting the Irish newspapers to these official communiqués from the promoters but in the days leading up to the fight they were becoming increasingly concerned at the way stories were leaking out of Dublin. Censorship, including the prohibition of certain films, had been put in place as early as June 1922 when it was decided that reporting on the military situation in Dublin should be censored. The importation, distribution or sale of any newspapers not passed by the official censor were banned. By this time the anti-Treaty IRA had left Dublin allowing the Free State government to present itself to the outside world as the lawful authority.

The press was issued with the following guidelines:

The Army must always be referred to as the 'Irish Army', the 'National Army', 'National Troops' or simply 'Troops'.

The Irregular Forces must not be referred to as 'Executive Forces' nor described as 'forces' or 'troops'. They are to be called 'bands' or 'bodies'.

Irregular leaders are not to be referred to as any rank, such as 'Commander,' etc., or are not to be called officers.

No news as to movements of troops may be published.

No news may be published as to movements of newly enrolled members of the army, movements of foodstuffs or trains, or transport, or equipment for army purposes.

Articles or letters as to the treatment of Irregular prisoners may not be published.

Censors may propose to substitute words or phrases, such as 'irregular' for 'republican'; 'fired at' for 'attacked'; 'seized' for 'commandeered'; 'kidnapped' for 'arrested'; 'enrolled' for 'enlisted'.

Letters, news, or articles, dealing with proposals for peace, or negotiations with the Irregulars should not be passed without submitting them to the Chief Censor.

The term 'Provisional Government' should not be used. The correct term being 'Irish Government'.

But the foreign press was much more difficult to control so on the eve of the fight the government tried, unsuccessfully, to cut off all unmonitored outlets. The *New York Times* reported: 'This evening the ban in Dublin on Irish news which was put on last night, was lifted to the extent that news of the Siki fight was circulated. Passengers reaching Belfast tonight from Dublin report that the tension in that city is extraordinary. Free State troops, with drawn revolvers, keep incessant vigil in the streets and challenge freely.

'The La Scala theatre, where the Siki fight takes place tomorrow, is guarded by troops, and the authorities are determined the fight shall not be prevented by the republicans. It is stated the ring for the fight, if it comes off at all, will be guarded by troops with fixed bayonets.'

In a cable to the *New York Times*, the *Daily Telegraph*'s correspondent in London wrote that 'so far as concerns publication of any news relating to Republican activities, Dublin has been completely in the grip of censorship since last night. No conversation with Belfast was permitted today, and inquiry brought the answer that the military authorities had issued orders that no communication or conversation was to be made by telephone.' A government official told the correspondent that 'all conversations about the trouble last night' had to be cut off.

The *Sporting Chronicle*'s correspondent fled to Belfast on the eve of the fight to make sure he got his story back to England:

I entered this troubled city yesterday as a sporting journalist and escaped stealthily this evening with something of the feelings of a war correspondent. I am in Belfast after some exciting adventures. Because a rigid censorship holds Dublin with a vice-like grip. I left behind me a chafing army of London and Continental journalists and photographers who were handing messages over the counters of the post offices, which are either refused, altered beyond recognition, or put aside altogether.

Not only are telegrams containing any reference to the

fight held up, but telephone wires are being tapped, and this afternoon I had dramatic confirmation of this soon after a call had come through for me. I was at the Herald office this afternoon. There was a sharp rap at the door. A soldier entered, handed a sealed envelope to the sub-editor in charge who opened it, and read: 'In consequence of publication of matter calculated to assist Irregulars in their campaign of destruction in the late edition of the *Evening Herald*, dated March 15, 1923, issue of today's edition of the paper is hereby suspended, by order of the army authorities.'

Soldiers with loaded rifles career about the streets in motorcars, and stop and search almost every passing vehicle. I was held up twice last night. You stand with upraised arms, whilst hands are roughly run over you.

These remarkable conditions have arisen because the Irregulars have, in view of recent executions, declared a ban on all amusements. The Free State reply has been to order all the theatres to open. Terrified managers have had to comply. Lights are blazing, doors are open, but there is no audience.

At the handsome La Scala Theatre, where this ill-conceived fight is to be put on, the manager last night refused at first to comply with the military demand. He was given three minutes to change his mind. Mysteriously delivered proclamations had previously assured him that if he did open, the place would be blown sky-high. Similar proclamations have been delivered to the fight promoters, and at the offices where the seats are being sold.

When I left Dublin yesterday evening there was a firm determination to hold the fight even though the audience be composed of those journalists brave enough to attend.

I do not think this fight – if fight there be – can be regarded as a good thing for anybody – fighters, referee, or the war correspondents who once were peace-loving sports writers.

If the McTigue-Siki fight takes place tomorrow evening in Dublin it will be literally at the point of the bayonet in a deserted theatre with armed guards surrounding the building. The history of the ring can never have known a contest with such an amazing setting as this promises to have. Dublin is in a state of war.

EIGHT

Machine guns to the right of 'em, steel-jacketed bullets to the left of 'em. Death threats. Milling mobs of belligerent Irishmen. Bombs bursting amid the ear-splitting din.

Jack Farrell, *New York Daily News*

At Dublin Port it was almost completely silent. The *Lady Kerry* had docked in the early hours with goods and passengers from Liverpool but there were no steamers from Glasgow, Heysham, or Holyhead. The *Hatteras* had come in from Baltimore, the *Havdrot* brought fruit from Valencia and the *Spinel* had arrived from Ghent. But all the shipping offices and official departments were closed. Guinness' cross-Channel steamers were idle on the Liffey and the steam lighters, barges and ferryboats enjoyed a rest in honour of St Patrick. It was an historic occasion, the first St Patrick's day to be celebrated in the Irish Free State. Masses at the Pro-Cathedral commenced at 5 am and were offered up every half hour for most of the day. At noon his Grace the Most Reverend Dr Byrne presided over Solemn High Mass.

Practically every shop, bank, office and factory in the city was closed for the holiday including almost all the public houses, with only the establishments run by the proprietors and their families remaining open. It was rare for pubs to be closed on bank holidays but the assistants, despite the protests of the owners, decided not to work that day. They paraded at the headquarters of their trades union in Parnell Square and then marched to mass, which they offered up for comrades who had fallen in the Irish War.

National Army troops were inspected and sent to religious services in various parts of the city. General Mulcahy addressed those assembled at Collins Barracks, where the colours were blessed and hoisted. The soldiers then took part in church parades and according to the *Evening Herald*, 'the general bearing of the men evoked expressions of admiration'. The morning edition of the *Cork Examiner* carried support for the day's big event from the clergy:

> Boxing is a fine, manly art. What is wrong with two fine men, who by hard work bring their bodies by lawful means to as near perfection as possible, agreeing under strict rules to exhibit their skill? They don't torture dumb animals under the name of sport; they don't wear ospreys or the skins and feathers of slaughtered birds. I can't speak for St Patrick, but I think if I were in his place, I should be proud that in the country I loved so much, after seven hundred years of slavery, I was free enough to welcome a stranger that dare not put his foot on the 'sacred soil of Britain,' and generous enough to give justice to a stranger. We all hope that our own countryman will prove that he is the best man, but if it should happen that the man of colour and the foreigner, after a fair fight, proves to the world that he is the best man, he will be assured of hearty applause.
>
> Father O'Ryan, Golden Bridge, Dublin

Georges Carpentier, still bearing the scars of his engagement with Siki six months previously, arrived in Dún Laoghaire by mail boat.

The fighter and his manager, François Deschamps, travelled with the famous London promoter, Major Arnold Wilson. The large crowd gathered on Carlisle Pier recognised Carpentier as the steamer berthed on the landing stage. As he stepped ashore the fighter was subjected to the usual search by the Marine Investigation Department and although at first he looked puzzled when an officer approached him, Carpentier submitted laughingly to the ordeal, making jokes in French. 'I have no financial or other interest in the fight and will be present only as a spectator,' he told a *Saturday Herald* reporter. 'I have never been in Ireland before, and this visit will give me an opportunity to see Dublin.' He also predicted that Mike would win. 'I never saw him fight, but I know his record,' said Carpentier.

The Frenchman's party moved on by train, in a specially reserved compartment, to Westland Row from where they took a hackney to the Shelbourne Hotel. Carpentier showed considerable interest in the hackneys as he had never seen the 'real thing' before, although he became annoyed when his party of six could not be accommodated in one car. On the way to St Stephen's Green, Carpentier pretended to be frightened when the vehicle swerved and he gripped the seat tightly.

In the afternoon Carpentier, along with thousands of race goers, headed for Baldoyle. The 'chosen leaf' was worn everywhere, invariably accompanied by the language flags sold by members of the Gaelic League. Camogie, Gaelic football, rugby and hockey matches were staged throughout the city. The National Championship Dog Show drew hundreds to the Royal Dublin Showgrounds in Balls-bridge and the booking office in Suffolk Street reported brisk business with many waiting until the last day to make sure there would be no hitch and that the fight would come off. The cheaper seats had been booked up for the past ten days and there was a steady stream of visitors picking up the remaining tickets throughout the day. The bookmakers had Mike as the 6-4 on favourite yet most of the boxing scribes predicted a win for Siki. 'Corinthian' wrote in the *Daily Chronicle*:

> A boxing champion at 11 stone 6lbs should not be able to beat another who is champion at 12 stone 7lbs. McTigue in this contest at Dublin has to concede that weight to Siki. There must be something in this Siki. He was able to render Carpentier helpless in six rounds. It has never been clearly made known whether Carpentier was so unfit as to be unable to complete six rounds against a man, who, according to a subsequent statement by the Frenchman, would not last three rounds in another contest.
>
> For the sake of the prestige of British boxing one naturally hopes the County Clare boxer will win. It will be a gloomy St Patrick's Day for all Ireland if the negro is successful.

Mike awoke early and took a short walk. At 8.30 he attended mass in Lucan and returned to his hotel where another letter had been mysteriously delivered. 'The Republicans sent me word that if I fought Siki for the title, I would be hanged. The Free Staters told me to go ahead and fight, and sent a regiment of soldiers to protect me to and from the ring and while I was in the ring,' Mike later recalled.

Mike stayed at the Spa Hotel until the afternoon when he moved to the Standard Hotel in Harcourt Street. 'Just fit and ready to go into the ring now if necessary,' said his trainer, Charles Brennan. 'McTigue is fit and well and in the best of spirits. We are quite optimistic and confident as to the result. I have yet to meet a more confident and crafty fighter than Mac, whether in attack or defence.

I am confident of the outcome, but should Siki beat our man, I will be the first to congratulate him. May the best man win.'

Siki did not get up until 10.30. He took no breakfast but had a good lunch at the Claremont after which he ate nothing until after the fight. 'We are all hopeful,' said Siki's manager, Brouillet, to the *Saturday Herald* reporter, 'and we will do our best.' He asked the reporter to print the following message in that evening's newspaper:

> There is one thing especially that I would like you to say, coming from me as Siki's manager. I am very thankful, indeed, to the Irish people for the welcome we have got from everybody since we got to Ireland.
>
> We are especially grateful, too, to the promoters of the fight, who gave my man the best chance a boxer ever got to train. Whatever happens – well, we are very thankful to everybody.

By the time the 'chicken coops' reached the Claremont, Ireland's Eye had already disappeared into the late-afternoon gloom. In the back of the Lancia trucks stood ten Irish Army soldiers brandishing Lewis rifles under chicken wire that offered adequate protection against grenades but did little to keep out the dank drizzle that had settled on Howth since morning.

Battling Siki believed the military escort to be yet another gesture of extraordinary generosity shown to him by his Irish hosts. The convoy made its way along the peninsula until it could see the bright lights across the bay at which point it headed south into Dublin. The church parades were over now, the football grounds empty, the pubs closed. 'Dublin is a city of furtive looks and sharp challenges; a city sitting despairingly on a volcano,' wrote the *Sporting Chronicle*'s correspondent. 'It is astonishing how sensation insists on following

Siki. The negro dishwasher god of the boulevards, for one night only, dragged reluctantly from his pet dogs to make a Dublin holiday. He knows nothing of the storm centre he has again become.'

When the Siki motorcade got within half a mile of the La Scala theatre it passed an improvised barricade from behind which a small band of gunmen started firing. A pitched battle ensued and as the bullets whizzed through the evening mist Siki, thinking it was a demonstration in his honour, stood up in his car and doffed his hat in gratitude.

While the world light heavyweight champion was delayed by a gunfight the promoters were trying to call the whole event off. Rumours of impending atrocities were rife and Tom Singleton was sceptical as to whether the authorities could provide adequate protection. But the Free State government insisted the fight go ahead and detailed a small fleet of armoured cars to carry five hundred extra troops to Sackville Street. The opening to Prince's Street was barricaded and guarded, leaving a channel just large enough to admit one person at a time. Another cordon of troops stood further down the cul-de-sac to perform a further inspection for guns and tickets.

The large glass doors of the La Scala opened, on time, at six o'clock, by which time the crowd at the entrance to Prince's Street was neither large nor enthusiastic. In the lobby 'a smart young gentleman whimsically inquired if I had a submarine in my vest pocket or a Lewis gun up my sleeve,' wrote 'Jacques' of the *Irish Sunday Independent*, 'and adeptly proceeded to satisfy himself of both matters'. Mike arrived early and stepped out of the car, wrapped up in a brown leather coat and flanked by his manager and seconds. He acknowledged the crowd with a wave and shook hands with people he recognised. He appeared fit but deadly pale with a look that betrayed nervousness and the cheering seemed to disconcert him.

Siki arrived just five minutes later; he too was cordially received and smiled and laughed with the crowd. His wife and a lady companion, both of whom took their seats in the dress circle, accompanied the champion.

The house filled up slowly until a few minutes before 7 o'clock when the preliminary contest was announced, by which time virtually every seat was taken. Crowds had congregated in Sackville Street and people were jammed shoulder to shoulder from the northern end of Parnell Square down to the Liffey. It was an orderly gathering and trams were allowed to travel as normal. Members of the St John Ambulance were on duty in the streets as motorcars tried to make their way through the throng.

'It was with a sensation of relief that one pushed through the dense crowds and escaped into the theatre,' wrote Gertrude Gaffney of the *Irish Independent*. 'Only one living under the same roof as one of the boxers can grasp the anxiety and uncertainty of those two days preceding the fight. Yet here we were at last, in the rapidly filling theatre, within sight of the goal, and all had gone well so far.'

The stage of the La Scala had been converted into a gallery, in front of which stood the ring. It was built with four wooden props hitched together by canvas-covered ropes: blue, white and red at one side, green, white and yellow on the other. A rig supporting massive arc lights hung precariously overhead. Free State troops with fixed bayonets were posted around the ring, in every aisle and at all entrances and exits. The *Boxing Blade*'s correspondent, who had sailed from New York for the fight, described it as 'the most unusual setting that ever surrounded a prize ring contest'. Platoons of pressmen filled the ringside area and there was a constant clatter of typewriters throughout the evening. Telephones and wireless sets were installed to get the story back as quickly as possible and a corps of messengers was employed to convey round-by-round accounts from the theatre to the Central Telegraph Office, from where a specially augmented staff of operators flashed updates to the ends of the earth.

All the London daily papers were represented, as well as several weeklies; four Paris papers: *Le Journal*, *L'Auto*, *Sporting* and *Echo de Paris*; three Italian newspapers: *Nuovo Giornale*, *Nuovo Della Sera* and *Nuovo Sport* and the four leading New York dailies: the *Tribune*, *Herald*, *Times* and *World* all dispatched their leading boxing writers to Dublin. It was rumoured that a number of the English journalists had been insured for considerable sums by their newspapers. 'The precaution appears to have been the outcome of alarmist rumours current in England,' claimed the *Irish Independent*.

About fifteen hundred of the two thousand tickets had been sold. It was an eclectic audience with nearly everyone sporting a shamrock. An English earl sat near ringside in company with a Curragh owner-trainer, an esteemed industrialist and an ex-MP of the Parliamentary Party. Hugh Kennedy, the Attorney General, sat in the gallery as did J. J. Walsh, Postmaster General, Joseph McGrath, Minister of Trade and Commerce, Dan Murphy TD, Chief Government Whip, Emmet Dalton, Chief Clark to the Senate and Colonel Edgeworth Johnstone, an ex-heavyweight champion of the British Army.

Many in the crowd had come straight from the Baldoyle races; 'one wore an outsize in waistcoats with a gold chain that would hold a barge'. Men sucked on oranges and cracked nuts and one 'well-fed man of foreign appearance who had made a fortune in rat-traps during the war' sat beside a 'coloured visitor with a head as bald as a basin' who had been known in the fight days of old as Bobby Hobbs. A fierce looking man sat a few seats away with a broken nose on a pug face and looked 'as if he could hold up the traffic, bark at bicycles and bite at motor cars'. Most of the women in the audience sat up in the circle. One was described by the *Irish Independent*'s correspondent as wearing a 'Pavlova blouse of striped organic cut on the basque and trimmed with trimming; a skunk squash coat with bobs all over it and a hat à la mode finished with a green gull's feather and crystallised shamrock'. Another was a 'well-known figure at matrimonial court trials and restaurant tea tables'. One American reporter was heard to say: 'can you imagine any one of these Janes with her head in a bag, rushing around the house doing the spring cleaning with a mop in her hand?'

The *Irish Independent* sent Gertrude Gaffney to get a woman's view of the big fight. 'They told me I would never sit it out,' she wrote, 'that I would feel faint, that I would certainly not enjoy it; and finally that it was one of the things that 'wasn't done' by a woman of taste. Being a woman, the last mentioned was enough to make me go, even if I hadn't wanted to, and I did happen to want to – very badly indeed.'

While the audience took their seats, Mike sent Eddie Eagan into Siki's dressing room to watch the champion bandage his hands. 'It was the first time I had actually met the negro and he seemed like a big, overgrown boy rather than a terrible pugilist sports writers had pictured,' Eagan recalled. 'He spoke only a patois French, and when he heard my name he smiled and said to me: "Paper said you fight for nothing. Me, I no fight for nothing. I get *beaucoup* money."'

The arc lights were switched on just after 7 o'clock and the theatre was flooded with a golden light. The first fight was announced: Stuber, Siki's sparring partner was matched with Tom Ireland from London. It was a slow, ponderous ten-round affair and the only excitement came during the third round. Stuber and Ireland were slugging away when a huge cheer boomed around the La Scala as Georges Carpentier, prizefighter, war hero and movie idol, was shown to his seat just a few yards away from the officials' table. A few minutes later the walls of the La Scala theatre began to shake.

It was 7.30 pm and by now twenty to thirty thousand people had gathered in Sackville Street. This was the hour that the big fight had been scheduled to start so exited crowds surged towards the approach to Prince's Street. Then came a deafening explosion. A mine had been laid at the end of Henry Place, just off Henry Street, a mere fifty yards from the back of the theatre. The bomb had been placed next to the Pillar Picture House where the cinema orchestra, which was composed of two young ladies and a gentleman, were seated less than a dozen yards from the hole in which the mine had been planted. The force of the explosion blew two large exit doors into the picture house. The two young violinists were thrown from their seats but sustained only cuts and bruises. The cellist was also thrown from his seat and his instrument blown from his grip and shattered into pieces. Large chunks of ceiling plaster rained down on the audience. The screen, which was suspended above the two blown-out doors, remained intact and the film, a five-reel spectacular called *Peggy Puts it Over* continued running despite the gaping hole beneath and the smoke and dust.

The cinema was crowded at the time of the explosion yet no-one was killed. The only casualty was Bertie Duffy, a two-year-old boy who had been struck by flying glass from a blown out window, while standing by his mother's fruit stall. 'The first thing I heard was a fearful bang, and the smoke came down the lane,' said Mrs Duffy as she carried her bleeding son to Jervis Street hospital. All the windows in the Tower Bar, at the corner of Henry Place, were blown out as were those of Messrs Dundon & Co, tailors. The windows of all the neighbouring houses were smashed.

CID officers and troops were quickly at the scene but there was no sign of the bombers. Tom Webster, the celebrated English sports cartoonist, was making his way to the La Scala at the time of the explosion. He jumped into a cellar and landed on a prostrate figure. He lit a match and saw it was Joe Beckett, the English heavyweight champion, who according to a *New York Times* reporter, 'was reclining in his usual horizontal pose'.

The minelayers had been unable to get close enough to the La Scala so they had tried to cut off the supply of electricity to the theatre. The bomb had been placed immediately over a main power cable, but they got the wrong cable and the lights of the La Scala stayed on. 'We weren't to forget that we were in Ireland,' wrote Gertrude Gaffney. 'During one of the minor contests the big, round boom that we know so well sent its dread message echoing dally through the walls. A bomb? The note of interrogation rippled over the black mass of people from the floor to roof and spent itself. We shrugged our shoulders. We had meant to see the fight – in spite of everything.'

The crowd outside stampeded. From Sackville Street, looking through the narrow entrance to Prince's Street, it appeared that the La Scala had been blown up and the smoke could be seen rising above the General Post Office. But the panic on the streets quickly subsided and inside the theatre, as soon as it became clear that the walls weren't about to collapse, the second fight was announced. Johnny Sullivan of London and Bandsman Cullen of the National Army stepped between the ropes. Loud cheers went up during one of the rounds but it wasn't to acknowledge either of the boxers currently fighting. Joe Beckett had made his way out of the cellar and into the arena. He shook hands with several acquaintances at ringside before taking his seat and as he walked to the stage the applause spread to all parts of the house. He slipped past Carpentier without a sign of recognition even though he shook hands heartily with Dick Smith, the referee, who was sitting beside the French champion. Carpentier had knocked Beckett out in a single round a few years previously.

Then, dramatically, the arc lights were switched off and the theatre was plunged into darkness. The glare of a searchlight pierced the darkness and the arc lights spluttered forth streams of purple light as the carbons got contact. Jim Harris, the master of ceremonies came forward. 'We have received an order from the military that you must keep your seats until 11.30 pm,' he announced. It had been thirty minutes since the mine exploded. 'None of us dreamed that his coming forward now had anything to do with that,' wrote Gertrude Gaffney, 'it had almost been forgotten by the audience and when he began to talk we thought it was to announce the contest we had all come to see. What happened? Many displayed signs of nervousness, but many others laughed. They thought it was a joke, and, anyhow, did not seem to care, for the next fight was to be for the championship.'

Harris then introduced several famous fighting men to the audience. Joe Beckett got a loud reception and there was a round of applause when it was announced that the British champion had been approached by the promoters with a view to a match in Dublin in the near future. Frank Moran, Eddie Eagan and Tom Webster were also introduced to the crowd. Pride of place was given to Carpentier who came forward to acknowledge the cheers of the crowd. The silver stitch in the cut he got in his fight with Siki shone in the glare of the lights. There were loud cries of 'Speech!' but he bashfully retired to his seat and whispered to Harris to thank the crowd for the wonderful reception. 'Carpentier,' announced Harris, 'has made the journey from Paris to challenge the winner of tonight's contest.'

'Carpentier. I don't wonder that he took his ovation as if it were his right. He is the most beautiful man I have ever seen, and I use the word beautiful advisedly,' wrote Gertrude Gaffney. 'The picture people knew what they were doing when they lured him from the ring to the studio.'

The crowd was hushed in expectation of the main bout. It was the first time that many in the audience would see a black man, or for that matter, a prizefight. A betting man's voice cracked over the ring, 'I'll take five-to-four McTigue.' Up and down the hall the odds were being announced; 'even money Siki' was a popular price. The gambling was temporarily suspended at 8.17 pm when Mike stepped between the ropes, dressed in a thick, white-grey gown and went straight to his corner. He looked ghostly pale as he sat statue-like in the off-right hand corner surrounded by his seconds. 'Now Mac' shouted an admirer from the back of the hall. Mac smiled.

The world champion was in the ring soon afterwards. Draped in a deep purple robe, Siki walked over to the Irishman to shake his hand before returning to the left hand corner from where he waved extravagantly at the audience. Siki's gown made one writer 'want to guard his eyes and ring up the ambulance. It struck the colour tone of a burglar's alarm.' In contrast Mike's robe looked 'the poorest thing that ever draped a human frame'.

'As they stepped into the ring,' wrote Gertrude Gaffney, 'I wondered how many among the great crowd thought past the contest into the personal issue for each man: of Siki who was risking a world reputation for small gain; of McTigue, who had sought fights in vain for the past year and who had been crudely told to go and make a reputation. Now he tells those same promoters who are after him to go and make theirs.'

A cardboard box was taken into the ring, one end opened and two pairs of gloves, both labelled, fell onto the canvas. Mike extended his hands to Siki who inspected the bandages and had his own tested at the same time. They shared another warm handshake before returning to their respective corners to don the gloves. Ted Broadribb, Bartley Madden, P. Farrell, Charlie Brennan and Johnny Curran worked Mike's corner. Siki was seconded by Stuber, Murphy W. Deane and Brouillet who kept a close eye while Mike's gloves were adjusted.

There was another audible hush as Siki, having discarded the robe, stood up clothed only in a narrow hip cloth. The arc lights glared down revealing a shocking contrast between the fighters. 'He was a figure of ebony, beautiful but formidable to look at,' wrote one scribe at ringside. Siki played his muscles under his glossy skin for the benefit of the crowd and such was the difference in size and physique between the two fighters that the odds shifted towards Siki before the fight even started. The champion appeared several stones heavier than Mike who, according to the *Sporting Chronicle*'s correspondent, 'presented the appearance of an underdeveloped stripling, although thoroughly trained, but he lacked the muscular development of his opponent'.

The troops, forbidden from watching the contest, stared out to the audience as one of the American radio announcers began his commentary:

'Good evening, ladies and gentlemen. This is WGN bringing the Mike McTigue-Battling Siki fight to you direct from the La Scala theatre in Dublin, Ireland! And what an evening it's going to be! Excitement is running high in Dublin because of the troubles between the republicans and the Free Staters, and when we came into the building we were searched thoroughly by a couple of policemen for concealed weapons. Everybody who's coming in is being searched ...'

There was a sense of foreboding as the timekeeper signalled the beginning of the fight – was the bell tolling for Mike McTigue? Siki rushed at Mike and made a motion as if to shake hands before launching a bull-like charge as he pushed his opponent back onto the ropes. 'Steady, Mac,' came a shout. Mike looked pale and almost indolent. The audience feared for the Clareman but it feared even more for a short contest. There was a feeling it could have been all over in the first minute and there was a roar of relief when the Irishman escaped from the ropes. And so the pattern for much of the fight was set. The champion, bigger and stronger, charging after the challenger who just managed to keep himself out of harm's way.

After the first two rounds no one at ringside believed Mike had a chance against this barrage of punches; no defence could last twenty rounds against such an onslaught and the layers who had been offering to take 5-4 on Siki refused to take any more. The only one who failed to see the position was Mike who laughed and smiled at his opponent's efforts to get home a blow. Then, when Siki paused for breath in the third round, Mike straightened his left arm and speared a jab onto the world champion's nose and the mood changed. Mike's confidence picked up and he came in with another straight left. Mike kept flicking his left glove like a cat's tail mesmerizing a mouse. In and out went Mike – feinting and stabbing, jabbing and stepping away, jabbing and circling; pop-pop-pop, three left hands in a row. But Siki seemed bewildered as to why, when Mike had opened him up with a left jab, no right hook came crashing in after it. The Irishman dabbed his opponent's nose twice, often three times in succession with a left. 'Sometimes this would be varied by a tap light as that of a lady's fan on each eye or the neck,' wrote the *Sporting Chronicle*'s correspondent. 'This would annoy the coloured man. He would dash in bull-like, and by sheer weight force Mike on the ropes and try to batter down his defence, but all to no purpose. Right and left punches were taken and warded off in machine-like fashion, while the Irishman smiled at the aggressor.'They made a constant duet of sounds, Mike's nasal breathing accompanied Siki's foot stomp. Whenever Mike shot out the straight left he accompanied it with a heavy exhalation. When Siki let fly a punch or a swipe he signalled it with a bump of his foot like a band conductor keeping time.

The next six rounds were fought in much the same way. Siki standing tall, launching fearsome attacks, punches flying through the smoky air; Mike standing small and sideways with his abnormally long left arm jabbing away at his opponent's nose. Then Mike's right, which was always swinging warily, came into play, and Siki rapidly covered up, clinched or sprang back. Mike's right hand seemed to fascinate Siki. He was always watching for it, and he had good cause, for every time it landed it shook the champion. Mike first used his right in the third but narrowly missed with an uppercut. He used it again in the sixth and he caught Siki with a blow to the head.

'Get his goat, Mac,' yelled someone from the top circle.

But Mike pursued the plan he had laid down. Siki was always on his toes, crouching low and springing at Mike with his whole weight behind swinging punches. Siki did most of the attacking throughout the fight but his efforts to do so were crude, while Mike's defence was masterly. He ducked, weaved and swayed away from Siki's punches. Even on the occasions when he was backed into a corner the Irishman managed to work his way out without taking any punishment.

But to the audience, most of whom had never seen a boxing match before, it looked like the fight was Siki's from the very beginning. What they saw was the champion smashing blows onto Mike who was forced back to the ropes in every round. 'Mike fought defensively throughout, and although he easily scored on points, his Irish supporters were disappointed,' wrote Eddie Eagan. 'They thought an Irishman should achieve murder at least.' The disapproving screams of the uninitiated proved too much for one 'case-hardened legal gentleman of much might and considerable reputation' who sat in the centre of the circle. According to one reporter 'he looked again and again as if he would like to commit every one of the vocal snipers around him for contempt.' The boxers themselves were the only ones saying anything fit for publication, for they were saying nothing.

On it went, round after round, each session much like the last. A tired moth struggled lamely upward toward the lights. By the midway point the *New York Times* correspondent relayed to his newsroom that the most exiting feature of the whole affair was the possibility that Irish Irregulars would interrupt the proceedings with a bomb but 'with soldiers stationed at various points around the theatre, and beyond one explosion a short distance from the battleground, there was no trouble, and the fight proceeded on its long and tiresome way.' Mike led with a few light lefts and Siki caught them on the nose. They lumbered, feeling for openings. They clinched, their interlocked bodies swaying under the white glare of the arc lights until the referee danced in and parted them.

It was when Mike's eyebrow was split open and pumped blood in the eleventh round that the crowd's emotions reached the highest pitch. Siki pressed forward, anchored to the canvas floor like a sturdy tree and threw a short, sharp, murderous punch, whipped to Mike's forehead that opened up a deep gash over the Irishman's eye. It was a terrible cut and Mike's face was deluged in blood within seconds and his green shorts were a dark crimson before the bell sounded to end the session. He returned to the corner with his head cocked back to control the bleeding. In between each remaining round Mike's seconds worked their dark arts and potions to stem much of the claret. The injury only served to sharpen his defensive instincts and he managed to protect the gaping wound from any further goring. Siki honed in on the cut but Mike was clever enough to offer the champion an opening elsewhere before closing it when the inevitable attack came.

'Let me tell you that boxing isn't any of the awful things people tell you about it, but the cleanest, most scientific, and by a long way the most thrilling of all forms of sport,' wrote Gertrude Gaffney. 'It stands apart from other sports as a king stands from his subjects, and my only regret is that there were only about a dozen and a half of my sex there to realise that for themselves.'

Then, in the thirteenth round, came a pivotal moment in the fight. Mike speared a left jab onto Siki's mouth and then threw a vicious right hook at his chin. The champion ducked and Mike's hand crashed on top of his head. A snapping, cracking sound could be heard back in the cheap seats. Siki's legs stiffened but the Irishman was the real loser in the exchange. He'd slightly mistimed the blow and broke his thumb on impact with Siki's skull. Georges Carpentier jumped up from his ringside seat and yelled to Mike in French, 'You've got him now.'

The Irishman did not understand him but Siki did, and he staggered over to where Carpentier was sitting and invited him to get in the ring. 'I could have "murdered" him when he turned his back on me,' Mike said a few years later, 'but I waited until he turned around.' In his anger Siki failed to see his opponent's distress. 'Oh, if Siki had only known of this, would the fight have ended differently?' mused the *Sporting Chronicle*'s correspondent.

Once in the thirteenth and again later, Siki missed with such a wild swipe that he nearly fell over. Mike was politely applauded every time he made the champion miss and landed a counter of his own. Each time it was accompanied by shouts of 'Bravo, Mac!' But generally the spectators appeared to be dumbfounded by the ease and certainty with which their favourite and representative was being outpointed. Out in Sackville Street the excitement grew as it became apparent that it would be a protracted fight. By now the street was virtually impassable as people overflowed into Westmoreland Street and as far away as College Green. The rumours from ringside were disconcerting. At about 10 o'clock a story circulated that Mike had been knocked out. It had a depressing effect on the spirits.

Siki resumed the attack in the fourteenth. Frustrated by his inability to land a clean punch on the challenger he changed his approach and tried to strike downwards at Mike's wrists and arms as if to batter the Irishman's defences away. But Mike was a gambler by nature and he'd risked all on Siki's fitness failing in the later rounds. The Clareman figured that the champion would surely pay at some point for months of wild living on the Paris boulevards. He was right. By the end of the sixteenth it was apparent that Siki was getting very tired; his legs were no longer springy, moving only with a dull flexibility. One ringside scribe remarked that as the French seconds poured water on their man it sizzled like a horseshoe in a farrier's bucket as it hit Siki's head. He was very weary and as the bell rang for the seventeenth round the champion had to be pushed out of his corner.

Mike knew he could protect his broken thumb no longer and shocked Siki by using both hands for the first time in several rounds. His stance changed abruptly, hands held down at belt level near to his body. He shuffled closer to Siki and braced himself as each right-hand blow sent his broken thumb smashing into Siki's face and body. He whipped in the punches and the crowd roared to its feet. The Irishman landed a heavy right on Siki's jaw and followed it up with two further, heavy punches. The attack brought wild cheering from the crowd and each burst of applause inside the house was taken up by the many thousands outside in the street. Mike sustained his attack for the next two rounds but as the bell sounded for the end of the nineteenth both men appeared to be exhausted and their eyes were glazed. The referee said: 'Last round.' They touched gloves, pushing, and the last round began amidst intense excitement.

A hush of expectancy fell on the crowd with only the occasional isolated cheer to break the silence in the packed hall. The cigarette smoke drifted towards the lights that illuminated the soiled canvas as the two weary warriors fell into a clinch; needing each other to remain upright. Mike won the twentieth round because he was marginally less tired than the champion.

And so the bell sounded for the last world title fight to go twenty rounds and the fate of both men would be determined by the referee, Jack Smith, who according to one ringside scribe 'had the look of a man who was qualifying for Fox's Book of Martyrs'.

It was at least ten minutes before the official announcement was made and when Smith reached for Mike's hand the noise was deafening. Most of the crowd rose in their places; seconds and supporters rushed into the ring and shouts of 'McTigue! McTigue! McTigue!' filled the arena. Hats were thrown in the air, men jumped up on their seats and embraced each other. Mike was almost in tears when the crowd finally made way for his father to enter the ring. Looking very little older than his son, he lifted the victor and tossed him up in his arms as he would have done a baby.

Meanwhile Siki sat in his corner. 'The black could not make himself intelligible in English; he only smiled a sad smile,' reported the *Evening Herald*. 'He seemed to envy the cheering that greeted the announcement that McTigue was the winner. He expressed surprise to his manager that he had lost.'

The new world champion was lifted shoulder high and carried around the ring. So great was the excitement that Charlie Brennan fainted and was carried back to the dressing rooms. Mike was released from the grip of the mob and walked around the ropes to thank the crowd. His appearance triggered further cheering and hat-waving and he was eventually carried out of the ring. 'The most tremendous thing that could happen had happened,' wrote Gertrude Gaffney. 'But it left one cold. That was the queer thing about it. You see, it was the unexpected climax. And few mortals are capable of enjoying the unexpected, however much they appreciate it on examination. But nobody stopped to think just then, and the figure of the pale young boxer, almost staggering with fatigue, hoisted in his father's arms before a house gone mad with joy was a great spectacle.'

When the crowds outside heard the verdict it had an electric effect. A roar worked its way from Sackville Street back into the streets further away. 'Some people became so delirious that they took to embracing people who were total strangers to them,' commented the *Irish Independent*. At the banquet of the Knights of St Patrick at the Shelbourne Hotel the guests all rose to their feet and sang 'For He's A Jolly Good Fellow' when the result was announced by the chairman. Alderman Byrne, acting Lord Mayor of Dublin, congratulated Mike on behalf of the citizens of the city. At the offices of the *Irish Independent* in London, a huge crowd gathered to hear of Mike's progress. A special edition was printed just minutes after the fight. 'It was not picturesque, not at all spectacular, commented 'Jacques' of the *Irish Sunday Independent*. 'That must be said about this performance. But it was a remarkable occasion.'

Back in his dressing room Siki told one of the French writers: 'I believed I was winning easily. My seconds continually told me so. I was never in danger, but this is the last time I will box in a foreign ring. I am going back to France at once.' Many scribes agreed with Siki and the beleaguered referee, Jack Smith, was compelled to justify his decision.

I understand that there is considerable controversy over my decision. Some, I believe, think that a draw should have been the verdict, but McTigue had secured a sufficient lead on points which left me in no doubt as to the winner. Granted that Siki was the aggressor for the greater part of the contest, yet in his retreats and evasions the Irishman was continually scoring and generally out-boxed his opponent. Siki was the better fighter, but as a boxer he was distinctly outclassed. Except when he caused McTigue's eye to bleed, Siki never had his opponent in any real difficulty.

There were other contests after the main fight but nobody was very interested and though the crowd was ordered to stay in the theatre under military guard, nobody seemed to mind very much. The boxers were allowed to leave, however, and when the crowds saw Mike approach the door of the theatre he was lifted up on the shoulders of the throng as they reeled and swayed towards the waiting motor car and the new champion was driven off through a frantic salvo of applause. 'I caught sight of his face as he left the theatre twenty minutes after the match and he looked a sick man,' wrote the *Sporting Chronicle*'s correspondent, 'but it may have been the effect of the flaring electric lights on a skin naturally sallow.'

Mike did not return to his hotel as planned. He was taken to hospital where an x-ray confirmed to Surgeon McArdle that Mike had broken his right thumb. 'To tell the truth I only knew something had gone wrong in my hand,' said the new champion. 'I did not know exactly what it was, but half-way through the match I was convinced that whatever my injury was, it was something that could not be treated lightly. There were occasions when I nearly groaned with pain as, for example, when now and again I sent my right to Siki's face just to convince him that I was still inside the ring and not outside.'

Finally, nearly an hour after the big fight had ended, the audience was allowed to leave the theatre. Among those leaving at about 11.15 pm was Joe Beckett and as soon as he was recognised there was a rush in his direction. A huge crowd had gathered outside the barrier and along the pavements towards Abbey Street and the Free State troops had great difficulty in clearing a passage for those leaving the arena. As the last of the audience made its way into Prince's Street several volleys of a revolver screamed across the vicinity of the theatre. The crowd charged from the corner of Middle Abbey Street from where the rapid fire was heard and it triggered a stampede as the crowds fled. Many were knocked to the road and were trampled by the mob. As the shots continued many threw themselves onto the ground – better to be trampled than shot. The only casualty of the attack was James O'Shea of Harcourt Street who was shot in the leg in Westmoreland Street. It all added to the drama of the evening, especially for the newspapers. Several correspondents were telephoning their accounts of the fight at the time and the sound of rifle fire could clearly be heard back in the newsrooms. Another burst of firing tore around the city as two parties of CID officers met each other in a dark back street and opened fire by mistake. It was rumoured that one policeman was injured.

Amidst the wild celebration and gunfire there was a great deal of sympathy for Siki. The American boxing writers in particular were surprised at the referee's decision. 'He smiled, that genial, good-natured smile of his,' wrote one scribe. 'He remained dignified and good-humoured. He took it as few white men would have taken it, considering that he came over here to risk his all for a paltry two thousand pounds – a mere nothing to a boxer with world titles, and remembering that his manager questions the decision. He was game – game right through, and McTigue admitted that to me. If he is coloured outside, he is white through, as well as game.'

The American writers conceded that a heavy percentage of Siki's punches were taken on Mike's arms, the sides of his body, kidneys and the back of his head. They also accepted that three or four, or perhaps six of the former champion's wild blows landed below the belt but they argued that enough punches did reach legitimate targets and despite Mike's protestations they were by no means all delivered by the inside of the glove. 'Siki is pugilistically uneducated enough to slap far more frequently than he need, but his knuckles do connect at times, and to the best of my vision of the contest – and I have pretty good eyesight – his knuckles connected not only more frequently, but every time with far greater force behind them than McTigue's,' wrote James McAnerney, in *Boxing*. 'I take no stock in the black brotherhood, or the coloured races at all. I am an Irishman and I am always pleased when an Irishman wins, but I do like to see him win before I hear that he has won, and with the best will in the world I am unable and was unable to make McTigue a winner last Saturday night.'

The *Irish Independent* was also sympathetic to Siki's complaints. 'From what we saw of the coloured man among us he was nothing like so bad a fellow as was made out by press reports. If he did not get the verdict over McTigue, he did more than the Irishman to satisfy the spectators who paid a high price to see the fight.'

Later that evening Siki sent a telegram to the French Federation from his hotel:

I protest energetically against the blind partiality and the unreasonable decision given by the referee. I would like the French federation to make inquiries before an Emergency Committee, with a view to taking all possible measures against a renewal of an unjustified decision.

'His was a common fate in the boxing world – up today, down to-morrow,' wrote Gertrude Gaffney. 'Thus has Siki gone down and McTigue gone up, and with him Ireland, our country.' Mike McTigue was the new light heavyweight champion of the world who could now look forward to taking his precious title to the United States and earning the purses that a black champion couldn't dream of getting. The title of 'world champion' was a valuable trademark; it meant easy money, free advertising and the right to dictate terms. As for Siki, Frank Moran in the following morning's Dublin *Evening Herald* accurately predicted his prospects:

Siki, the much-abused, not to say ill-used negro, passes out and passes out for good, for after all that has happened, he will not be given the chance to return. His reign has been brief, and in some aspects inglorious, and it is better for boxing, better for everybody that he has gone. Yet the man fought fair in the ring, whatever his other faults, and I could have wished that his finale had been more appropriate to that spectacular debut (for such it was as far as first-class boxing went) when six months ago he dethroned Carpentier. McTigue has settled the Siki problem.

NINE

Every ambitious fighter dreams of winning a title some day; the man who has one dreams only of keeping it until the last dollar has been squeezed out and then retiring undefeated.

Charles E. Van Loan, *One-Thirty-Three-Ringside*

Bonfires blazed around Kilnamona; tongues of fire shot up on distant hills until the whole county seemed ablaze. 'Cheers for McTigue, for Kilnamona and for Clare filled the air,' reported the *Clare Champion*. Large crowds arrived in Ennis and from 8.30 pm onwards rumour and counter-rumour filled the air. The announcement that Mike had won came just before 10 pm. Throngs lined the streets outside the offices of the *Connacht Tribune* in Galway to wait for the result and when it finally came through people tore papers from the boys. The Clareman had been heavily backed at short odds and when the result was announced in the town's Empire Theatre the film had to be stopped for the cheering to subside.

The verdict rendered by referee Jack Smith was the main topic of conversation well into the night. Carpentier, Deschamps and the rest of the French contingent maintained that Siki was the victim of a bad error of judgement, a contention supported by more than one Irish writer of repute. Nonetheless, according to *Time* magazine, 'Siki's name is henceforth listed in the 'Who's Through' of pugilism.'

Siki's term as champion had been a very short one; he took the title away from Carpentier only to lose it in his very next contest. 'Even his championship season yielded him practically nothing at all, since most of his time was spent in exile and in wrangles with the French Federation. He considers himself the most harshly used of mortals and would seem to regard the adverse decision against him as the unkindest cut of all,' wrote *Boxing*. 'We shall not be at all surprised if Siki lodges a protest with the French Federation. His previous performances demonstrate that he has a natural gift for public sensations, and, by general consensus of the reports, he did do most of the attacking in Dublin last Saturday.'

Siki certainly felt like the most harshly used of all mortals after the fight. 'I protest that I won the fight,' he said. 'I won at least seventeen of the twenty rounds. McTigue might have won the other three, but I won the fight all right.' He was not alone in that opinion. Brouillet, his manager, unsurprisingly described the decision as the worst he had known in his long experience. Even Tom Singleton disagreed with Jack Smith's verdict, although this may have had much to do with generating publicity for the promoter's plans for a rematch.

'The contest was most disappointing, for seldom has a battle of this class proved so tame, whilst the verdict in favour of McTigue, though popular with his countrymen, came as a surprise to many in the house,' commented the correspondent for the *Sportsman*. 'True, McTigue's science, ringcraft, and generalship were superb, and allowance must be made for the breaking of his right thumb which greatly handicapped him, but except in three of the twenty rounds he boxed on the retreat; and though Siki was very wild with some of his right and left swings, he nevertheless had run up a lead on points … which to my mind did not wipe out.'

Siki's defeat received a mixed reaction in France. From the boulevards of the French capital an *Associated Press* reporter commented that, 'Battling Siki's defeat by Mike McTigue caused much rejoicing among the enemies of the Senegalese fighter in Paris and was received with the keenest of disappointment by his admirers. The defeat of Siki, sporting men declared, will end the Siki boom, which close followers of boxing in France assert, has been "smoked up" with an intensity totally unwarranted by the negro's fistic ability.'

But many of the French boxing writers were convinced Siki had won. *Le Matin* was of the opinion that the decision would disturb the harmony of international boxing. 'Siki beaten by the officials,' it stated. The special correspondent in Dublin of the Paris *Le Journal*, Jacques Marsillac, wrote:

> I have seen many boxing contests, but I can say I have never been witness to a decision so iniquitous as that which has given victory to McTigue on points over Siki. There was none among the boxers or experts seated at the ringside that was not indignant at the decision. As Carpentier said to me – 'This victory of McTigue's ought to give me pleasure but I must say, being before all a sportsman, that I find the decision incomprehensible and indefensible!'

The argument was one of interpretation. Was Siki's great physical advantage and punching power more impressive than Mike's clever boxing? 'Straight Left' writing in *Sporting Life* described it as 'not so much a boxing contest as a struggle between a hunter, deadly cool and grimly watchful, and an animal, striking out fiercely everywhere and anywhere'. If points were awarded for hitting on the back, kidneys, hips, back of the neck and sometimes very dangerously low, then Siki would have won clearly; but as the referee, though showing the champion every leniency, could only count clean blows, delivered by the knuckle part of the gloves, Siki's tally of points was not very big. There was no doubt however that a man less watchful and resourceful than Mike would have been brought down by Siki's whipping, crashing arms. Messrs Pathé Frères privately exhibited a film of the fight to a select few, a film which, according to the *Sportsman*, completely vindicated the referee. What the film shows clearly is how many of Siki's punches missed.

'My critics do not realize I was giving away nearly twenty-eight pounds in weight to Siki,' said Mike. 'Neither do they sufficiently consider the tremendous disadvantage under which I laboured as a result of the cut over my eye in the eleventh round and the breaking of my right thumb in the thirteenth round. If it had not been for the broken thumb there would have been no need for the referee to award the decision.'

Mike was in a bad way after the fight with his head swathed in heavy bandages to stem the blood from the cut over his left eye. Back in his hotel room the new champion gave his view on the evening's events:

Siki did not hit me one clean punch in the whole of twenty rounds. He was rushing all the time, but he had only two punches, left and right leads, and I blocked them. It was an old cut which he opened up over my left eye in the eleventh round, and I think it was caused by the lace of a glove. But it was in the thirteenth that I knocked out the thumb of my right by a punch which I drove to Siki's head. I was very cool and confident of the result, but the injury to my thumb prevented me from using my right with the effect that I would like.

Siki is a tough fellow, but he does not know much about boxing. He is a tough, strong fighter, but he has no judgment at all. I had no doubt as to the result, and as I said before the fight I would not disappoint the Irish people as to how I would perform.

Ennis was the scene of great celebration again the following morning as crowds anxiously awaited the return of motorcars from Dublin. Frank Lyons arrived at 9 o'clock carrying the father of the new champion as his passenger. When McTigue senior arrived in Kilnamona he was met with blazing bonfires, handshakers and backslappers. But by the time he had made the journey west, most of the Sunday newspapers were reporting that, while his son may have won the fight, he wasn't the world champion. The contract for the fight did not call for a formal weigh-in and because Siki didn't do so, no title could change hands. The American publication, the *Boxing Blade* commented:

The failure of the Dublin promoters to insure that Battling Siki and Mike McTigue were up to the required poundage for their recent ballet – advertised and announced as being for the world's cruiser title – stamps them as novices in the game of fight promoting.

The rules governing title battles are clear enough on this point and both men should have weighed in at least eight hours before the scheduled time of the scrap. As they failed to do this it is clear that no title was involved. Siki may have been under the limit, but there is no evidence to show that he was, a remark that also applies to McTigue. We know that Mike poses as a middleweight and possibly can make

160 pounds, yet the fact remains he did not go to the scale for the Dublin fight.

James McAnerney wrote in *Boxing* that Mike and the promoters 'were guilty of a gross oversight in not stipulating that the Senegalese must mount the scales before he entered the ring. In America, I imagine that the neglect of this ceremony would not have mattered – though New York rules would have insisted that both men should weigh in, irrespective of any prize which might be at issue – but as National Sporting Club rules governed the contest, and there was no definite evidence as to Siki's weight, McTigue will have to fight the negro again before he can secure official recognition as a World title-holder.'

The National Sporting Club rules did call for fighters to weigh in for a championship match but there was no real danger of Mike losing his claim to the title because of this technicality. There had been great consternation over an ever-swelling system of protection for titleholders – who, in order to steer clear of risks, made matches at a pound or more above the championship limit, lost decisions and then claimed to have lost nothing more. It was obviously unfair that champions should annex the advantage in weight and at the same time secure protection against the penalties of defeat and the custom was developing farcical proportions. It was generally agreed that Siki underwent a thorough preparation for his match with Mike and that he was consequently inside the light heavyweight limit. He wasn't going to be allowed to preserve his title merely because he omitted to mount the scales. Besides, Mike was regarded as having provided a service to both France and England. According to the *Chicago Tribune*, 'ring championships are becoming too complicated and their effect on international affairs too serious. Mike has saved the British and the French a great deal of trouble. The former appreciate it more than the latter. Every time a Senegalese fighter knocks a European on the chin and breaks his shoelaces the great white idol in Asia and Africa totters. It does not appear then as a God, but as a piece of porcelain that a brick could shatter. The British carefully kept Joe Beckett out of Siki's way; but an Irishman has done the empire a good turn and he has helped the French colonial administration recover what Carpentier lost.'

Mike told American pressmen that he wanted to make it known in the States that at three o'clock on the afternoon of the fight he weighed in before witnesses and tipped the scales at 159 lbs. They did not permit champions to ride off on odd weight conditions in America and it was inevitable they would accept Mike as champion. Every American fighter knew that if he fought to a referee's decision with anyone at his own weight or less and lost the verdict, he automatically lost his title. He also knew that if he was knocked out, even in a no-decision contest, he lost the title. There was no safe-guard in insisting that they were allowed to enter the ring at a pound or two above the championship limit, nor was there any protection in refusing to disclose their actual weight. An editorial in *Boxing* on 28 March stated:

We know quite well that the self-protecting champions' apologists claim that a titleholder must be permitted to make some profit out of his new crown. But we do fail to see why he should be permitted to make this in false pretences. Either he is a champion or he isn't. If he is one, he should be prepared to defend his title. He may say that he should only be expected to defend it when he is sharing in a championship-sized purse. Well, wouldn't he stand a more reasonable chance of sharing in them if it were known that his title was at stake? He tops the bill on the strength of his fame and honours, doesn't he? Isn't it obvious then that if he takes the trouble to advertise that he is only giving a more or less serious exhibition of himself that the public interest will be merely moderate?

By the following day talk had turned from the weigh-in that never was to the possibility of a rematch. Battling Siki showed up at the promoter's office on Suffolk Street to pay over the stakes but he spent most of his time signing autographs. Siki was the centre of attention wherever he went. One evening he was spotted on Abbey Street handing out coins to a group of children, one or two of whom he lifted up playfully. His manager, Brouillet, challenged Mike to a rematch over twenty rounds for a side stake of £500 and any purse offered by the Irish promoters. Brouillet said Siki would be happy to fight for the purse on a winner-take-all basis.

'I think it is only fair for McTigue to give me a return contest, as I was the first to give the Irishman an opportunity of boxing me,' said Siki. 'My side stake will be immediately deposited with any sportsman in Ireland as soon as McTigue accepts this challenge.'

When he was told of Siki's challenge Mike said, 'If he wants it I will fight him again if any promoter will put up a purse in accordance with my expectations, which are reasonable. I beat the Senegalese with one hand and one eye. A picture of my broken right hand has been taken. I was with a surgeon today to whom I was taken by Dr McCartan, TD. I have no immediate plans, for I intend going to see my wife. There is not a mark on my body except my back and my kidneys. I assert positively that Siki did not land half-a-dozen direct blows on me in twenty rounds.'

As soon as the challenge and its acceptance was made public, Tom Singleton issued a statement to confirm that he would put up a purse of £2,000 for the return match to be staged in Dublin, even though he had lost money on the first fight. Mike knew, however, that a rematch in Dublin was unlikely. As the *Boxing Blade* reported:

> We doubt very much if the Free State authorities would welcome another big bout in Dublin. They had an anxious time in securing reasonable peaceful conditions for the St Patrick's night affair, which could not have been pulled off without the presence of a huge armed force. As it was, the Irregulars exploded a landmine within a few yards of the La Scala theatre and kept up a lively fire with rifles and revolvers outside the building whilst the bout was being decided.

Mike was swamped with better offers. Carpentier's manager Deschamps, Major Arnold Wilson and Jim Harris visited the new champion at his hotel in Lucan the morning after the fight. The English promoter and French manager were already negotiating a Carpentier-McTigue fight at the Olympia in London at a date to be determined. According to *Boxing*, 'McTigue will, of course, have to rest up for a week or two, his broken thumb will need all that time to heal. But once it has healed he may then sign up for a long list of matches and look forward to the amassment of a substantial fortune.'

Since he had arrived in England Mike had been clamouring for matches with Jack Bloomfield, Joe Beckett and Ted 'Kid' Lewis, and they had all ignored him. But suddenly Mike had the title and was an attractive proposition. Jack Bloomfield, who held the British cruiserweight (light heavyweight) title, had boxed Mike in ten-round no-decision fights in the United States and still had the newspaper clippings to show he had the better of the contests. But Mike could pull out another batch of reports to the contrary. 'So the two ought to have a grudge to work off against each other, as well as a couple of championship titles to throw into the pot,' wrote *Boxing*. 'The Irishman is champion of the world, but would like to be champion of the United Kingdom (or now Disunited Realm, we suppose we ought to call it) as well.'

The *Boxing Blade* commented: 'The fact that Mike McTigue never did anything of much account in the American ring, prior to his defeat of Battling Siki in Europe, left rather a vague idea of his true value as a light heavyweight fighter, especially to the followers of the game in this country.

'Over in Ireland they think Mike is the goods, and will back him against Siki for a return battle or with any man of his weight in the world.'

The Americans considered the light heavyweight title to be damaged goods as it was held, in their view, by second-raters. The weight division was essentially the invention of promoter Tex Rickard who had awarded a belt, which according to Westbrook Pegler was 'set with a cupful of slightly spotty diamonds' as part of the promotion of the so-called 'Battle of the Century' between Jack Dempsey and Georges Carpentier in July 1921.

Rickard thought the fight would have greater appeal if Carpentier took a title into the ring. So he crowned Battling Levinsky, an old two-a-day fighter who had actually retired, light heavyweight champion by reason of having been beaten least often at 175 lbs. The promoter induced the International Sporting Club to offer Levinsky a sum of money to defend his title against Carpentier. The aged battler returned to the ring and duly conveyed the title to the Frenchman. The famous American boxing writer, Bob Edgren commented:

What is done with a title 'taken away' seems to be a mystery. Carpentier couldn't very well have it back, for Carpentier was knocked out [by Dempsey] in the ring, no matter what ethical conditions of the match may or may not have been violated.

Dempsey must have softened 'Carp' if Siki could beat the Frenchman under any circumstances, for Siki's right to be classed among the soup-kitchen fighters was shown when he couldn't beat Mike McTigue – a fair second-string middle-weight.

McTigue didn't have to weigh in to prove he isn't a heavyweight. He never weighed 175 pounds. Whether Siki weighed or not makes no difference; he could lose the title if he scaled a ton. As for the French Boxing Federation, it couldn't 'take away the title' from Siki on the ground that he was a roughneck or that he said he had double-crossed Georges. It could keep Siki from boxing in France; there its authority stopped.

That leaves McTigue light heavyweight champion. He can keep the title by staying abroad where the picking is soft, or lose it quickly by returning and meeting [Gene] Tunney.

Tex Rickard had once been described as 'a gambling man with a sur-passing appreciation for the lure and nuances of money and a sense of promotion that might serve as a model for post doctoral seminars at the Harvard School of Business'. Rickard was the key figure in making boxing popular and fashionable in New York in the 1920s. Within twenty-four hours of Mike's victory, Rickard informed the American press that he held an option on the Irishman's services and was negotiating a fight in the coming summer in the United

States for the light heavyweight title. Rickard got his option through Mike's American manager, Joe Jacobs, who had visited the promoter at his office. Rickard sent Mike a congratulatory telegram and told American reporters that the new champion had agreed not to take any more fights until returning to America for a match with Gene Tunney, Carpentier or the world middleweight champion, Johnny Wilson. The promoter planned to stage the contest at Boyle's Thirty Acres, Jersey City, or the Yankee Stadium, New York, probably in June.

The most lucrative opponent for Mike was Gene Tunney. 'I think I will go to work on it,' said Rickard. 'I am not sure I will make the match, but just now it appears to be a logical one to promote. Mike won the world's light heavyweight championship when he defeated Siki. Tunney is the American light heavyweight champion. To match them ought to be a good move. I think the public would support such a bout. That is what I am in the business for – to please the public.'

Rickard spent most of the following day cabling Mike with 'something pretty' to lure him back to the United States to defend his title. But the Irishman did not reply. The *New York Daily News* speculated: 'The impression here is that Mike is having his own troubles with the Irregular faction among the Irish folks for having engaged the Senegalese battler. At any rate, Mike hasn't come through with any response and the chances are that it will be several days before anything is heard from the tall Celt.'

When Mike failed to respond to Rickard's telegrams over the next twenty-four hours, one newspaper issued a public plea:

Speak to us Mike McTigue, Plaintive Wail of Promoters

Where in the world is that guy Mike McTigue keeping

himself these days? Lot of anxious folks would like to know whether Mike is coming over here to show us how he plastered that dark-skinned Battling Siki or whether he has made up his mind to stick on the other side where the going is much softer. One report has it that Mike is going to take a few theatrical engagements before starting for these shores. Just like the rest of the mob. The moment they grab off a championship, they hop on the stage. No matter what the matter is, Mike just won't answer any of the anxious Yankee kids on this side of the pond. It might be that Mike has fallen into the hands of John Law and cannot creep as far as a cable station to send his greetings to his pals in America.

Mike had other priorities that week however. On the morning of 22 March 1923 he left the Spa Hotel, Lucan, for Liverpool to see the Grand National the following day. He gave his new address to reporters as the Imperial Hotel, Liverpool. He said that he would return to Dublin on Monday or Tuesday of the following week and that he intended to remain in Ireland for some time. He claimed to have received many attractive offers for exhibitions in England and the Continent, including Paris, but so far had not made any definite decisions. The champion said he was charmed at the reception he had received in his native country. Mike also spoke highly of Rickard as a man and a promoter and added, 'I think you will be hearing something very interesting from me in the not-too-distant future.'

The news was that he had that accepted an offer to box Carpentier in the United States. On 23 March, under the headline 'McTigue Wants Our Titles and Money' the *New York Daily News* predicted that Mike would 'crease a groove across the Atlantic Ocean in his haste to get back to the land of the large money with his new title of world champion light heavyweight.' The following day the same newspaper reported the following story:

Mike The Champ He's Coming Back Soon

Just as we predicted, Mike McTigue will return to America just as fast as the big ship can carry him. What chance of Michael staying over on the wrong side of the world, when he can wrap himself around a chunk of Uncle Sam's coin of the realm for doing a few little boxing stunts? Now watch the scramble to get first rap at the young Irishman. Funny racket, the old boxing business. One day a hero and the next just a piece of camembert.

The American press was not impressed with the choice of Carpentier as opponent, however. 'If they pass up Gene Tunney and give Georges Carpentier first crack at McTigue, we think the fans will put up an awful squawk,' commented one New York paper. The *Washington Post* wrote that the 'defeat of the Senegalese battler proves beyond peradventure that he [Carpentier] has been greatly overrated, and that he never will be recognised except in France and England as a real champion. European titleholders, with few exceptions, are counterfeits.'

Carpentier, Rickard and the host of American fighters would have to wait a while. Mike's broken thumb ruled out any more boxing in the short term but it certainly didn't put an end to his winning streak. When he had landed at Dún Laoghaire to complete his training for the big fight, he had been presented with a sprig of shamrock containing one 'four leaf for luck'. The donor was a little girl dressed in the Irish national costume, who spoke in Irish, and wished the big Clareman every luck during his stay in his native land. On St Patrick's night he won a world's boxing title from Siki, then on Monday 19 March he drew White Bud in the Lincolnshire Handicap Sweepstakes. The following day he backed the same horse 'for luck' with a bookmaker; White Bud won at 66-1. On Thursday 22 March, he told a press interviewer who asked him about his Grand National choice, 'Sergeant Murphy is good enough for me; he carries my money.' The horse won at 100-6 and Mike won a 'tidy purse'.

'Is there any limit to Mike's good luck?' asked the *Irish Times* and, after news of Mike's success in the Lincoln and the Grand National, *Boxing* wrote that, 'a man who can enjoy a run like this may well be excused for believing that he is in the vein and can go right ahead after anything in sight. He has plenty of temptations to do so.'

But Mike was soon to get his first taste of the downside of being a world's boxing champion. In all the years he'd been a journeyman fighter in the United States he had received nothing worse from a largely disinterested press than an occasional word of criticism for a poor performance. Now he was champion it was different and the first publication to lead the attack was *Boxing*, which questioned the sincerity of Mike's oft-pronounced patriotism.

Before we leave the subject of the general consideration of all the possibilities to which the Siki-McTigue verdict has given rise, we feel we must give our promised explanation for styling Mike McTigue a cosmopolitan,' commented the publication. 'The label is not ours, Mr McTigue, so don't lay the blame on us, please. We were merely quoting an American summary of your nationality.

'The writer, a correspondent of the *New York Morning Tele-*

graph, was commenting on you as the representative of Ould Erin prior to your contest with Siki. He wrote: Not that McTigue is permanently Irish. If he were fighting in Siam on the day of a national fête, McTigue would probably find some line of argument to prove himself a homing Siamese of the purest breed returned to uphold his country's honour in an urgent pugilistic crisis. He was once an ardent Canadian, champion of Canada. Finding himself in New York somewhat later on, there was none so star-spangled as Mickey himself when he bowed himself into public notice and there was a claim against the American middleweight championship. When he beat Panama Joe Gans, the coloured middleweight champion, Mickey was in quite a bucket of tea for a few days because he wanted to claim the coloured title for himself. So Mickey called himself champion of Africa. Within the last year McTigue did some fighting in England as a 'Britisher', which is an ambiguous term covering a multitude of racial strains, but carelessly accepted as meaning English. The sun never sets on Mickey McTigue's numerous patriotisms.

According to *Boxing*: 'We haven't a doubt that you, Mr Michael McTigue, were duly born in Ennis, County Clare, and that you are a true blue, dyed-in-the-wool Irishman, but it would seem as though there are a few Americans around who seem to think that you have not consistently advertised the fact. We remember, however, that you were most insistent on your Irish nationality when Boy McCormick was disporting himself in New York. As we read it, you expressed annoyance that McCormick should be seeking to enlist all the Irish sympathies – seeing that he was born in India and not in Ireland – as you then declared you had been.

'Despite this, however, McCormick remained deaf to McTigue, and so Mike wasn't able to make all the splurge he wished out of his Irish origin. Nor, apparently, was he able to impress it on the New York Pressmen. It is, however, not impossible now that he can put in a more or less recognizable claim to the world's cruiserweight crown, that McCormick will be more attentive. The 'Boy' has always felt that he was unlucky when Carpentier got matched with Levinsky before he could himself get signed with that Battling person. McCormick won over Levinsky a few months too late, and has ever since felt that he ought to have been given a shot at the Hebrew's conqueror. It was for that very reason that he was so eager to meet Beckett. And we have all noticed that the ex-Dragoon is showing signs of a desire to get and keep busier than when he first came back from the States.'

Mike returned to his temporary home in Sheffield after successful forays on Battling Siki and the Lincoln and Liverpool bookmakers. He told local reporters that he would meet any heavyweight or middleweight in the world except Jack Dempsey. Dempsey was excluded from the challenge because Mike thought there was too great a disparity between the heavyweight champion's 13 stone 6lbs and his 11 stone 5lbs. He had hoped to meet Carpentier about 17 May but because of his injured thumb the match would now have to be put back until July. There was a great deal of speculation in England that Mike would fight the new British middleweight champion Roland Todd for the middleweight championship of Great Britain and Ireland. 'McTigue is, I understand, ineligible to compete for a Lonsdale challenge belt,' remarked the *Irish Independent*'s boxing writer, 'because only British-born boxers are qualified, and it is argued that Ireland is now in the same category as the Colonies.'

Battling Siki, who had greatly enjoyed his stay at Howth, re- mained in Dublin for twelve days after the fight. He finally left on

29 March after presenting a silver-mounted walking stick to Mr Bourke, the proprietor of the Claremont Hotel. He told writers that he was anxious to return to Paris where he owned a gentlemen's out-fitting establishment.

Siki took the morning train from Dublin to Cork where he was soon the centre of attraction and he got a particularly cordial reception from National troops stationed in the Custom House. He was due to take a steamer direct to Le Havre but as the ship carried the British flag Siki wasn't allowed on board. So he stayed in Cork for a few days and then took passage on the small cargo steamer, *Finula*, to Le Havre. Siki said he would return to Ireland in the course of a couple of weeks to meet Mike's sparring partner Bartley Madden in Dublin on 26 April and maintained that he believed he deserved the verdict in the recent bout. 'If I didn't,' he added, 'he would not be bandaged up; still, I got five hundred pounds out of it, and three hundred more is sure to come from film rights.'

According to the Communist newspaper, *L'humanité*, Siki met a group of strikers at Le Havre on his return and gave them two thousand francs. The strike was settled the same day and the money forwarded to the Marseille miners who were still out.

'I was robbed,' said Siki on his return to Paris, 'I will never go to Ireland again unless I can cross by way of England. I lost so much weight during the ocean trip to Ireland and back that I am now a middleweight.' He also claimed that his best and truest friends were the Irishmen in Paris who had advised him not to go to Ireland. A few days later Siki was called to a police station in Montmartre after a fight at the Rat Mort restaurant. Siki said he had been ridiculed and assaulted by the diners but he was formally charged with assault and battery. According to the *New York Times*, 'Siki, apparently back in form, knocked out a diner in one of the best-known Paris restaurants early this morning during a brawl.' Siki managed to side-step trouble over this incident when the complainant, a waiter in the restaurant, withdrew a charge of assault against him. The boxer appeared in court and agreed to pay indemnity and was let off with a warning. Siki's run of misfortune continued however. He had dragged a lion cub into a Paris café and was attempting to feed the animal when he was bitten. He had to cancel a bout planned in Marseilles after the wound became infected.

Mike was deluged with offers to induce him to stay in Europe for at least one more fight, but acting on his manager's advice, he turned a deaf ear. Joe Jacobs met Tex Rickard at Madison Square Garden on 21 April to sign up for the Carpentier fight. A cable was sent to Mike:

> Am signing tomorrow for Carpentier. Book passage immedi-
> ately and cable me time of departure and boat.

The following day Carpentier cabled Tex Rickard agreeing to take the fight with Mike, providing the promoter would stake him something in the neighbourhood of $75,000. 'Not so bad! The request of the Carp is under consideration, but the chances are that he will get what he asks for. Funny stunt about that guy still being a drawing card, but is he?' asked the *New York Daily News*.

Under instruction from Mike, Jacobs declined several offers of theatrical work, among them a proposition for three weeks of stage work that would have netted him $9,000. In a letter to Jacobs, Mike wrote that he preferred fighting to theatrical work because of 'the greater benefits, from a standpoint of physical preparedness, resulting from actual ring combat'. He then cabled Jacobs that he would sail for America on 5 May.

Mike booked passage on board the Cunard liner, *Berengaria*, which was expected to arrive in New York in time for him to be in the ring at the Milk Fund benefit show run by Tex Rickard at Yankee Stadium on 12 May. He wrote: 'I am sure I will KO Carpentier and then for Tunney. I fooled all the wise fellows here [Dublin] who thought Siki would KO me!' While waiting for his passage Mike put on his gloves for the first time since the Siki fight for an exhibition at the Free Trade Hall, Manchester. The exhibition did him little good, however, and he stepped onto the ship with his right arm back in a sling.

While Mike and his family were sailing to the United States the strength of public support for the Free State in Ireland was becoming overwhelming. Anti-Treatyism had lost but the mopping up was bloody and protracted. Kevin O'Higgins summed up the attitude of the government in an often-quoted phrase: 'This is not going to be a draw, with a replay in the autumn.'

The attitude of the Irregulars also hardened and 'military necessity' as Mulcahy described it, was used as an excuse by both sides to justify the brutality. From January to March 1923 republican forces were losing the war but most of them never gave a thought to surrender, despite the hardships. The official executions continued relentlessly and the unofficial ones too. IRA men were secretly court-martialled and shot, usually in groups of three or four throughout the twenty-six counties. The Free Staters took on the outward trappings of the Republic: the tricolour flag, the claim to the 1916-21 tradition, even the name of Dáil Éireann for the Leinster House parliament. They claimed that Pearse and Connolly would have backed the new state.

Although the Civil War was dragging on, it was obvious that the Free State forces were massing to end the conflict. Few of the original republican army leaders were left alive and the round-ups were more effective daily. The Free State army numbered around sixty thousand men, properly equipped and paid. An IRA brigade typically numbered around twenty and had to share a few rifles between them. Liam Lynch was mortally wounded on 10 April and his replacement, Frank Aiken, declared a universal ceasefire a few weeks later. On 24 May Aiken ordered his men to 'dump arms' and the war was over. Eamon De Valera addressed a message to the 'Soldiers of the Republic, Legion of the Rearguard':

> The Republic can no longer be defended successfully by your arms. Further sacrifice of life would now be vain and continuance of the struggle in arms unwise in the national interest and prejudicial to the future of our cause. Military victory must be allowed to rest with those who have destroyed the Republic. Other means must be sought to safeguard the nation's right.

He reassured his men that much had been accomplished and that the people, exhausted by seven years of intense effort, would rally again to the standard.

TEN

If you didn't see Mike fight when he was light heavyweight champion of the world, you can have no idea how terrible a prizefighter can be.

Westbrook Pegler, *Washington Post*

A whiff of bootleg Scotch and speakeasy smoke drifted down 'Jacobs Beach'. The babbling little strip of sidewalk populated by thugs and bent-nosed pugs, mobsters and their molls, cops and conmen led to the 49th Street office of Joe Jacobs, the most colourful fight manager in town.

Known along Broadway as 'Yussel the Muscle', Joe was a tailor's son from Manhattan's west side. He had made and spent a fortune, but win or lose he was always a jaunty figure with a cigar tilted at the corner of his mouth. *Boxing* writers loved his keen knack for making a headline. He coined the phrase 'We Wuz Robbed' following the second fight between Schmeling and Jack Sharkey, when Sharkey was awarded the decision and with it the heavyweight title. His other famous saying, 'I should of stood [have stayed] in bed,' was said in the press box at Detroit during the 1934 World Series between the Tigers and Cardinals on a cold, damp afternoon.

Jacobs had been a familiar figure in gymnasiums around New York from the age of fifteen, whether guiding one of his own fighters or passing judgement on others. Joe had graduated from neighbourhood fighters to genuine contenders and on the morning of 11 May 1923, he made his way down the Great White Way with its gaudy lights, through the clanging of skyscraper steel, the noisy streetcars and jazz horns, to Pier 54 to greet his first world champion. He hadn't played much of a part in landing the Siki fight but Mike McTigue was his fighter and Joe could smell the money.

The *Berengaria* arrived in quarantine at about eleven o'clock. She carried members of the Czechoslovakian Debt Funding Mission who were travelling to America to negotiate a settlement of their country's liability to the United States. Baron Bornemisza, head of the Cunard line in Budapest was also on board. But the shipping reporters were only interested in one passenger and they'd been invited on board to watch Mike McTigue box a few rounds with George Mason, who was in charge of the ship's gymnasium. The new light heavyweight champion was unaware of the elaborate reception that awaited him on the pier. It was in sharp contrast to his departure less than a year previously when he had to push his young family through crowds of longshoremen who had gathered for the 'shape up', where the boss chose who among them would get to work that day.

As Mike and his family stepped down the gangplank, more than a thousand people boomed their welcome and the Sixty-ninth Regiment Armoury Band played home the new hero. Murray Hulbert, president of the Board of Aldermen, officially welcomed him back to the United States after which representatives of various Irish societies and athletic clubs descended on the champion, all wanting to shake his hand. Pier 54 was a big, three-storey-high shed, like a train station on water with waiting rooms, luggage holds and an extravagantly frilled Edwardian-style concrete façade. Somehow a way was cleared through the crowds that packed the building and the McTigue family appeared from under the Cunard-inscribed arch-way and were escorted to a waiting motor car. Over twenty vehicles followed in a procession headed by the band of the Sixty-ninth. It made its way slowly up Broadway to Fifth Avenue and on to the Pennsylvania Hotel where the McTigues would stay until they found an apartment. 'The Irish middleweight was visibly impressed with his reception and grew enthusiastic under the greeting,' reported the *New York Times*.

'I'm back in America now, prepared to defend the title I won in Europe,' said Mike. 'I want to be a real champion. If I have not the ability to qualify as a real champion, then I don't deserve the title. I'll box any middleweight, light heavyweight or heavyweight who is selected for me. Tom Gibbons, Gene Tunney, Harry Greb, or any other man who seeks the title I hold is welcome. My manager, Joe Jacobs, will arrange my matches. I'll do the rest. I would like particularly to get a match with Johnny Wilson. I'll guarantee to make the middleweight limit for him, and I am confident I can beat him.'

The Americans thought Mike a fluke champion and virtually every leading middleweight, light heavyweight and heavyweight in America had posted a challenge at Joe's office. 'Jack Dempsey has lost a record,' wrote Bob Edgren, 'He is no longer the most challenged champion in the world. Mike McTigue, recently returned from Ireland and greeted by bands, parades, flowers, speeches and a procession of dinners that would fatten him into a heavyweight if he ate them all, has had to requisition a couple of ten-gallon waste-baskets and put them outside his bedroom door to receive wired and written challenges. Fighters who never indulged in such intellectual pursuits before have taken pen in hand and scribbled defiance to Mike.'

Among the gentlemen now engaged in annoying Mike and filling Joe's waste-basket were the best light heavyweights in America, Gene

Tunney and Harry Greb, and a ring-full of other leading boxers who had avoided the Irishman for years. Now it was Mike's turn to tell them to go get a reputation. 'It is easier to haul a multimillionaire before an investigating committee than it is to get a champion of the world into the ring with a fighter who has an even chance to defeat him,' wrote Charles Emmett Van Loan. The world title meant Madison Square Garden, the big dough and security for Mike's family. The Irishman's first title defence had already been signed and Georges Carpentier was due to follow Mike to the United States in a matter of weeks.

It was a good time to be handling a champion. Joe Jacobs had started managing in the old days of the Horton and Frawley Laws when boxing was disreputable, attended by only a few sports and their 'broads' and purses were paltry. But the 1920s was an extraordinary decade during which previously unheard-of sums were bestowed upon champions of every class. Joe was thinking big numbers. The biggest draw in New York was the American light heavyweight champion, Gene Tunney. The Greenwich Village fighter had posted a challenge to Mike with the boxing commission and a match between the world champion and the American champion was a lucrative proposition.

Just days after Mike's arrival in the United States, Joe showed up at the Garden to accept the challenge on behalf of Mike, but 'there wasn't anybody around to talk turkey'. Tunney's manager Billy Gibson had promised to be on hand to talk over a match but got lost somewhere in the wilds of the Bronx and never showed. A match with Tunney suffered a further blow when the American champion damaged his hand on Jimmy Delaney's head so Joe turned his attention to Harry Greb. He secured Greb's signature for a ten-round no-decision bout at the Cubs' baseball park in Chicago on 20

June and matched Mike with Tommy Loughran in an eight-rounder in Philadelphia just five days later.

Mike wasn't allowed to fight a championship match until he'd boxed Carpentier so the no-decision bouts would make his waistline thinner and his bankroll thicker until the Frenchman arrived. More 'soft money' came from Dave Marion and his Big Burlesque and Vaudeville Show. Mike put on an exhibition twice daily at 2.15 pm and 8.15 pm for a week at the Columbia Theatre in New York. 'The gang is all ready to greet the tall Celt when he breezes across with his stuff,' commented the *New York Daily News*.

Mike resumed training at Sprague's Gymnasium in Harlem where several hundred fans watched the new champion work. Those 'in the know' believed him to be a greatly improved fighter compared to when he had last been seen around New York. But it wasn't long before the curse of the injured hand struck once more. Georges Carpentier suffered the damage during a one-round knockout of Marcel Nilles in Paris and the Frenchman's summer schedule had to be rearranged. He had a prior engagement to keep with British champion Joe Beckett and the match was postponed from 14 June to 4 July. The title fight with Mike had been slated for 14 July so this was put back to 11 August to give the Frenchman time to prepare. Carpentier's manager Deschamps was quoted as saying: 'Carpentier and myself have the greatest appreciation for the wonderful way we have always been treated by the British sporting public, and we fully realise our first duty, when fit, is to fulfil our obligation to the public, to Beckett and to Major Wilson.'

Mike's $100,000 payday was in jeopardy but Joe Jacobs had a plan: the upcoming no-decision contest with Harry Greb could be elevated to a championship match. Greb used to sport the American honours among the light heavyweights until he lost to Tunney and according to one scribe he was 'a dangerous bird to be flirting around when you have one of those pet titles'.

The sports writers believed that Joe was taking a big risk with Mike's newly won title. So did Mike. He and Greb had fought three times previously and the Irishman had not got the better of the encounters. Mike was publicly claiming that if he wasn't a real champion he wanted to find out right away, but he wasn't about to risk his precious title without a big financial inducement. If he lost to Greb he'd lose the Carpentier match and the big purse attached. Unfortunately for the Irishman the New York promoters didn't think a McTigue-Greb match would justify that sort of outlay. Yet another fight fell through. Mike had only been back in New York for a few weeks but the new champion's reputation was tarnished already. When he had stepped off the *Berengaria* back in May he was hailed as a hero for beating the 'black menace' but by the end of June he was being portrayed as a lucky champion with a greatly exaggerated sense of his own worth.

Tom O'Rourke, matchmaker at the Polo Grounds Athletic Club, was trying to arrange a match between Mike and the fit-again Gene Tunney for Independence Day. Tunney's manager Billy Gibson had agreed terms but doubted whether Mike would do likewise: 'I think McTigue will insist on too much money. Tunney would like nothing better than to meet McTigue in the ring for Gene feels sure he would emerge the world's light heavyweight champion.'

Joe was charged with countering the allegations and conveniently, he was able to announce that he had signed a contract with Dr Patrick McCartan for Mike to meet Battling Siki in a return match in Dublin. Dr McCartan was the former editor of *Irish Freedom* and a close friend of the publication's founder, Thomas Clarke. The two men fell out on the eve of the Easter Rising when McCartan sent word that the Tyrone volunteers would wait until they received confirmation that the Pope had been informed of the action and that German guns had landed in County Kerry. He was elected for Laois Offaly in 1921 and initially gave the Anglo-Irish Treaty his reluctant support, but he soon became disillusioned and quit politics. According to Joe Jacobs he had taken up prizefight promotion. Joe claimed to have agreed with Dr McCartan a guarantee of $100,000 with the privilege of taking 45 per cent of the gate receipts for a fight to be staged at the Gaelic Athletic Association's ground that was capable of seating 35,000 people with tickets selling for $5 to $15. The New York boxing writers were keen to discuss the big fight with Dr McCartan in person but Joe informed them that the contract had been signed out at Mike's training quarters at his brother-in-law's estate at Babylon, Long Island. He claimed the doctor was to sail to Ireland the following day and go immediately to France to sign Siki.

'There's a stranger in town by the name of Dr Patrick McGilli-cuddy Cartan from Dublin,' reported the *New York Daily News* on 14 June 1923. 'The stranger's mission is to sign up Mike McTigue for another jam with Battling Siki, the peace-loving citizen of Senegal, at the Irish capital on September 7 … According to Joe Jacobs, Patrick McGillicuddy Cartan has offered Mike £20,000 or almost $100,000 in American currency. Joe says he will not let Mike play unless the visitor raises this to £25,000.'

The press believed that Joe was following the lead of champion Jack Dempsey and others in boosting Mike's price for matches. The *Boxing Blade* published a letter from a former American writer based in London:

The story published in New York papers that Mike McTigue

was cabled an offer of $75,000 to box Joe Beckett in London is sheer bunk. Purses of this dimension are not obtainable on this side, and in any case, McTigue has done nothing to justify such an offer. His victory over Siki was not particularly striking, granting that he did win, a point still disputed by some witnesses of the bout. Even more absurd is the alleged offer of $100,000 for another McTigue-Siki bout in Dublin. In the first place there is no building large enough in the capital of the Free State to stage a contest with profit. Secondly, Siki will not fight again before the Carpentier return match next September and lastly, I doubt if the Free State authorities would permit another scrap in Dublin.

Outdoor boxing is not flourishing in Ireland, most of the Belfast promotions resulting in loss to the organisers. It is therefore difficult to see how Dr Patrick McCartan proposes to raise the amount of $100,000 for McTigue, pay Siki, preliminary boxers and other expenses and leave himself a profit.

In Scotland, there are several spots where big bouts can be pulled off, but a McTigue-Siki would not appeal as a great attraction to Scotch fans. London promoters are out of the reckoning as Siki is definitely and permanently barred in this country and on his performances in Paris, it is safe to say he is not wanted.

The British boxing writers were also sceptical about the venture. They'd been told that Dr McCartan was in New York to line up a fight between Mike and Joe Beckett. Most of the newspapers voiced their suspicions that the story was a ruse to up Mike's purse with American promoters. *Boxing World*, *Mirror Of Life and Sporting*

Observer, under the headline, 'Mike McTigue and Big Money', reported:

> Mike McTigue appears to have come to the conclusion that there is money to burn in the boxing game. He must be seeing pictures of himself entering the boxing ring in the midst of a shower of dollar bills or English treasury notes, for it is said he has had an offer of $75,000 to fight Joe Beckett in London, and may accept it later on.
>
> We are prepared to believe that Michael is in line for all this 'dough' if he feels disposed to accept it, I suppose, but the tales will not go down very well in Great Britain or Ireland where promoters are not exactly what you'd call munificent 'mugs'.
>
> McTigue is, or has to meet, Greb in a ten-round no-decision bout, and he hasn't received nor will he receive, anything like the fabulous sums mentioned above, nor will his end for tackling Carpentier run into so many thousands, so the opinion to be ventured as to why he hesitates to accept £15,000 to £20,000 offers is that he hasn't had the chance to grab them.

Within a few months of returning to the States Mike picked up another title, the undisputed champion of unpopular champions. The previous holder was Al McCoy. In February 1914 McCoy had fractured contender Joe Chip's chest bone during a no-decision bout. A rematch was scheduled for April but Joe was injured and his brother George was sent in as a replacement. George Chip was the world middleweight champion but the match was a no-decision affair and his title could only be taken away by knockout. Less than two minutes of the first round had passed when the referee tolled the doleful count of ten over the champion. Al then kept the title for three years by limiting himself to countless no-decision bouts or matches he knew that he couldn't lose. The scribes christened McCoy the 'cheese champion' for being a poor fighter who had lucked into the championship then hidden it away.

Mike would now replace Al as the most fromagenous titleholder in town. At best he was an accidental champion, the result of a memorable coup d'état in Dublin on St Patrick's Day. Now it looked like he would retain a steadfast hold on the title by heading off to favourite stamping grounds where decisions were not permitted. The purses for such bouts were much smaller than for championship matches but Mike wasn't putting his title in any real danger and by now he needed the money. He had made a loss on the tour of Britain and Ireland and hadn't boxed at all since beating Siki. Joe signed him up with Tommy Loughran in Philadelphia on 25 June but the match only served to reinforce the suspicion that Mike was a poor fighter holding on to the title any way he could. The majority of newspapermen at the ringside credited the champion with only two of ten rounds against Loughran. 'McTigue appeared listless and was hit almost at will by the Philadelphian,' reported one newspaperman. 'McTigue appeared awkward and displayed anything but championship form. In the first two rounds he landed only four blows and they did no damage.'

More bad news was to follow when the *New York Times* reported that 'Georges Carpentier's third invasion of the United States is off indefinitely.' The Frenchman's fight with Joe Beckett had been postponed once more and the most recent information was that it would be staged on 26 July. Tex Rickard had planned to stage the McTigue-Carpentier bout at Boyle's Thirty Acres in Jersey City on

11 August but now the promoter announced it would be held, if held at all, some time in the autumn. It had been an on-off affair all summer, so much so that interest in the fight had been knocked groggy and almost counted out. So Mike took another no-decision fight.

He was upset and angry over what had been written about his bout with Loughran so he signed to meet the Philadelphia man once more. 'Mike McTigue has a grievance,' wrote one boxing writer. 'He is not peeved with anyone but himself ... Mike has contended ever since that inactivity prevented him from doing justice.' He realised that his showing was 'not of a champion' the first time he fought Loughran and was anxious to regain lost prestige.

The return was duly arranged by John M. Tenney, matchmaker of the All-Stars Alliance, for twelve rounds in Harrison, New Jersey on 19 July. Mike trained for the fight at Grupp's Gymnasium on 116th Street, Harlem where he worked before a big crowd every day. It used to be *the* fight gym in New York until Billy Grupp launched into a drunken anti-Semitic tirade, blaming the Jews for the First World War. World lightweight champion Benny Leonard and a contingent of Jewish fighters stormed out and Grupp's lost most of its best fighters.

Mike was training for the return with Loughran when an interesting visitor arrived in town. Major J. Paul Jones was the athletic director of the Charles Harrison Post of the American Legion and he had a proposition. He offered Mike $10,000 to fight William 'Young' Stribling of Macon, Georgia for the light heavyweight championship. The fight would take place in the South on Labour Day, the first Monday in September.

Stribling was still in high school but had boxed professionally since he was sixteen and was regarded as the best boxer to have emerged from the South in many years. He was the son of professional athletes; his father was his trainer and manager while his mother looked after his diet. 10,000 dollars was far below what Mike and Joe had been asking for a championship match in New York but Stribling was only a schoolboy and it was easy money. So the match was made.

Meanwhile the Loughran fight at the West New York Ball Park was generating some interest with the customers. The *Daily News* ran a campaign on behalf of the 'two-dollar boys' and a large number of cheap tickets were made available. Mike had loafed on the job while training for Loughran before, underestimating the ability of a clever, hard-hitting biffer from the sleepy burg. This time he promised to display a brand of milling that would prove a revelation to those at ringside. 'Indications are that it will be a battle of the Tabasco variety with one or the other taking the count before the final bell,' wrote one pundit.

Not so. It was a slow, tedious affair with Loughran generally credited with six of the twelve rounds, Mike three, with three even. Loughran threw straight lefts into the Irishman's face throughout and it wasn't until the closing rounds that Mike made a fight of it. The championship wasn't lost as there was no decision but the value of Mike's title had slipped a little further.

Kid Norfolk, the 'coloured' light heavyweight champion, posted $5,000 with Jess McMahon of the Commonwealth Sporting Club as a forfeit if the matchmaker could arrange a match with Mike. Norfolk was preparing for a match with Jamaica Kid and if successful he was going to demand a match with the world champion. He argued that since Mike won the title from a black fighter he could not draw the colour line. Norfolk beat Jamaica Kid but a 'unification' championship bout between black and white was never going to attract the sort of purse Mike was looking for.

It didn't get any better. Young Stribling broke his arm in a fight with Happy Howard and the Labour Day fight in Georgia was off. Another attempt to make a match with Tunney floundered with both camps blaming each other for the breakdown in negotiations. 'All attempts to complete a match between Mike McTigue and Gene Tunney failed yesterday and Joe Jacobs is running around with an awful squawk against Billy Gibson and his charge Gene Tunney,' reported the *New York Daily News*. 'Sore to the quick, Jacobs says that Gibson and Gene are running out on Mike. Nothing short of an out is the way Joe feels about it. According to Jacobs, Tunney has been telling the folks that he is anxious to fight McTigue, but when they came to talk turkey Gene and his manager, Gibson, demanded nearly everything in sight and the prospects of a fight blew up. This is the way it is with these fighting fellows. They can stir up more trouble than any other racket in the world.'

Then it got worse. An x-ray examination revealed that Mike had broken his left hand in the Loughran fight and it would keep him out of the ring for several weeks. Negotiations for future fights were put on hold. But at least there was an old friend in town with whom Mike could trade his tales of woe. On the morning of 1 September 1923 Mike and Joe elbowed through the crowds on Pier 54 and walked up the gangplank to meet Battling Siki in the main saloon of the *Berengaria*. The *Washington Post* reported that there was considerable trepidation at the Battler's arrival. 'The residents of New York as a whole have no desire to become the centre of Siki's playground. The coloured fighter combines the abandon of a true Frenchman with the idiosyncrasies of an Aborigine in the pursuit of his profession.' In a brief and tragic spell in the city, Siki would do little but live up to his reputation.

Siki's presence did mark an upturn in Mike's fortunes however.

He travelled to Columbus, Georgia to sign a contract for the re-scheduled Stribling fight and after another bout of hard negotiating a match with Gene Tunney for the light heavyweight title was finally made. On 4 October 1923 Joe Jacobs and Billy Gibson, respective managers of Mike and Gene, posted forfeits guaranteeing the weight and appearance of the boxers for a championship match at Madison Square Garden on 10 December. The weight was to be 175 pounds at 2 o'clock on the afternoon of the bout. Tunney opened training quarters at Red Bank, New Jersey, while Mike went to Georgia to swell his bankroll before beginning his training in earnest. The injury to his hand was said to be healing nicely.

ELEVEN

McTigue invaded the stronghold of the Ku Klux Klan with the dust of Dublin still on his shoes, to measure his reach with Young Stribling, a Macon high-school student.

Los Angeles Times, 9 October 1923

Like the deep green waters of the Chattahoochee River, champion boxers never stopped in Columbus. This was the proud State of Georgia where Grand Opera had been taxed out of existence as a useless luxury and the biggest draw at the picture houses was D. W. Griffith's racist epic, *Birth for a Nation*: record-breaking crowds cheered on the hooded and robed crusaders as they rode into town to save the young white heroine from rape by castrating and lynching her black would-be assailant. But on 4 October 1923 an Irish Catholic fighter and his Jewish manager arrived in town with the light heavyweight championship of the world in tow. They even reckoned on accompanying the title back to New York. Joe Jacobs had spent six months negotiating six-figure purses on the East Coast but ultimately settled for a 10,000-dollar guarantee in hostile territory.

Joe planned on a routine ten-round contest to get the champion ready for the glamorous matches lined up for the winter season at Madison Square Garden. He even took along his own referee, Harry Ertle, for a little extra insurance. Mike's critics like Westbrook Pegler of the *Chicago Tribune* believed the champion's reign was about to come to an untimely, but deserved, end:

> [Jacobs and McTigue] went to Columbus, Georgia, to fight a homeboy or townie by the name of William Stribling, intending to jumble the townie around the ring for a harmless manner for ten rounds, collect their honorarium, and be on their way. Although Michael was a champion, he was a very demure prizefighter and did not enjoy meeting rough characters in the arenas of the larger cities.
>
> That was why he was touring the country, meeting townies at the rate of three or four every week, and jumbling them around in bouts that were devoid of danger and also devoid of interesting incident. At the end of each contest the spectators would cry, 'Boo! McTigue's a bum,' but Mr Jacobs would have the money and the pair of them would catch the late train out of town, ignoring all such remarks.
>
> But what was their surprise on arriving in Columbus, Georgia, to discover that this townie, Willie Stribling, was a rough, slippety-slap young man who could not be jumbled around because he could outjumble any man living. He was not much of a prizefighter, you understand, but gracious, that young man would jumble. Their surprise was A1.

Mike sensed there was something bad in the air and it wasn't coming from the river known to locals as the 'Chattanasty'. This was no place for an Irishman. Anti-catholic and anti-semitic fervour swept through the Southern states and Catholics were leading the militant anti-Klan group known as the Red Knights or Knights of the Flaming Circle. Mike had no desire to be a Red Knight; in fact he had no desire for any sort of combat. He set up training quarters at Camp Benning, the military base just outside Columbus, where he sparred with local soldiers in the days leading up to the match with Stribling. The champion was lethargic and the scribes attributed his stupor to a cable from Georges Carpentier. The Frenchman had knocked out British heavyweight champion Joe Beckett in one round and sent Mike a challenge for a bout in America. Carpentier had signed with a syndicate of sportsmen from Phoenix, Arizona and Mike could expect 100,000 dollars for the match; if he still had a title to defend.

It was at dusk, during the hush just after the sawmills had closed down, that the world champion walked into the matchmaker's office. The pine smoke still hugged the town as Mike, with his right hand in plaster and an x-ray photograph under his arm, said he was out of the following day's fight. He claimed to have re-broken his right thumb earlier that afternoon. Whether the injury was genuine or not only Mike and a Dr Blake, who was paid for the examination and prognosis, really knew. The promoters, the Charles Harrison Post of the American Legion, suspected foul play and had the champion's hand examined by several reputable Georgian doctors.

Mike refused to take the cast off but the medical party accepted that the x-ray examinations showed an 'imperfectly healed fracture of the metacarpal bone of his right thumb'. Major J. Paul Jones, an athletic director with the Legion and a man Mike described as 'one of those stay-at-home war heroes,' called both fighters and their managers to a meeting. It lasted until midnight. An *Associated Press* dispatch sent out from Columbus at 3 am stated that two local boxers, Joe Lohman and Captain Bob Ropur, had been named as potential substitutes. Mike placated the promoters by returning the guarantee paid him the previous day and agreeing to fight Stribling in Georgia within ninety days. But the Georgians were not to be cheated of their gore.

It was 5 o'clock in the morning and the early trains had shaken the thick dust of the road before Mike got to bed. He was a contented man. There would be no fight and his bags were already packed. Then the first editions hit the newsstands and an angry crowd gathered at his hotel. They jeered and bayed for the 'yellow' champ. Mike had had barely two hours' sleep when two men, one armed with a pistol, broke into his room. 'Some banker of Columbus told me my life wasn't worth two cents; to take that statement any way I wanted and that if I didn't go into the ring, I would know what that would mean,' Mike later recalled. Jacobs called the police who escorted fighter and manager to Major Jones' office where a reception committee lay in wait. A gun was placed under Jacobs' nose who, as was pointed out by one newspaperman, was 'no Hibernian nor even slightly eligible for Klan membership.' He has warned that the people of Columbia had no patience with un-American or unsportsmanlike tricks and that the fight would go on. Mike and Jacobs were told that the crowd at the fight would be Klansmen down to the last man and by ingenious forethought, the ring ropes had been strung to the corner posts in quick-detachable fashion.

'See those trees out yonder,' asked one of the hosts as he manoeuvred Jacobs to the window. 'Just name the one you and your fighter would like to hang from. There is one tree apiece and there is plenty of rope.' Jacobs is reputed to have replied: 'If you hang me, there will be some guys down here from New York that will blow this dump off the map.'

Westbrook Pegler wrote an alternative account of the conversation in the *Chicago Tribune*:

'Tree?' Mr Jacobs said, 'why should I wish that I should have trees?'

'Because,' the committee advised him, 'if your gentleman should chance to beat our native son, we will call for you promptly at the ringside, and we shall then hang you from your tree and Mr McTigue from his tree.'

'Oh, in that case, I will just select a modest tree. Please get me something about four feet high and, if convenient, pick out a small shrub for my gentleman too. However, I would like to insist that whatever you do, you give him the larger one because we always divide everything on a basis of 66 2/3 per cent to him and 33 1/3 per cent to me.

'And furthermore, do you think you could find a rubber tree for me – something that will bend easy? All my life I have thought that if anybody wished to give me a tree I would like to have a rubber tree.'

Despite the bravado Mike and Joe had been made an offer they couldn't refuse. Losing a world title was preferable to swinging from a noose and the fight was back on. 'A lot of quarrelling, scrapping and rioting followed, during which I was backed up with revolvers to my stomach and told that I would not leave that town alive unless I fought Stribling that night,' Mike recalled. 'I was charged with being a yellow quitter, that got my goat, so I finally announced that I would go on and fight Stribling with one hand, if he would bind himself to fight me a return bout for the title before he fought anyone else, if he beat me.'

'In Ireland McTigue was condemned to death because he wouldn't call the fight off,' wrote the *Los Angles Times*. 'In Georgia he was threatened with a similar fate because he did.'

With fighter and manager taken care of, the mob turned its attention to the referee, Harry Ertle. Major Jones came up to

Ertle's room two hours before the fight to warn him against leaving Columbus. 'He said that McTigue, Jacobs and myself, as long as we were in town, were being watched, and that every railroad station was covered,' said Ertle. The press, especially the local contingent, believed the blame lay with the champion. Even Julian Harris, editor of the *Columbus Enquirer-Sun*, who won a Pulitzer Prize in 1926 for his efforts in reporting Klan violence and exposing the public officials who were members, had some sympathy for the mob on this occasion. 'There is no question but that McTigue and Jacobs were aware of the condition of the champion's thumb when the contract to fight Stribling was signed,' wrote Harris. 'Undoubtedly the thought of endangering the champion's title, with the possibility of a $100,000 fight with Carpentier in sight, caused the injured thumb to take on exaggerated proportions.'

Back in New York the celebrated boxing scribes thought the whole matter highly amusing. 'Discussion, pro and con, as the boys say, arose and the local Ku Klux Klan held a conclave to debate upon the advisability of suspending Michael from the top branch of a Southern pine,' wrote Bill McGeehan in the *New York Herald Tribune*. 'When the proposition was placed before Michael, he pleaded a sore throat and voted in the negative. Since that time Michael has been unpopular in Georgia, and it is held that he committed a breach of Southern hospitality in refusing to accept the tree that was offered him. Georgians are very sensitive about such matters. Mr McTigue denies that any offence was meant or that his refusal to be hanged was due to any sectional prejudice. He says that he would object to the same extent on principle to being electrocuted.'

The crowd was the greatest seen at a fight south of the Mason-Dixon line since the defeat of John L. Sullivan by Jim Corbett in the Great Fistic Carnival of New Orleans in September 1892. New

Orleans was a refuge of corruption and depravity and had been an ideal setting for boxing to thrive illegally in the years after the Civil War. But the boxing boom in the South did not last. Three men died in New Orleans prize-rings in quick succession and the love for pugilism left the city. The big title fights moved to Chicago, Buffalo and especially to New York. The last champion to defend his title in the South, John L. Sullivan, left a beaten man and the next to try, Mike McTigue, would fight with one hand and at the point of a gun.

The Irishman's broken thumb was numbed with Novocaine and soldiers with fixed bayonets escorted him to the ring. The referee, Harry Ertle, was already there. 'Before he got in, some of those crazy Georgians stuck guns into his vest buttons and told him that he must be mighty careful who he gave the verdict to in the ring. He laughed at them, for he is a game man,' Mike recalled. The challenger, William 'Young' Stribling had proudly boasted to have never been knocked off his feet. Stribling couldn't stake such a claim after the fight. For the first nine rounds the champion, using his right hand exclusively for defensive duties, was content to stay away from the Georgian's rushes. Then, just as he had in Dublin against Siki, Mike started to attack in the later rounds and he floored the challenger in the ninth round. Stribling beat the count and answered the bell for the tenth and last round. The real drama of the day was about to begin.

The boxers shook hands and referee Ertle said: 'You boys are all right; don't work too hard.' Ertle decided to call the fight a draw before the tenth round started. He scored it four rounds to Mike, Stribling three, with the others even, but he took a diplomatic decision. As the final bell tolled Ertle pointed to both corners to signify a draw. Major Jones leapt into the ring and demanded a verdict for Stribling. 'I told him that my decision was given,' said Ertle, 'then he said to me that I'd better get back in there and give that decision to Stribling, and I said my decision was given and that I could only give it a draw; that if he wanted to give the decision to Stribling, he could.'

'How do you call a draw? Don't you have to raise both arms?' asked Jones.

Ertle explained that it wasn't necessary, pointed to both corners once more and repeated his decision. Instantly the ring was filled with 'scowling citizenry' and though none of them wore white robes or brandished flaming crosses, they were mighty persuasive. The decision did not correspond with the Georgian concept of justice and as Ertle climbed through the ropes to begin his escape he was surrounded by a mob showing a 'very Klannish spirit in their preference for home talent'. The press area was invaded as the crowd rushed over the tables and several writers were trampled under stomping feet.

Mike watched the riot develop from his corner. 'When Ertle started out of the ring, somebody struck a gat [gun] in his stomach and ordered him to get back and give a decision. When Harry refused to do this, somebody, I'm pretty sure it was Captain Bob Roper, spat in his face,' claimed Mike.

Rather than continue his getaway through the crowd, Ertle opted for the relative safety of the ring. A military policeman escorted him back through the ropes while other officers tried to clear the ring by throwing the invaders back onto the crumpled heap of boxing writers. 'Then he [Major Jones] said I would never leave that ring alive,' said Ertle. 'He called several newspapermen into the ring and said he would ask them for their decision, and I said no matter what they say I cannot reverse my decision; I have given them a draw.'

The master of ceremonies announced that the referee had asked the newspapermen into the ring. Those who weren't crushed under broken chairs, tables or Klansmen were told by Major Jones that the referee wanted their opinion of the fight. They unsurprisingly and unanimously proclaimed Stribling the winner. Jones instructed Ertle to shake hands with the young Georgian, who had been sitting in his corner, weeping, throughout the commotion.

Ertle reached out to Stribling then Jones stepped up and raised both Ertle's and Stribling's hands in the air. The journalists were climbing back through the ropes when they saw Stribling and Ertle's hands flash above the throng in the ring. The official announcer yelled that Stribling was the new world champion. 'They take their fighting seriously in Georgia, and heaven help the referee who doesn't consider the just claims of the home-town boy,' commented the *New York Times*. 'Mr McTigue, having won his championship in Dublin, where he was the home-town boy, should be broad-minded enough to appreciate this sentiment.'

A detachment of troops was called in to break up the mêlée. Soldiers pushed through the crowd with pointed bayonets shouting orders of shoot-to-kill. 'That quieted the boys down,' recalled one scribe. Ertle was escorted to a safe house in Columbus. Willie Pfeiffer, Mike's sparring partner, was to fight Stribling's sparring partner Jimmy Findley straight after the main event. Pfeiffer refused.

It was a 'blood-burning moon' and the air was heavy with the scent of boiling sugar cane. Columbus was packed with angry men deep into the night. Ertle, closeted away from the baying mob, issued a signed statement that he'd declared the fight a draw and hadn't reversed the decision even when told he wouldn't leave the arena alive. Mike and Joe sped out of town guarded by four military policemen from Camp Benning, immediately after Ertle issued his affidavit. 'I've been in jams,' Mike recalled, 'but none so tough as that one.'

Mike released his own statement describing how he'd been

forced into the ring with a broken thumb at the point of pistols. 'It was never known in the history of the ring to have a referee's decision reversed,' claimed the champion. 'I will meet Stribling in a return match when my hand is well again, any time, any place, where I am sure I will receive a square deal.' Joe Jacobs was telling anyone who would listen how he had been threatened with hanging by a mob that held him responsible for the fight being called off earlier in the day. 'In Jacobs there was capsuled a mocking parody on the policies, aspirations and pretensions of nations,' wrote Westbrook Pegler. 'Great was the amazement of the prizefight profession,' he added, 'when there came over the wires the shocking news that Michael McTigue, an Irish Catholic, owned and operated by Yussel Jacobs, a New York boy of the most conspicuous Jewishness, had lost the precious title by a close decision to Willie Stribling, a native son in Columbus, Georgia, where the Ku Klux Klan was seeing blood in the moon.'

With Mike, Joe and Harry Ertle safely on board trains to New York, back in Georgia Major Jones claimed the trio had succeeded in pulling 'a colossal fake'. The promoter produced a contract, signed by Mike, showing the referee was in the employ of the world champion. Ertle was promised $250 and expenses for his services. Mike agreed to pay $125, with the American Legion posting the remainder. 'He told me that if both boxers were on their feet at the end of ten rounds, he would call it a draw, because of McTigue's supposedly broken thumb which was paining him,' Jones told the *Chicago Tribune*. 'I told Ertle frankly that such an arrangement would not do, that we had entered into no such arrangement with McTigue. Then, when the fight was over, Ertle spread out both hands in the fashion of an umpire calling a man safe at first in a ball game and started to leave the ring. In fact, he had crawled through the ropes when, afraid of the crowd or something, he crawled back and lifted the hand of Stribling and said, "You win." McTigue paid half of Ertle's fee of $250, and I don't know how much more, to get that draw decision with Stribling.

'There was talk of violence, and a tree was even pointed out to McTigue as a good spot for a hanging if he did not fight Stribling,' said Jones. 'But McTigue and everyone else was aware that such talk was made only in a joking manner – in fact most of it was made by McTigue's own camp followers, including his manager, Jacobs.'

Jones sent a telegram of complaint about Ertle to the New York State Athletic Commission. The Commission had no jurisdiction in the matter because he was not a licensed referee in New York but it indicated that Mike and Joe could be 'called in'. Though no official announcement was made, the Commission supported Mike's claim to the title, despite the fact that it disapproved of the champion taking his own referee to Columbus. Most referees gave the champion the edge in a close fight and public opinion, as a rule, acquiesced in this. But there was a growing feeling that too many champions had got into the habit of carrying 'tame' referees around. 'If the Georgia episode puts a stop to this practice, it will not have been in vain,' commented the *New York Times*, 'though it doesn't seem likely that there will be any more championship fights in Georgia.'

There was no changing a decision once it was given. Mike was still champion, at least technically, but he'd left the prestige of such a title behind in Georgia. Harry Newman of the *New York Daily News* tried to 'simplify' the confusing sequence of events for his readers:

If that man Harry Ertle don't stop tossing around decisions on that jam between Mike McTigue, the big broth of a boy from home, and Young Stribling, he'll drive us plum nutty.

What a nice racket that fuss between Mickey and Stribey turned out to be. First crack out of the box Ertle tries to square matters and save his own neck by calling the bout a draw. But he don't get very far with that kind of stuff down in Georgia. They drag him back for another verdict and this time Harry gives the decision to Stribling. Great! But you ain't heard nothing yet. Harry hauls off once more when he gets away from the boys who were going to give him one of those necktie parties and this time Harry allows that Mike is still the light heavyweight world's champion. So what are you going to do about it?

All of which makes that title a sort of jigsaw puzzle. The age of the old gal Ann never had anything on that light heavyweight situation. Up this way McTigue is still the champ, but down in Georgia, Stribling is the fair-haired child. Now, will you have ice cream with your onions?

The man with most to gain from the affair was Tex Rickard. The promoter had an option on Mike's services for a bout at the Garden later that season, and a return with Stribling couldn't fail at the box office. Rarely could a match have received so much publicity. Lurid tales of hanging, shooting and lynching generated great interest but they further damaged a reputation already in decline. The Irishman, through bad advice and handling, had failed to capitalise on his good fortune. He could have taken a chance and boxed one of the leading Americans, Tom Gibbons, Harry Greb or Gene Tunney, immediately upon his return to the United States. Fresh from his victory over Siki he might have received $75,000 for such a fight. Now he'd been discredited. Mike may have been world champion but he wasn't even rated as one of the best light heavyweights in New

York and his market value plummeted. 'If McTigue gets $25,000 in a guarantee now, he will be receiving a lot of money,' commented *Boxing* magazine.

Mike knew the scribes were right and the word on Broadway was that the boxing firm of McTigue & Jacobs was in trouble. Joe admitted that, while everything was satisfactory at the moment, it was probable that he would sever relations with the boxer when their contract expired the following August. The reason for the break, according to the manager, was Mike's desire to return to Ireland to start a business career. In the meantime he intended to keep his fighter busy. A match with Gene Tunney had been agreed before the fateful trip down South and Jacobs was also negotiating with Jim Coffroth, the promoter at Tijuana, Mexico, for a match with either Siki or Tommy Gibbons. 'Never let it be said that Mike McTigue and his manger, Joe Jacobs, are afraid to take a chance on their lives,' commented the *Los Angeles Times*. 'After their thrilling experiences in that series of mob scenes in Columbia, Georgia, not long ago, it might be supposed that Mike and Joe would want to stick close to little old New York. Not at all. Jacobs and McTigue are considering an invasion of Mexico, for a trip to Tijuana to be exact. Having successfully defied the rope and the automatic pistol, Mike and Joe evidently figure they need to have no fear of knives or whatever other weapons the irate customers do business with across the border.'

But all talk of future fights ended on 7 November with Mike's announcement that he had cancelled the fight with Tunney and split with Joe. The boxer claimed he'd never signed a contract with his manager and that the only document that bore his signature was a blank piece of paper which Joe later filled out after the two men had talked over the general terms of an agreement. Mike's understanding was that the arrangement was for two years; a period of time which had already elapsed. It was obvious, however, that money was at the root of the problem. Mike believed he was getting $10,000 to fight Stribling in Georgia but all he got after expenses had been deducted was $3,800. He also accused Jacobs of signing for the Tunney fight without finding out if his injured hand had recovered. Joe retaliated by instructing his lawyers, Shapiro & White, to proceed with a 50,000-dollar damage suit for libel and defamation of character. Papers were served on Mike and filed in the Supreme Court.

Joe produced the contract for the Stribling fight which stipulated a guarantee of $7,500 not $10,000, along with a photograph showing Mike watching the document being signed. He also denied the charge of signing up for the Tunney match without consultation. Joe said that on the morning of 15 October, the day the articles were signed, he had spoken with Dr Phillip Jordan who was treating Mike and was told the fighter would be ready to box in early December. Jacobs emphasised that he was still Mike's manager and would continue to be so until 31 August 1924 when the contract expired. 'Until that time McTigue will fight for me and nobody else. I signed him to box Gene Tunney, and he will box Tunney under my management either in December or January. He will also box in other engagements for me, or he won't box at all. I hold a legal contract with him and he cannot break it. At the same time, however, I have instructed my lawyers to go ahead with the suit.' It had been insinuated in the sports' pages that Mike was afraid to meet Tunney. Now his manager seemed to confirm the story.

On the day Joe served the writ on his fighter both men were forced to share a room at the New York State Athletic Commission. All the recognised world champions and their managers were invited to a meeting to discuss a new rule requiring boxers to defend their titles against sanctioned challengers or suffer suspension in the

State. It was introduced following the cancellation of a succession of championship fights, usually over money.

William J. McCormack, Chairman of the License Committee of the State Athletic Commission, believed the public squabbling and bickering over terms for bouts was helping the 'chronic antagonists' who wanted the sport banned. 'I want you to realise from past experiences that if boxing is killed in this State, it will be killed all over the country,' said McCormack. 'You have the chance to build boxing up to the position in sport which it deserves. You can be constructive or destructive, that is up to yourselves. Bigger crowds are now being attracted to boxing matches than ever before. Boxers and champions particularly are making more money now than ever before. Your champions are holders of honours conferred upon them by the boxing public in recognising them as the best men in their classes. Titles are not fragile things to be won and hidden away beyond the reach of a challenger. Only through activity of champions can there be stimulated competition, for title-seekers have an incentive in active champions.'

After his address McCormack yielded the floor to the boxers and their managers. Seven champions, either there in person or represented by their managers, made pledges of activity. Mike told the meeting that when his hands had healed not only was he willing to defend his title against Gene Tunney, but he would also box Tom Gibbons, Kid Norfolk, Battling Siki or Georges Carpentier. Mike said he would even fight Harry Greb for the middleweight title. It was an uncomfortable afternoon for the Irishman who was certainly one of the guiltiest champions in terms of not defending a title. He kept a discreet distance from Joe Jacobs throughout the proceedings.

Mike countered Joe's legal action with one of his own and filed a suit in the Supreme Court to compel his manager to account for money he'd received under the terms of their contract. Joe countered once again and dispatched several process servers, 'each one laden with a good deal of court literature,' to hunt for Mike, who had 'developed into one of the most elusive humans imaginable'. When the servers arrived at Mike's home they were told he was visiting his sister at some place in Long Island.

'Under the lash of McTigue's suit against him,' reported the *New York Times*, 'Jacobs, through his attorney, Louis A. Shapiro, yesterday announced that he intended to press action against the boxer in two civil suits which heretofore have been mentioned as merely contemplated.' Joe said he was instituting his threatened suit for $50,000 for slander in the Supreme Court and a further suit for $1,966.84 representing 30 per cent of the money Jacobs alleged Mike earned in five bouts in Europe. Attorney Shapiro said he would start his own suit against the champion for $1,000 representing that which the lawyer claimed was due to him for legal services in drawing up contracts and legal documents.

Mike's troubles continued. The State Boxing Commission threatened to strip him of his title if he didn't meet the challenge of Gene Tunney. The Irishman eventually satisfied the boxing bosses that his hand was still injured and was granted a postponement on condition that he boxed Tunney at a later date. He may have convinced the doctors, but the scribes were growing increasingly sceptical about Mike's injured hands. 'Mike McTigue disease is the scientific name for an injured hand,' wrote Westbrook Pegler. 'This ailment was named in Mr McTigue's honour in his days as light heavyweight champion of the world, when all of his bad fights were explained away on the grounds that his hand was hurt. Nowadays any prizefighter who has been guilty of a particularly bad prizefight is assumed to have been suffering from McTigue disease, although most cases are presumed to be rather mild inasmuch as few prizefighters ever fight as badly as Mike McTigue does when he is hurted.'

It had been seven months since he'd won the world championship and Mike had barely made a dollar. The only work he managed to find was a couple of hundred dollars for a boxing exhibition at the annual football smoker at Fordham's College. Mike refused to box anybody under Joe's management again and vowed not to fight in America until the contract expired. 'I do not feel that I can consistently accept any matches here in view of the situation existing between Jacobs and myself,' said Mike. 'I will not engage in any bouts he arranges for me and I will not be able to arrange any matches for myself, I suppose. I have informed Tex Rickard that I will not box in Madison Square Garden in January.'

Mike wanted to manage his own affairs and he contacted his old friend Tom Singleton in Dublin to negotiate a match with the English heavyweight, Joe Beckett. He intended to sail for Europe after the Christmas holidays and would not return until his contract with Joe ended in August 1924. His plans were laughed off as a publicity stunt in New York. Dispatches from London the previous week reported how Beckett had abandoned the British title after a humiliating defeat by Carpentier. Beckett's manager later confirmed that his fighter had retired following the one-round knockout.

Mike and Joe kept fighting into 1924 until eventually, on 24 January, a solution was found. The boxer was released from the contract by paying his manager about $10,000 and they agreed to drop the various lawsuits they had threatened each other with. The Irishman had interpreted his liberation from Joe as a release from all contracts that his former manager had signed on his behalf. But this took him into conflict with the boxing authorities once more. William J. McCormack of the New York State Athletic Commission said Mike would be compelled to fulfil the Tunney contract before he engaged in any other fights. The Commission had seen a copy of the release agreement and concluded that Joe couldn't discharge Mike from a contractual obligation with a third party. Jacobs had signed his man to box Tunney at the Garden and Mike was obliged to fight unless the other two parties to the agreement, the promoter Tex Rickard and the challenger Gene Tunney, consented to a cancellation. They didn't. Mike was in with an opponent he had no hope of beating.

There wasn't a boxing body in the world with as much legal power as the New York State Athletic Commission and it wasn't about to let a 'lucky champion' challenge its authority. The boxing bosses could suspend non-fighting champions but their jurisdiction extended only to fighters who'd won their titles in New York State. Mike became champion in Dublin and was immune to any direct punishment but such was the power of the Commission that it got around this technicality. It notified other boxers that they would be banned from fighting in New York if they engaged in contests with blacklisted champions. It was a sanction that no leading boxer could afford to risk.

Mike celebrated his first Christmas as world champion with no money, no manager and no prospect of work unless he submitted to the will of the dark forces controlling boxing in New York. The *Ring* concluded that all Mike's woes could be attributed to the poor Senegalese fighter from whom he'd taken the title. 'A dark cloud has followed this crown,' wrote the magazine's editor Nat Fleischer, 'Siki must have put a bad luck sign on it.'

TWELVE

Champions have run from bad to worse. The various elimination tournaments have resulted in the survival of some of the most terrible looking titleholders in the history of the cauliflower industry.

Bill McGeehan, *New York Herald Tribune*

Paddy Mullins never shirked a challenge. He was the manager of the black heavyweight Harry Wills, the New Orleans-born fighter who was an obvious contender for the heavyweight title for much of the 1920s. It was a time when racism was rampant and a black champion would have been a financial disaster, so Wills never got his shot. Undeterred, Mullins took on another outcast, although whereas Wills' only 'crime' was to be born the wrong colour at the wrong time, Mike McTigue's status was largely self-imposed.

Billy Gibson, Gene Tunney's manager, demanded the Commission compel Mike to honour his contract and defend the title against his charge. The Three Dumb Dukes, as Bill McGeehan dubbed the Commission, told Mike he'd only get a licence to box in New York if he fought Tunney. The biggest market in boxing was closed to the world champion. So the Irishman turned to a compatriot whose job it was to find fights for one the most difficult boxers in the world to match. With a typical piece of opportunism

Paddy came up with a solution. The circus was in town and Madison Square Garden was the big top for a few weeks, so Mullins offered Mike's services to the National Sportsmen's Club in Newark, New Jersey. Newark was barely an hour's train ride from New York and with a dearth of big shows in the city the customers could be lured out of State. The choice of opponent was obvious: the sensational events in Columbus, Georgia just a few months previously were still news so Mullins called Pa Stribling.

On 9 February 1924, the *Boxing Blade* announced that the National Sportsmen's Club in Newark offered Mike $100,000 for matches against Young Stribling in March and Georges Carpentier in June. Mike countered with a demand for $150,000 for the two bouts. The story, hacked around Broadway by Paddy's press agent, wasn't true. Mike barely cleared $10,000 and was paying the price of incurring the Commission's wrath.

The Stribling bout, a twelve-round no-decision affair, was to be staged at the First Regiment Armoury in Newark on 31 March. Both fighters agreed to weigh in under the light heavyweight limit of 175lbs and the Irishman could lose his title if knocked out, disqualified or if he failed to respond to the bell. If he was on his feet at the end of the twelfth, Mike was still champion, regardless of the newspaper decision. This New Jersey law had led to a succession of poor fights involving champions who were content to do very little for a purse. The customers were not happy and neither was Platt Adams, New Jersey's chief boxing inspector. Adams issued a warning to both men that unless they tried their best and put up a satisfactory exhibition they would be 'fired' out of the ring and their purses held up. 'In time the boxers, big or small, will begin to realise that when they fight in New Jersey they will have to do their best or suffer,' Adams announced. 'No fighters are going to come into this state and get away with anything. They are paid to do their best and will be compelled to live up to their contracts.

'McTigue is to receive $12,500 for boxing Stribling, Monday. For $12,500 he ought to open up and fight,' Adams added. 'What do we care of he loses his title? He's getting paid for taking that chance. There will be none of this fol-de-rol on the part of McTigue. He has been warned. The same goes for Stribling. He will be treated likewise.'

Mike's publicity campaign did not start well. He was booked to appear on WGY, the General Electric-run broadcasting station at Schenectady, to talk boxing. According to chief announcer, Kolin Hager, 'he was the last man in the world that we expected would suffer a case of "microphone fright", but he did'. Mike stepped up to the pick-up device but could not talk. 'I would rather face Dempsey than talk into that thing,' he said. His trainer read the pre-written address. Mike was a mild-mannered man of few words but he did his best to stoke up some bad feeling by threatening to punish Stribling for the way he had been treated in Columbus and that he didn't think much of the so-called Southern hospitality. The Irishman was an unconvincing bully and Westbrook Pegler once described him as a 'domestic soul with the social traits of a corner grocer'.

Despite the contrived advertising the promoters expected a crowd that would tax the capacity of the arena with over $30,000-worth of tickets sold by the day before the fight. Mike was a 'cheese champion' but there was a grudging admiration of his craftiness and defensive skills. The crowd was boosted by a large delegation of fans from Atlanta and Macon who arrived in two special carriages attached to the New Orleans Express and a block of 150 ringside seats was reserved for the boys from the South.

There was one other reason for the busy box office. The under-card featured a young light heavyweight by the name of Paul Berlenbach,

Mike McTigue,
Chicago 1925.

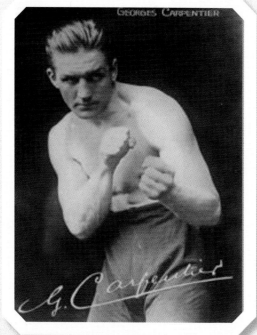

Georges Carpentier,
Light Heavyweight
Champion of the
World 1920-22.

'I will fight and make Georges kneel before me.'
Battling Siki winning the world title in Paris, 24 September 1922.

Battling Siki and his entourage arrive in Dublin.

Mike in training for Siki.

The opening
exchanges,
McTigue-Siki
17 March 1923.

Siki continues to
chase the Irishman
around the ring.

The new world light heavyweight champion on board the *Berengaria*.

Mike striking a fight pose in MacLevy's gym, where he trained for his bout with Young Stribling.

The champion in training.

Mike weighing-in for his match with Billy Vidabeck
15 November 1926 in Brooklyn.

The blood-soaked
encounter with
Jack Sharkey
3 March 1927.

A ten-round defeat
against Leo Lomski
3 February 1928.

Another defeat, this time against Armand Emanuel on 7 June 1928.

'Show me a better business than this one I am in, and I will quit.'

a darling of the New York boxing writers because he was the best knockout puncher the city had produced since the days of Knockout Brown twenty years previously. Berlenbach was originally booked to box in a main event at the Armoury but he'd lost a recent bout to Jack Delaney and was looking to re-establish himself as a leading contender for Mike's title. By the time of the weigh-in at 2 pm on the afternoon of the fight every ticket had been sold. Promoter J. Frank Black claimed that 11,000 people got in while another 7,500 were turned away after the police and fire department insisted on closing the doors. The net receipts were announced as $40,139.10.

Stribling entered the ring first and was wildly cheered; Mike followed a minute later and was equally loudly applauded. Harry Greb, Mickey Walker, Gene Tunney and Harry Wills were introduced in the ring, as was Mayor Briedenbach of Newark. Paddy Mullins was chief second for the champion; Pa Stribling acted in a similar capacity for his son.

The crowd grew impatient as the gloves were tied on the hands of the boxers. The Newark promoters had imported Madison Square Garden announcer Joe Humphries for the evening who called the champion's weight as 166 ½ pounds, the challenger 165. The bout started promptly at 10 pm and from the opening bell the atmosphere was very tense with intermittent battles breaking out among rival factions in the audience. 'The greatest and "fightingest" mob that ever thronged the Newark Armoury was jammed into the building,' reported *Boxing*. 'Because of the racial feelings that had been aroused over the bout, an extra large force of special police was on hand. They were kept busy stopping the incipient free-for-alls that kept starting up all over the building. At the ringside one could look back over the crowd and see the disturbances start and ripple over the floor like splashes and ripples made by jumping trout in a millpond.'

The Southern deputation was enraged as the champion made his intentions clear in the early rounds. The first session was even but thereafter Mike clinched and stalled his way through the fight. 'He was the poorest apology for a champion and for an Irish fighter we ever have seen,' wrote one scribe at ringside. 'He didn't show the courage of a chipmunk and was about as belligerent and aggressive as a rabbit.'

Time after time Mike held Stribling in a vice-like grip and was hooted and jeered by the crowd. The referee tried to break the clinches but he wasn't strong enough. The champion landed a good right in the second that almost knocked Stribling off balance, then the challenger returned the attack with renewed fury and landed a-plenty before the bell sounded. In the third session Stribling staggered Mike with a hard left and right to the jaw. Again in the next Stribling caught the champion with a right to the jaw and then rushed him to the ropes where he drove in four solid left hooks to the face without return. Stribling hit Mike so often and promiscuously it would have needed an adding machine to tabulate the blows. The two men clinched in the fourth round and Mike's left arm was wrapped around his opponent's neck pressing his head onto the champion's chest. Stribling braced himself and while Mike retained his grip the challenger lifted the champion off the ground without using his arms or body, just the muscles in his neck.

Mike smothered Stribling when danger threatened but as the fight progressed the Irishman tired badly and his strength gradually failed him. Unable to hold his opponent any longer Mike retreated and the crowd was incensed. Stribling used his elbow, forearm and forehead in his frenzy to score a knockout. Mike was tossed around the ring and now he was in trouble. Stribling was faster, cleverer, more aggressive and more accurate than the champion. 'Mike hung on to Stribling as if the pair were honeymooning,' commented one scribe, 'he showed himself to be the champion hugger of the universe'.

Mike was stung again in the sixth by a left hook to the jaw followed by a left and right on the chin. The only round the champion won was the eighth, although it was very close and Stribling was conserving his energy for a final onslaught. When Mike got the chance to throw punches of his own, he didn't, because according to one writer, he had 'the heart of a chicken and a brain of solid ivory. Mike was so scared he was white.'

The challenger nailed the champion flush on the jaw with a right hook in the ninth. Mike's mouth sagged, his knees trembled and he shook 'as if with the palsy'. But Stribling stood back before continuing his attack and the champion recovered. By the time the young Georgian resumed firing, enough of Mike's strength and senses came back for him to ward off the youngster's assault and stall to the bell. A knockout would make the nineteen-year-old world champion and it almost happened in the tenth. According to the *New York Daily News* Stribling plastered 'the plastic and classic Celtic countenance of Mike McTigue with such a choice assortment of jabs and jolts that he made the gossoon from County Clare look like a battered old punching bag. Believe us, Shamus, this is no April Fool joke.

'Ochone! Ochone! What a b'atin! What a b'atin!'

A left hook sent Mike careering into the ropes and as he bounded off the strands, he was met with a right to the jaw. It spun the Irishman completely around and he staggered across the ring and almost fell through the ropes in the opposite corner. He collapsed onto the canvas but got to his feet before referee Henry Lewis could reach 'two'. Had Mike been in his senses he would have stayed down until the count reached nine, but he rose intuitively to be battered by a furious onslaught. Amazingly, one jolt in this crazed attack seemed to bring him around somewhat while Stribling flailed away like a wild man.

Mike clinched and hung on while Stribling shook him like a terrier would a rat. The champion clinched tenaciously and retreated steadily but he had still to shake off the effects of the blow when the bell ended the round and he walked on unsteady legs to a neutral corner. Referee Lewis had to direct the champion towards his frantic seconds. But he was still on his feet.

The sight of Mike on the canvas had thrown the crowd into a frenzy. The blood cry of the pack rose from a throaty rumble to a turbulent roar. Ma Stribling leaped from a ringside seat behind her son's corner and yelled her encouragement. Pa Stribling was also screaming and both parents kept up the barrage for the remaining three rounds. Mike looked all but out and the customers sensed a knockout. It didn't come. What should have been the round that ensured fame, fortune and a place in boxing history for Young Stribling was, according to the *Newark Evening News*, 'his most dismal'.

Stribling resorted to back-alley fighting and missed the flat-footed and brain-fogged champion by yards. Instead of measuring his punches, Stribling got so angry that when one spectator shouted an insult at him, he took time to see who it was and stuck out his tongue at the tormentor. He then head-butted Mike under the chin, rocking the Irishman's head backwards. Stribling's fury deprived him of the title. The wise old champion had a reprieve and he kept out of trouble until the final bell.

'With his rosy cheeks, curly hair and blue eyes, Stribling twice had the world title in reach' wrote one observer, 'only to fail to seize opportunity by the forelock, and let the coveted titular honours go flying and skittering away in the smoke clouds that hung as thick as a London fog over the ring.'

When the fight was over, chairs were hurled back and forth across the arena with wild abandon before the police intervened. It took twenty officers to restore order. Another dozen were sent to escort Mike from the ring and judging by the torrent of abuse hurled at him he needed all the protection he could get. 'One Irishman on our right vowed to heaven Mike ought to be sent back to County Clare,' wrote one reporter at ringside. 'A Tipperary man in the second row declared that if Mike attempted to go back to Ireland they'd kill him.'

The champion left the ring still holding his title although his right to call himself so was considerably clouded by his poor show-ing against a youthful challenger. According to the *New York Daily News*:

We have seen McTigue in about half-a-dozen fights. We have never seen him in a good one. Last night's bout was decidedly the sorriest of all the sorry contests we have seen Mike put up. The sooner Michael is knocked off the championship perch the better it will be for him and the game. Boxing doesn't want champions unless they are real ones.

About the only thing that will bring the crowd to see McTigue fight hereafter is to see him licked. Nine-tenths of the crowd that will go to see him hereafter will be hoping to see him whipped. Those be harsh words Granma, but once more they're the truth.

Had referees' decisions been permitted in New Jersey, a new world light heavyweight champion would have been crowned in the First Regiment Armoury. Mike did have an excuse, however. The following day a Dr Meylackson confirmed the champion had a fractured arm. It was an easy diagnosis; the limb had swollen to nearly twice its normal size. There was the inevitable clamour for another rematch. Paddy Mullins rejected Pa Stribling's offer of $35,000 to sign articles for a return fight in Georgia. It wouldn't be enough to lure the champion south of the Mason-Dixon line again. An oil syndicate from Tulsa, Oklahoma reportedly offered the champion $100,000 to defend the title against Young Stribling in a fifteen-round contest on 4 July. Promoter Barry McCormack said the consortium was 'composed of reliable citizens of the town, who believe another meeting between McTigue and the man who outpointed him in Newark a short time ago would be a great attraction for the Western berg'. The story was not without its flaws; for one, boxing was banned in Tulsa.

Mike took his family to stay with old friend Jack Britton at a cottage in White Sulphur Springs to recuperate and get himself fit to fight again. The village in upstate New York was near to Saratoga, a resort and racetrack town popular with prizefighters. The famous writer Paul Gallico described it as a place with 'sparring partners with bent noses and twisted ears; handsome state troopers in grey and purple uniforms; doubtful blondes who wandered about and blondes about whom there was no doubt at all.'

A few months out of the city had a rejuvenating effect on the Irishman and he declared himself ready to defend his title any time, anywhere for any number of rounds against any opponent considered suitable by the public and the press. 'Mike McTigue weighs in with the announcement that he is now ready to take Gene Tunney, Tom Gibbons or any other member of that set,' commented the *New York Daily News*. 'Mickey says he is gosh-dinged sore at his tormentors and proposes to chastise them one at a time. 'Just throw them in one at a time,' avers the handsome Irishman, 'and I'll crush them as fast as they can peg 'em in.' Sounds rather fierce for a mild-mannered person like Mike, but he's sore and so is his manager Paddy Mullins, and they are loaded for bear and won't stop until they have wiped the whole works.'

On 22 August Young Stribling set up camp at Tom Luther's place in Saratoga Springs, just a mile from Mike's training quarters. Stribling was preparing to fight Paul Berlenbach and arrived at the camp to meet Mike who was there to greet him. The Irishman wanted to gossip but Stribling donned his running shoes and went on the road for a brisk run. Mike probably wanted to exchange notes on Berlenbach, who had been second on the card during his bout with Stribling in Newark. During his Saratoga summer Mike had become convinced that the New Yorker was the perfect challenger for his title.

Paul Berlenbach was a great favourite of Tex Rickard. The promoter had plucked this awkward, sluggish taxi driver out of the smaller fight clubs and put him on at the Garden at regular intervals over a period of years until he eventually made Berlenbach half a million dollars. Born in Astoria, New York to French and German parents, he was a deaf mute as a child and suffered that affliction for eighteen years. Then one day he was knocked unconscious by an electric wire while dislodging a kite and his proper faculties came to him for the first time. Or so the legend goes.

Berlenbach became a wrestler and in 1920 won the middleweight mat championship for America at the Olympic games. He then entered the amateur boxing ranks and gained a string of thirteen knockouts before becoming a prizefighter. Berlenbach was one of the most popular fighters in New York with a reputation for being brave, with few skills but vicious punching power. There was no compromise with the Astoria Assassin and he either succeeded or failed in spectacular fashion. He was just the type of boxer the customers loved and as Rickard once said, 'I can put Jeff Smith or Mike McTigue in there and nobody will lay a glove on them, but they won't draw enough business to buy the heat.'

Mike believed him to be the ideal opponent. Berlenbach would ensure a massive gate and the champion thought he'd been 'built-up' as a terrible puncher by battering an endless supply of palookas. But it did no harm to paint a challenger as a man-killer even though the best man he'd fought, Jack Delaney, had beaten him into a 'helpless inert heap' in one of the most sensational fights held at the Garden. Mike knew that a championship fight against such a popular challenger would attract a huge guarantee and he asked Paddy to strike a deal. On 16 September Tex Rickard announced that he had signed Berlenbach and McTigue for a fifteen-round match at the Garden in the coming winter season. But as soon as Gene Tunney's manager, Billy Gibson, found out he cried foul.

The Commission had to decide whether to compel Mike to fight Tunney before the champion was allowed to fight Berlenbach. Billy Gibson argued that he held a prior contract with Mike and exhibited the document signed by Joe Jacobs. The Commission ruled that this contract had expired and advised Tunney to file a new challenge along with the required forfeit of $2,500.

Mike still didn't hold a licence to box in New York, and until the champion applied for one, he was outside the jurisdiction of the State body. Under those circumstances the Berlenbach fight couldn't go ahead. When Mike did apply for his licence Tunney's challenge would be called to the champion's attention and he would be requested to accept or reject it. In cases where challenges had been rejected or ignored in the past, champions had been denied the privilege of fighting in New York. So it was a stalemate. The promoters weren't stumbling over one another to get the McTigue-Tunney scrap and there was big money in a Berlenbach challenge. But Tunney was the Commission's challenger and Mike had to fight him or no one.

Rickard wasn't going to risk losing a precious date at the Garden and gave up on the Berlenbach fight and he planned to put on Argentinean heavyweight Luis Angel Firpo in its place. The *New York Times* reported that a source close to Mike said the champion was arranging an extensive tour of the United States that would begin at Providence, Rhode Island against Frankie Carpenter. Paddy Mullins then met with Babe Cullen and Nick Kline, the Newark promoters, about moving the Berlenbach fight across the Hudson. The plan was to stage the fight under the auspices of the National Sportsmen's Club at the 113th Infantry Armoury. Neither plan was realistic but the stories had the desired effect. Tex Rickard met the Commission on 18 October and the board agreed to endorse any agreement satisfactory to Gene Tunney.

Just a few days later it was announced that Tunney had allowed the McTigue-Berlenbach match to go ahead under guarantee of a fight with the winner. Mike and Paul had to post $10,000 with the Commission in cash, certified cheque or bond, guaranteeing Tunney a match with the winner within sixty days of 14 November. The arrangement also stipulated that the winner was not to fight anyone else until he had boxed Tunney. The offender would forfeit his $10,000 if he didn't comply. Tunney was in Hot Springs, Arkansas when his manager, Billy Gibson, told him the news. 'That agreement is perfectly satisfactory for me and I am perfectly willing that the McTigue-Berlenbach fight go on. The boxing commission has protected me as a challenger in every way, and the entire arrangements meet with my approval,' he said.

Rickard had persuaded Tunney to accept the compromise and now he had to re-sign the title contenders. Mike agreed immediately but Berlenbach demanded a five-month gap between the title fight and a match with Tunney, should he win the championship. 'If I'm willing to withdraw my man in favour of Berlenbach I've got to have some protection for him,' said Gibson. 'McTigue was willing to sign the agreement but Berlenbach refused: in the event that he won, he could go around the country exploiting the title and Tunney could wait until he had white whiskers before he'd get a shot at the title to which he has first claim.' The match eventually dissolved amid a general conflict of interests.

The Commission then issued Mike with an ultimatum, that unless he agreed to defend his title against Gene Tunney he would also be banned from boxing in New York for a year. He would be prevented from boxing any fighter licensed by the Commission, unless the opponent wanted to suffer suspension himself. Mike's sense of injustice was heightened when Tunney refused to meet the challenge of Tom Gibbons for the American title, yet he wasn't suspended. 'He is mad clear through and wants the world to know all about it,' commented one New York paper. Mike's attorney started a suit against the Commission claiming $250,000 damages on the charge that the champion was prevented from obtaining a licence and boxing in the state. On day the suit was filed Mike knocked out Frank Carpenter in six rounds at Providence, Rhode Island. He arrived back in New York late the following afternoon and went directly to a meeting with his lawyer, Alexander R. Tendler. A 'writ of mandamus' ordering the Commission to issue Mike with a licence when he wanted one was completed and the damage proceedings were instituted for $250,000. 'All the boys are hooking up with John Law these days,' wrote Harry Newman in the *New York Daily News*. 'Michael hasn't told anyone what he wants to do with the licence when he gets it, but he doesn't like the idea of the commission telling him he can't have one and that to hold good for a year ... But wurra wurra, Mike wants to see anybody keeping him from battling in New York, if he feels like pulling on the mitts for a little dough,' wrote Newman. 'Hence the law horrible.'

Mike's case was based on precedent. He was barred while other champions like lightweight Benny Leonard and heavyweight Jack Dempsey had turned down sanctioned challengers. Paddy Mullins put down a $2,500 forfeit for Harry Wills' challenge to Dempsey; but the Commission never forced the issue. Leonard flunked out of a match with Mickey Walker and had not fought a decision fight for over a year.

'We don't give Michael much credit as a champion,' commented the *Boxing Blade*, 'and think he is a detriment to the division. However, if all the information we have is true, we believe Sir Michael has a strong case and perhaps a just grievance. But the question is, how far can he get with it? Most of the open-and-shut cases and grievances against the moguls of the game in New York are usually squashed, hushed up, no cause for action, died from natural causes, or some other OK terms are applied and that is all we ever hear of them thereafter.

'However, if McTigue is successful in getting his case properly before the courts he may make things very interesting for the New York Boxing Commission before the winter boxing season is over.

'But the betting is against him.'

So with New York closed for business for the foreseeable future the partnership of Mullins & McTigue looked out of state to make a few bucks. There was an intriguing proposition from promoters in Newark for a fight with the world welterweight champion Mickey Walker. Even though the men were two weight divisions apart, it was a natural match: both were world champions and both were banned by the New York State Athletic Commission because of their failure to defend their respective championships. In Walker's case, the Commission ruled that he could not fight in New York until he consented to defend his title against the Californian Dave Shade.

The critics were unconvinced. 'Well! Well! Can you beat it?' wrote Charlie Rose in *Boxing*. 'Mike McTigue and Mickey Walker, the welterweight title holder, have signed to fight twelve rounds in Newark, New Jersey on January 7. Why not April first? "All Fools Day" would be the most appropriate setting for such a ridiculous match.'

It wasn't the first time a leading light heavyweight had been matched with a welterweight. Joe Choynski, one of the outstanding light heavyweights at the end of the nineteenth century, had a famous scrap with welterweight Joe Walcott at the Broadway Club in New York. The customers thought it was a joke but Walcott knocked Choynski stiff in seven rounds and the boxing writers wondered if history was going to repeat itself. Rarely did a good little man beat a good big man. But Mike wasn't regarded as a good big man and Walker had a fearsome reputation. 'It doesn't always prove profitable to spot another guy plenty just to get a shot at him,' commented one scribe, 'but it must be borne in mind that Mickey Walker is a rough socking lad.'

Mike got $15,000 for his end, Walker $10,000 because the Irishman was the only one taking a risk. Although it was a no-decision bout, according to New Jersey law Mike's title, but not Walker's, was on the line in the event of a knockout, disqualification or injury.

Walker's title wasn't at stake because Mike could get nowhere near the welterweight limit. But if the Irishman was knocked out or disqualified or injured he would lose his championship because Walker was well under the light heavyweight limit. 'And what is more it will show the cautious Michael actually taking his crown into the ring,' commented one newspaper. 'True he's fighting a little fellow but, gee whiz, supposing Mike hits up against a ring post and knocks himself out!' It was a hazardous undertaking but Mike figured he could take Walker's punches for twelve rounds and even if he lost the popular decision, he'd still retain his title.

Both men intended to take interim fights before the Newark clash. Mike accepted terms to fight Young Marullo in New Orleans over twelve rounds with no official decision on 22 December. Referees' decisions were allowed in New Orleans but there wasn't enough money on offer for Mike to risk his title against a hometown fighter, especially after the Stribling fiasco. However, on the morning of the fight Mike was on the train back to New York – the event had been cancelled due to the extreme cold in New Orleans. Mike stopped off in Atlanta, Georgia, on his return journey where he boxed an exhibition with local fighter Johnny King. The world champion was very impressive and appeared to be much faster than in recent outings. Mike moved on to Madame Bey's training camp in Chatham, New Jersey, to prepare for the Walker fight. He said he was tired of being called a poor champion and hoped that a victory over Walker would stop such talk.

I will win decisively. And I will teach Mickey something about the finer points of boxing while winning. You can rest assured that Mickey isn't going to knock me out or even come within the proverbial mile of winning. The business of knocking out and winning will be taken care of by yours truly, have no fear. And I might as well go on record right here as saying that I can lick any light heavyweight in the world and will prove it as soon as I am through with Mickey. Come early and watch me show Mickey something about boxing which he never knew.

Walker was everything American boxing fans of that era admired about a fighter. He was a relentless, courageous boxer, always throwing punches, never taking a step back. Walker planned a tireless body attack with which he hoped to weaken the Irishman and pave the way for a knockout. When the National Sportsmen's Club first suggested the match many within the New York State Athletic Commission believed it to be a publicity stunt. The Commission had practically driven Mike and Mickey out of the State's rings and it prompted further discussion in New York as to the body's role. It was rare to see two world champions in the same ring and the city's promoters could only look on in envy as the National Sportsmen's Club made elaborate preparations for a capacity crowd at the Armoury. The Hudson Tubes arranged special trains between New York and Newark both before and after the fight to cope with the demand.

Walker entered the ring as favourite even though he was the smaller man; not that there was any vast difference in their physical proportions, however. Walker was heavy for a welterweight and Mike very light for a light heavyweight. Walker entered the ring at 149 ½ pounds, Mike at 160. The announcement of weights sparked a murmur through the crowd. It was thought that the Irishman would be closer to 170, but a very hard training regime had taken him into the ring as fine as he'd been for many years. He fought Walker as a middleweight not a light heavyweight.

It was exciting for the first four rounds with Walker carrying out his promise to attack Mike's body with right and left hooks. The Irishman was on the defensive from the first bell and was forced back against the ropes. But Walker's energy store was emptying rapidly and he made a furious attempt to finish the fight at the end of the fourth. A left hook and a right to the jaw staggered the light heavyweight champion who managed to clinch and clear his head. Mike was never flustered, even during the moments when Walker jumped in at him with both feet off the ground, desperately looking to land the one punch that could take the Irishman's title. Walker drove his opponent to the ropes once more and lashed out with both hands but failed to land another effective blow before the bell tolled to end the round.

That bell also sounded the end of any possibility of a title changing hands. In the fifth the action slackened. There were innumerable clinches and from there to the finish the crowd booed and stamped its feet. The fight got slower and slower and Walker's only other fleeting chance came at the end of the eighth when a sharp left to the jaw briefly turned the jeers into cheers. According to the *New York Times* it became a 'listless bout which grated on the nerves of the crowd which witnessed it'.

The bell rang for the eighth and the boxers ragged languidly into action amid a salvo of boos. After a bit more flaccid action, some clinching, a little pushing, one raucous customer started a rendition of 'Every Hour I Knead Thee'. Mike drew Walker into a clinch and said: 'D'ye hear them bums out there – don't pay any attention to them, Mickey, remember our titles are not at stake.'

Mike out-pointed Walker in the last two rounds. The Irishman was certain that he had no more to fear from his opponent and he cut loose a little, throwing several right hooks to the chin and the side of the face. He continued to attack until the midway point of the tenth when he came out of a clinch with a small cut under his right eye. When the bell rang for the end of the twelfth both men, still champions, retired to their corners. Tony Polozzolo, Mike's trainer, leaned through the ropes to vociferate that his man had hurt both hands early in the fight. Walker was said to have entered the ring with a heavy cold that caused the dramatic slackening in the pace of his attack. It wasn't a good night for the Newark promoters. The gate at the Armoury dwindled considerably from the estimate announced prior to the fight. Instead of a $43,000 house it was only $26,000 and the club lost about $6,000 on the venture.

It was inevitable that Walker would receive the plaudits of the pressmen but there was a grudging respect for Mike, whose re-markable defensive skills kept him comfortably out of harm's way for twelve rounds. Mike knew Walker was a good opponent for him. Apart from the physical advantage he held, ten pounds in weight and a considerable height and reach advantage, Walker was the type of fighter who threw few, if any, straight, off-the-shoulder punches but relied largely on roundhouse swings. For a master defensive boxer it was easy to pick these punches right out of the air, blocking them with gloves or elbows long before they reached their intended destination. Mike was able to counter with straight lefts speared into Walker's face. 'Science to Walker is a foreign word,' wrote the *Newark Evening News*, 'science to McTigue means something. A less cagey fighter than McTigue would undoubtedly have been battered down by Walker's wallops.'

After the fight Mike went to see the man known as the 'master mender' and 'bone-setter extraordinary', Dr William Fralick. The surgeon removed a five-inch long sliver of bone from Mike's hand and told him to 'go out and stall no more'. It saved his career. The injury had handicapped him since the night with Battling Siki in Dublin. He had injured it again training for Walker and it was aggravated early in the match. Dr Fralick worked his magic and after a series of 'special treatments' Mike declared the hand 'as sound as ever'. He believed his 'finishing punch' that was lost on Siki's head had been restored and he promised to knockout Tunney, Gibbons, Berlenbach, Delaney and any other challenger. There was a story circulating along Broadway that Mike was looking to insure his newly healed hands for $50,000. It amused the boxing writers who believed his 'injury' was an excuse. The *Washington Post* commented:

Mike M'tigue's Joke; Why Should Boxer Insure Idle Hands?

The catch in the announcement is that Mike McTigue has seldom used his hands except for normal every-day purpose since he succeeded in getting a Free State decision over Liquid Siki in Dublin on St Patrick's Day some time since.

The light heavyweight titleholder ought, therefore, to be one of the world's best risks for the policy that he is seeking. He is, if anything, more interested than the insurance company possibly could be in seeing that no untoward incident in the prize-ring shall mar either the fight or his hands.

Why insurance on McTigue's hands? It would be a most unusual departure for the holder of the policy to use them in an offensive manner, and no-one credits even Berlenbach with such a punch that his gloved blows will harm the gloved fists which McTigue employs only for the purposes of self-protection.

During his recuperation Mike met up with one of his old adversaries. Battling Siki was in training in Summit, New Jersey, for a match with Berlenbach. The Irishman stopped in at the Garden to collect his tickets for the fight and told reporters there that he was so sure that Berlenbach was going to be flattened that he was going to take 5-1 that the Senegalese fighter would score a knockout. 'This fellow is going to be right and he is no chump when he trains for a fight and it looks to me like it will be another Carpentier-Siki sensation,' said Mike. 'He has had two fellows over in Jersey fighting in the style of Berlenbach and he has every move of Paul's down to a fine point. I won the title from Siki and should know a bit about him.' He didn't know Siki as well as he thought and Berlenbach won the fight easily.

By now Mike was a free agent once more. The contract under which Paddy Mullins managed him jointly with Charlie Rose expired on 13 January 1925. Mike wanted be his own manager and according to the *New York Times* he supplemented 'his recently announced intention of returning to the ring with a large-sized chip on his shoulder' as he disclosed plans for his re-entry into boxing. 'McTigue is not entirely in accord with the idea of splitting his ring earnings with a manger which accounts for his decision to look after his own interests in the future.' Free of managerial control Mike received a boost to his hopes of that big-money fight with Paul Berlenbach. The Commission continued to insist on Mike boxing Tunney first, but then Tunney refused to box Gibbons for the American title and the light heavyweight division became tangled up in a series of contractual disputes. 'Looks like the boxing fathers should just let Mike go in with Paul just for the sake of getting his title into action,' commented the *New York Daily News*. 'Tunney isn't behaving in a manner that entitles him first shot at McTigue.'

But just as the light heavyweight class became too much of a puzzle for anyone to even try to straighten out, the situation suddenly became much clearer. Gene Tunney cast his lot with the heavyweights after either growing too big to be a light heavyweight or too tired of trying to get a match with Mike. The reason for putting Mike on the ineligible list had been removed and there was a bout in the offing that would make the sides of any arena bulge. The Mickey Walker fight had increased the public appetite to see Mike lose and the overwhelming favourite with the customers to perform the service was Paul Berlenbach. The Astoria fighter had recovered from his defeat to Jack Delaney with a succession of knockout victories and his ability to recover from the setback had made him even more popular. As Paul Gallico noted in a column entitled, 'Tis Fatal To Be Perfect'. 'The quirk in human nature is found in any sport. What made Paul Berlenbach a popular fighter? The fact that Jack Delaney knocked him out. All our best-loved champions have been on the floor at one time or another,' adding, 'of course, there's no sense in carrying it to the extreme that Mike McTigue does.'

THIRTEEN

The race does not always go to the swift, nor the battle to the strong – but that's who I'd bet money on.

Damon Runyon

The 'New York Cauliflower Cabinet', otherwise known as the New York State Athletic Commission, was a group of three earnest ministers, whose administration of the prizefight business regularly attracted more notice than the gladiators they purported to control. The Cabinet sat in the Flatiron Building, a limestone wedge just six feet wide at its rounded tip, that ploughs up the two great streets of Broadway and Fifth Avenue. It was said that the building's aerodynamic shape created unusual winds that caused women's skirts to lift up as they walked along 23rd Street. Young men would line up along the sidewalk to catch glimpses before the cops chased them away. It was an appropriate setting for the laugh-a-minute regime that presided within.

Boxing commissions were appointed all over the United States to keep the sport away from the gamblers and the criminals in which it grew up. Prizefighting was to be pulled out of the gutters and side-alley clubs and set down at the table with the dinner jackets. The commissioners were supposed to be sportsmen but in many states they were politicians only a cut above the very racketeers they were called upon to regulate. So politics came to dominate the fight game and the prize-ring was as corrupt as it was in the days when the roughnecks were in control and the customers were forced to sneak away to barges on the river.

James Farley, George Brower and William Muldoon had done well in their respective vocations before their tenure on the Commission and were never accused of clowning in their own affairs. Yet during their term of office in the mid-1920s there were many decrees spread, or smeared, on the records of the Cauliflower Cabinet that made them a constant object of ridicule. Farley often denied that political pressure was bought to bear on the State Commission; nevertheless, it was a rare thing when the Dukes made a ruling stick. Boxers and managers who had been indefinitely suspended were reinstated and a collapse of discipline gradually ensued as rules were violated with impunity and official reprimands held in contempt. But what went on behind the Gothic and Renaissance detailed walls of the Flatiron building on 7 April 1925 was extraordinary even by these standards.

The repeated failure of champions to defend their titles against recognised challengers had created a condition of chaos in boxing. By April 1925 four of the eight world champions had been suspended in New York: Johnny Dundee at lightweight, Mickey Walker at welterweight, Mike McTigue at light heavyweight and Jack Dempsey at heavyweight. The long-anticipated amnesty came in the most significant meeting held by the Commission since the elevation of James Farley to the chairmanship many years previously. Dundee, Walker and McTigue were restored to good standing and the conditions imposed were not likely to be too exacting or severe for any of the boxers. Dundee provided an adequate explanation for running out of a recent match in Paris, Walker denied that he'd ever said anything or authorised anything to be said that ridiculed the Commission and he expressed a willingness to box the challenger Dave Shade while Mike promised to fight a bona-fide challenger to be selected by the Commission and on the understanding that a title bout be held within sixty days. According to Harry Newman of the *New York Daily News*, 'when the cute Celt stepped on the carpet before the Commish yesterday afternoon and stated his case clearly, the boxing board didn't have the heart to turn him down.'

The reinstatement of three world champions 'brightened the pugilistic skies' considerably. With these fighters back in the good graces of the ruling powers, only one champion remained out in the cold – Jack Dempsey. 'As a result of the Easter gifts to the boxing world, New York and its vicinity will be humming with big bouts next summer,' commented *The Ring*. 'Indications point to the greatest activity since the passage of the Walker Law [the 1920 law which had legalised professional boxing in New York State].'

Upon hearing the news of the reinstatement of the three champions the *Washington Post* wrote:

> The boxing commission, at any rate, has narrowed the wide gap that existed prior to its action between corrals within which to herd the cash customer and fighters to serve as bait to separate the cash customer from his bankroll. A recent census indicated, counting the various craters, bowls, stadiums, arenas and mere ballparks, there were at least 800,000 seats yawning largely to be filled at so much per cash customer. The slogan of the prize-ring industry, 'Cash customers for hungry seats,' seems to have been answered.

As soon as Mike was restored to good standing, Paul Berlenbach's manager Dan Hickey posted the $2,500 with the Commission to uphold his challenge. In the event of other challenges being posted the Commission would select the 'most formidable candidate' but if none other appeared Berlenbach's name would be put to Mike with a request that he fight him for the title. The champion was in Saratoga Springs and sent word that he'd accept the Berlenbach challenge for $75,000.

Paul Berlenbach had already signed a contract with Tex Rickard for a match with Jack Delaney in an outdoor boxing carnival at the Yankee Stadium. It was a benefit show, the profits, after the boxers had been paid, going to the Milk Fund. Rickard persuaded Delaney to stand aside on the proviso that he would get the first fight with the winner. Mike was asked to return from Saratoga to talk turkey. He arrived back in New York on 13 April and went directly to Tex Rickard's office in Madison Square Garden.

Mike was without a manager once more but took Jeremiah O'Leary, an Irish barrister, as legal adviser. After a prolonged session of 'verbal dickering' with Rickard and the Milk Fund committee the champion signed the contract that also bound him to engage Jack Delaney should he beat Berlenbach. According to Rickard, who put his own money up to help things along, Mike was very liberal and signed for less than the 37.5 per cent allowed a titleholder in championship matches. The exact terms were not made public but Mike had proved 'an easy customer to do business with'. Mike had given what Rickard called 'a reasonable proposition' and agreed with the 'general idea of things'. Rickard countered with a proposition which was 'more reasonable from the fund standpoint' but not 'so remunerative to the McTigue family income'. Mike valued his title at $75,000, came down to $55,000 and finally agreed to a percentage arrangement that promised to net him at least $50,000.

The scribes thought he was getting way too much dough. Paul Gallico entitled his reaction piece, 'Aw! Lay Off Charity':

> The glove warriors are warming up for the summer season, and for the present, sweet charity is serving as the heavy punching bag and is taking many a sock on the whiskers from well-meaning pugs.
>
> Big-hearted Michael McTigue actually scissored $10,000 from his demand to fight Berlenbach for the benefit of the Milk Fund, leaving a mere $65,000, according to the Milk Fund show promoters, which Mr Rickard was to pay him out of the receipts or the overhead or the net or his own private bank account. Mr McTigue has no objection to the remaining $1.98 being used to buy grade-A milk for the little ones, bless their curly heads.
>
> Michael yesterday sent us a perfectly elegant picture of the bone that Dr Fralick took from his hand. I suspect that what McTigue needs now is an operation for gallstones or whatever it is that is giving him such unlimited crust.

Unsurprisingly, Mike was happy with the deal and said he welcomed the match as an opportunity to prove to the Americans that he really could fight. 'I intend to show the public in this match that I am not the unsatisfactory champion I have been pictured as over the past two years,' he said. He made the promoters and matchmakers shell out for his services and he was worth every dime he got. A fighter didn't have to be popular to draw a crowd. There were many cases of a boxer almost hated by the customers who proved to be a box-office attraction. They turned up to see the man plastered and they jammed every joint he ever showed at in the hope that he would be knocked dead. They flocked to see Mike knocked out and never cared who the opponent might be. Just 'kill that fresh guy McTigue' was the fond hope as they filed into the arena only to meet with disappointment. 'Mike is not very popular with the mob, but he is always in there helping himself to plenty,' wrote Harry Newman. 'McTigue is far from being anyone's fool. When they get Mike in there for a quarrel, they have to pay plenty.'

Fighters were proverbially careless of their obligations to managers, as many found out to their grief when the money finally came in. When news of Mike's $50,000 windfall was bruited about the managerial claims of Paddy Mullins loomed up like a ghost. But Paddy was more substantial than a menacing spirit and he presented his claim to the Three Dukes for adjudication. Mike admitted he'd been managed by Mullins but claimed to have procured a release. Paddy said it was a temporary arrangement granted when the champion said he wished to go to Ireland for a few fights. He didn't want to 'cut in' on any of the receipts that might accrue from such a trip and signed a paper that Mike had shown him; but he didn't read it. Paddy had the reputation of being 'one of those persons who takes everything for granted'. Mike never made it to Ireland but claimed the release Mullins had signed was permanent. Paddy found out he was no longer Mike's manager when he read in the newspapers that Jeremiah O'Leary had handled the Berlenbach negotiations. It was only later that he discovered that the paper he had signed gave Mike permanent release regardless of any tour of Ireland. Paddy was certainly a more popular figure than Mike along Broadway and the gang's sympathies were with the manager. Mike was regarded as the fighter who won an easy title and then managed to hold it by the use of rare diplomacy. In order to preserve his standing as light heavyweight champion of the world he had found it advisable to dispense with the services of two managers, Joe Jacobs and Paddy Mullins. The boys believed that when his managers moved him into tough spots by arranging fights that were not to his liking, Mike found a way of getting rid.

'Did Paddy shed bitter tears? He did not,' wrote Jack Lawrence of the *New York Herald Tribune*. 'Did he consider availing himself of the civil courts in order to hold McTigue to his original contract? He did not. Paddy merely tossed the contract into a dusty pigeonhole in his desk and proceeded to forget about it. No member of the fistic fraternity has ever heard Paddy Mullins squawk. He manages to retain a fine equilibrium – win or lose.'

The Cauliflower Cabinet confirmed that Mike was a free agent and the champion approached veteran trainer 'Doc' Bagley. 'Will you take a thousand dollars to be in my corner the night of the fight? And if I win, I'll not forget ye,' promised Mike.

The Commission's climb-down had made three world champions available to New York promoters again. Now they had the chance of getting big money in the only city where big money was on offer and the customers were looking forward to a busy summer. The *New York Times* commented that with 'one single application of its magic wand the State Athletic Commission has transformed the boxing outlook so that it now appears that one of the greatest outdoor seasons in ring history lies ahead.'

The McTigue-Berlenbach match was one of the events of the year in New York. The demand was extraordinary and Rickard managed advance sales of over $75,000-worth of tickets nearly a week before the fight. This indicated that the final receipts would exceed $200,000. To protect his investment the promoter ordered the fighters to stop training to guard against injury. According to Bill McGeehan of the *New York Herald Tribune*:

The first two chins to be laid on the altar of charity this summer are those appertaining to Mr Michael McTigue and Mr Paul Berlenbach. They will constitute the major part of the Milk Fund's offering at the Yankee Stadium. The lacteal philanthropy has done much for the advancement of the cauliflower industry, stimulating the interest when the market was at a low ebb.

Since he acquired the title of light heavyweight champion, Mr Michael McTigue has been most cautious and modest. He has been indisposed toward engaging in unseemly brawls with any of the contenders. Only the sound of milk bottles rattling over the stony streets succeeded in rousing Michael from an apathetic – not to say comatose – state.

Upon being offered the bout with Berlenbach in the interests of milk Mr McTigue recovered from his fit of temporary deafness and listened. He seems to have concluded that, even if he were knocked horizontal in such a worthy cause, he would come to in a clear conscience and about $50,000 in his fist. Then again, he might not even be knocked unconscious. But Michael is a pessimist. Every time he enters the ring he looks forward to the possibility of being carried out in a horizontal position. It is because of this in born pessimism that he does not enter the ring any more than is necessary.

Mike had seen all Berlenbach's fights around New York over the past two years and studied him carefully. 'Berlenbach can't box a lick and he knows it,' wrote Harry Newman, 'but he is a most effective hitter.' Mike thought his opponent was 'wide open' and a sucker for a right hand. In his younger days the Irishman was known as having a mean right that he threw straight from the shoulder. He felt sure he could stop the challenger and bet $5,000 against $20,000 on such an outcome. 'If anyone else wants some more money at those odds, I'd like to hear from them,' said Mike. 'I would never have taken the match if I hadn't been in perfect condition, for if I lose it means my title, and I value that at somewhere around a quarter of a million dollars.'

The betting began to show real signs of life a few days before the fight. Berlenbach had reigned as slight favourite since the match was made. The challenger was said to be a 6-5 favourite to get the referee's verdict while some of 'Punch 'em Paul's' backers were willing to take 2-1 on a knockout. But the champion's price shortened steadily and the first signs of even money on Broadway came a few days before the fight when one well-known sportsman wagered $500 at those odds. Several hefty wagers followed at evens. Mike's friends predicted that he would enter the ring as favourite, as befitting a champion. The boxing scribes were split in predicting the outcome. This fight was no no-decision affair; it was a fifteen-round battle with a verdict and Mike would be compelled to do his share of the forcing instead of concentrating strictly on defensive issues as he had done against Stribling and Walker. The Irishman was also taking on the most ferocious hitter he had ever faced. In the course of fifteen rounds Mike was going to be hit harder than he had ever been hit in his life.

The opinion held by a great many judges of 'fistic matters' was that the champion would be flattened for the ultimate and final count of ten. 'If it should happen, Michael will have to take it philosophically,' commented the *Herald Tribune*. 'He will be $50,000 wealthier when he recovers consciousness and he will have the satisfaction of having aided the milk industry.' It was the first time that Mike had placed the title in anything resembling jeopardy since he had won it from Battling Siki and his adversaries were relishing the prospect.

Somehow, Mr Michael McTigue is one of those unfortun-
ates who are loved only by their near relatives – if any.

The consensus of opinion seems to indicate that Mr
McTigue will be knocked horizontal this evening. Hence
there ought to be plenty of customers. They will turn out to
see a fighter of this sort knocked horizontal.

There is no use Michael pointing to the fact that
his record contains an impressive number of knockouts.
Michael has become unpopular and that is all there is to it.
The multitude is convinced that he is one of the conservative
ones, keeping the title by the simple expedient of keeping
out of the ring.

This state of affairs may work upon the mind of Michael,
or whatever he has in lieu of a mind. He may say to himself,
'Oh, well. If I am not flattened this evening they will insist I
keep fighting until somebody does flatten me.'

Bill McGeehan, 'Down The Line'

Of the nine leading New York papers, five went for the challenger,
two for the champion, with two abstentions. However, there was a
niggling suspicion that Mike was a better fighter than anyone had
been led to believe. 'If Mike McTigue leaves his little pal Inferiority
Complex in the dressing room at the Yankee Stadium tomorrow
night his followers can bet all the family silverware against a monkey's
chapeau that he's liable to beat the daylights out of Paul Berlenbach,'
wrote Jack Farrell, 'very few people know what Michael's pugilistic
limitations are.'

The *New York Times* predicted a crowd of 50,000 for the first
championship match of the outdoor season. Both boxers made
weight at 2 pm in the Flatiron building after which a doctor declared

them to be in good physical condition. Mike seemed the less nervous of the two. The champion's pulse was 68 at rest, 75 under exercise; his blood pressure 85-126. The gates of Yankee stadium swung wide open at 5 pm when the sale of twenty thousand one-dollar tickets started in the ball yard.

But just as everything was set for the fight the weather 'uncorked the meanest collection of showers'. The forecast was for clearing so Rickard waited until the last moment before deciding whether to postpone; but the longer Tex waited, the worse the weather got. The decision was made at 4.30 pm. Rickard wanted to wait a little longer but the fields and stands were drenched by the early-afternoon down-pour and the promoter was overruled. For the first time in his career Tex had lost a decision to the weather. The Commission granted per-mission for a twenty-four-hour delay but warned that in case of an-other postponement it would be necessary to seek a much later date or wait until there was an open date in the baseball schedule.

Mike returned home and slept for nine hours before taking a light breakfast of two soft eggs, a few slices of toast and a cup of tea. He then set off on a two-mile walk before resting up for several hours. Harry Newman caught up with the champion in the after-noon. Mike said he wasn't worried about Berlenbach and that he would 'lay the German stiff in a few brief rounds'.

The next day the multitude arrived early. The two-dollar cus-tomers started to assemble shortly after 2 pm and surrounded the Yankee Stadium during an early rainstorm. By the time of the first preliminary bout there were close to 40,000 people in the field, stands and bleachers. There were more women in the gathering than had been seen at such an event previously. According to the *Herald Tribune*, 'the front rows of the ringside section looked like an assembly of motion-picture extras, with here and there a star of the silent drama. They were not keeping anything like silence, however.'

Babe Ruth was an early arrival. He explained that it wasn't the combatants that drew him there but he just wanted to judge the distance from the home plate to the right-field bleachers. Battling Siki sat at ringside with what Jack Lawrence described as 'some poignant thoughts passing under his close-cropped dome' at Mike's purse of $50,000. Champion golfer Bobby Jones arrived during the preliminary bouts and took his place among the politicians, the 'notables' from Broadway and the 'dudes from Wall Street with their sweeties'. All the town was there.

There were plenty of overcoats around but it was a mild night. The announcer, Joe Humphries, was in 'fine form, using eighty-five-cent [verbose] words in introducing the battlers' and the crowd 'didn't quail under the punishment'. Berlenbach entered the ring first, bundled in a heavy bathrobe and a woollen sweater. He sat hunched in his corner waiting for the champion. Mike followed about a minute later. As the Irishman stripped off his check bathrobe to reveal a pair of red shorts a voice broke out, 'Bad luck to you Michael for wearing those colours, and you yourself that was born in County Clare.'

Mike was waiting in the centre of the ring when the opening bell sounded.

For five rounds it was a pursuit race. Mike was drifting around the ring, always just outside Berlenbach's slow, lumbering reach. The challenger couldn't catch the shadow but the champion was making too few threatening gestures of his own. Mike fell short with a succession of left jabs, such was his care to stay out of Berlenbach's reach. The champion was content to bide his time in the hope that Berlenbach would tire of his own exertions. Mike tried to throw the occasional right hook but never connected.

Then in the sixth round Mike suddenly abandoned his defensive ploy. Urged on by the increasingly desperate pleading of Doc Bagley, he emerged from his corner and slugged Berlenbach with his right. He had the challenger in trouble for most of the round and he drove several rights and lefts to his opponent's jaw in a furious rally that got the crowd roaring. Mike scored a knockdown when he dropped Berlenbach with a left hook as the round was coming to a close. The challenger got up before the referee and timekeeper could start a count but another right to the jaw had Berlenbach holding at the bell. According to Bill McGeehan, 'after that round Berlenbach, who always wears a blank and amazed expression, looked blanker and more phased than ever as he sat on his stool. Mr Daniel Hickey, who discovered and trained Berlenbach, applied the smelling salts and looked worried.'

Mike ran to the centre of the ring as the bell sounded for the seventh and continued his assault. He outfought and out-hit Berlenbach and staggered the challenger with accurate rights to the jaw. The champion sustained the attack until the end of the ninth but when he realised he had hit Berlenbach with his best shots, he got discouraged. Mike looked at Doc Bagley in the corner, but there was nothing Bagley could say; the effort had been too much.

As the bell rang for the tenth round Mike had very little left but a determination not to be knocked out. For the remaining rounds Berlenbach resumed his chase of the champion who drifted, slipped and weaved his way out of danger. Mike was content to throw long pounding lefts that kept bothering and upsetting the challenger's attempt to land his big punch. But the younger man was now much stronger and he staggered Mike with heavy lefts to the stomach. It was a typical Berlenbach performance. He plodded steadily, always on the attack, ripping and slashing with his left. Occasionally he drove home a right to the head or the ribs but those blows carried little power because Berlenbach was essentially a one-handed fighter. His left was best and he used it almost exclusively. The champion's red trunks were soggy and dark with sweat. Still he retreated, always faster than Berlenbach, ducking, rocking and pulling away and yet, amazingly, by the end of the bout it was the young challenger's legs that sagged. Mike bore the marks of an old fighter, his lips were puffed and bleeding, his nose trickled blood, there was a slash over his left eye and the claret poured from his right ear. But the fight was close and the Yankee Stadium grew quiet as the crowd awaited the verdict of judges Jimmy Collins and Charles F. Mathison and referee Eddie Purdy. Finally, Joe Humphries stepped into the ring.

At midnight, in the middle of a baseball lot on the outskirts of Manhattan stood a squat man in a blue suit. He lifted up his face toward the dark cave of a stadium risen out of cigarette smoke, peopled with 40,000 ghouls. Enormous lights concentrated their white, sterile fire upon his stubby head. On each side of him, in opposite corners of a roped square, sat a boxer. On his right was a young German, whose heavy, amazed face protruded from the folds of a bathrobe that concealed a torso bulging with incredible dorsal muscles, and a pair of clumsy thighs. On his left sat an old Irishman, tired and sly, with a streak of blood like a scarlet worm running down the corner of his mouth. The ghouls waited. This man in the blue suit stood before them to announce a decision. He did so, when he felt that the drama of his pause had reached its climax, by sharply raising one of his hands. Instantly, from the smoky caves, came a great hooting.

Time, 8 June 1925

Mike was more popular in defeat than he ever had been in victory and his dethronement was greeted with a roar of catcalls and hisses. He had never been a well-liked fighter, let alone a well-liked champion, but the majority of the 45,000 smoke-veiled spectators believed the Irishman had been unjustly deprived of his title. Mike had been the cleverer of the two men, he'd put up a gallant defence and championships weren't usually taken away on such a slight margin. As the customers walked to the exits across the transformed baseball diamond the booing could still be heard. They continued to boo even though the mistake hurt an unpopular boxer and benefited a New York favourite. Mike was given a rousing ovation as he left the ring.

The champion had been expected to make the challenger look foolish but the biggest surprise was that Mike appeared to be hitting harder than Berlenbach. 'The man who now holds the light heavyweight title,' commented the *Newark Evening News*, 'will perhaps have a harder time hanging on to the title than McTigue did.' The consensus of opinion at ringside was that Mike had been entitled to a draw at worst. The Irishman was generally credited with the honours in six of the fifteen rounds. Berlenbach's aggressiveness gave him a possible edge in five, but the challenger could get nothing better than a draw in the four remaining chapters. World championships were not generally supposed to change hands when the going had been as even as that. It may have been undeserved but it was not unexpected. Mike had been unlucky or ill advised since he became world champion on St Patrick's Day 1923 in Dublin. But he had also been too greedy. This, according to *Boxing*, had been his failing since beating Siki.

Mike may not have been so much to blame himself, may rather have suffered from injudicious managerial advice. In any case, Mike has failed to earn the dividends which should have come to him from his title. And now the title has gone and McTigue has no highly profitable assets to market.

FOURTEEN

The Californian who claims to have produced the largest lemon in
the world evidently forgets that Ireland produced Mike McTigue.

'Lanky Joe', *Washington Post*

'One day I'm looking out the window and I said to Toots, "Do my eyes
deceive me or is that Mike McTigue crossing the street?" He looked
and snapped, "Not only is it Mike McTigue but he hasn't a manager."'

'He doesn't seem to have anything on his mind,' commented
Sullivan, 'and he was a pretty good fighter too, in his day.'

'He could still be a good fighter with the right handling,' answered Johnston, 'Come on, let's go down and see him.'

Jimmy Johnston and his sidekick, 'Toots' Sullivan, ran onto
Broadway and caught up with Mike as he was entering the Putnam
building. Mike and Jimmy had barely shared a dozen words before
that afternoon, even though the Irishman had fought on several
bills promoted by Johnston, including his first professional fight at
Jimmy's St Nicholas Rink over a decade previously.

Jimmy grabbed Mike by the sleeve and said, 'Wait a minute
Mike, I want to talk to you.'

'I have a lot of errands to do, Johnston, so make it quick. My
wife's coming to see a picture with me and I have to get to the Rialto
theatre in a hurry.'

'Are you going to fight again?' asked Jimmy.

'I don't think so. I can't get any bouts, they all say I'm no longer a card and the fans don't want to see me. I've practically quit the ring. I figure on getting a job as an iron-worker on one of the Jersey bridge jobs.'

'Listen, Mike, you're still a pretty good fighter. I think you can still lick eighty per cent of the men around here right now. I saw your battle with Berlenbach and thought you won. Give me a chance and I'll get you some fights and we'll see what happens.'

'Guess it's no use, Jimmy, I'm through and I intend to accept things in a good spirit.'

'Michael, me lad, you're still a great fighter and you probably realise that I'm the best manager in the world.' Mike grinned and answered softly, 'I know it.'

'If you come up to my office tomorrow morning and sign a contract appointing me your manager, I'll get your light heavyweight title back for you,' offered Jimmy.

'If you do, I'll buy you a car. I'll be there at eleven tomorrow morning,' answered Mike, and he disappeared into the Putnam building.

Jimmy turned to Sullivan and said, 'That's the last we see of him.'

'Bet he shows up on time in the morning,' said Sullivan.

'You're crazy,' replied Jimmy.

The following morning Jimmy arrived late at his office. Mike had been sitting there for three hours. 'When's my first fight Jimmy? Where's the contract?'

Jimmy hadn't filled it in. But Mike grabbed the sheet of paper and signed the blank contract. 'Thus encouraged, I gave him two more to sign,' Jimmy recalled. 'Then he threw a thousand dollar bill at Toots and me.'

'Can you boys use any part of that? And if you want me to help you out any more just say the word,' Mike told the startled duo and suddenly he was gone. The old champion thought Jimmy had to be in dire straits to want to sign a fighter like him.

'Sullivan had never seen so much money before and he fainted,' said Jimmy. 'As for me, I remained cool, calm and collected. First of all I put the money in the safe and then I revived Sullivan. I hate to have to admit that I ever gave back money to anyone, but we kept it only until Mike's next visit.'

After he lost the championship Mike had disappeared for a time. The customers hoped it wasn't temporary; promoters and fans wrote him off as washed up and too old. Mike's friends told him to quit the ring or end up punch-drunk like the other old pugs that hung around Broadway. But fighting was the only thing Mike knew and he took to wandering the streets looking for any promoter who'd give him a match. Then he met Jimmy Johnston. It was an old axiom in boxing that a good Jewish fighter needed a good Irish manager to go places, and that an Irish fighter would be a total loss without a capable Jewish gentleman in his corner. Ring history is replete with such combinations.

But the Johnston-McTigue story is a tale of two Irishmen who found each other on the streets of New York and who together perpetrated one of the most extraordinary feats in boxing history. The legendary sportswriter Damon Runyon believed the story to be imbued with a magical, almost supernatural, element. 'Not until he dropped the title and fell victim to the hypnotic influence of Mr James J. Johnston, the man with the suspiciously black hair, did McTigue start to do some real fighting. Scientists are still endeavouring to discover the prescription Mr Johnston employed.'

The sceptics had a different theory. They believed Jimmy told

Mike he was a great prizefighter; Mike had no sense of humour and thought Jimmy meant it.

Jimmy Johnston was born in Liverpool, to Irish parents, on 28 November 1875. His father, an iron-moulder, moved the family to Hell's Kitchen, New York, which was full of Irish immigrants who hated the English. The neighbourhood children dismissed Jimmy's claims of Irishness and beat him up on a regular basis. But he was a tough kid and the other boys soon left him alone. He boxed as an amateur and a professional although his career in the ring ended prematurely when a future champion, Danny Dougherty, knocked him out. Charlie 'Handlebars' Harvey, a fight manager who looked after British boxers in the States, offered Jimmy a job as an assistant.

When Harvey was appointed to the newly formed New York State Athletic Commission in 1914, he turned his stable of boxers over to his young sidekick. Jimmy's business acumen and 'ballyhoo' set him apart from other fight managers and he had an uncanny knack of picking good, useful friends. One such friend was Damon Runyon and the two men would run together through New York. Jimmy, always dapper with a dark Derby perpetually cocked over one eye, owned a Stutz motorcar and with Runyon in tow he would cruise around the 'Roaring Forties' calling in everywhere there was anyone likely to be a source of gossip or scandal.

Jimmy began running shows out of the old Madison Square Garden in 1915, and it's here the Johnston legend really began. The staff at the Garden had been terrorised by a number of infamous gangsters: men like Gyp the Blood, Dago Frank, Whitey Lewis and Leftie Louie. The story went that on his opening night at the Garden, Jimmy approached Gyp the Blood, who was sitting in someone else's seat, and asked him to leave. Gyp refused. Jimmy pulled the chair backwards throwing the gangster to the ground and proceeded to kick and punch one of the most dangerous killers in New York unconscious. He then threw him out into the alley. Leftie Louie came to the aid of his accomplice and Jimmy beat him up as well. Harry Perry, a cousin of Tammany Hall boss 'Big Tim' Sullivan, was told of the incident. Perry went to the Garden and when he saw how small Jimmy was he asked Gyp, 'is this the fellow who's been kicking you around?' and began to laugh. 'If you can't handle a little guy like this, it's a cinch I ain't gonna help you do it. Okay, Jimmy, from now on you won't have any trouble with my boys. I'm for you.'

Jimmy got good currency from the story for years. It ingratiated him to the press and ticket holders who had been bullied at the Garden and they returned to his shows. It also discouraged anybody from moving in on him. It's a good yarn, and it worked for Jimmy, but it wasn't true. Gyp the Blood, Dago Frank, Whitey Lewis and Leftie Louie had been executed at Sing Sing before Jimmy Johnston took over at the Garden. He was just the sort of man Mike needed. Within days of his defeat to Berlenbach the former champion had walked into the offices of the Commission to demand a rematch and file his challenge. But his efforts with the paperwork were described as 'tardy' and he was told to go away and try again. Even though he'd put up a brave performance in defence of the title, most of the city's sportswriters celebrated the demise of a fighter they'd always disliked. 'Berlenbach took the title from the most pathetic figure of a champion that has imposed on the patience of the paying trade since Al McCoy, in whose honour the term "Cheese Champion" was invented,' commented *Boxing*. And when Tex Rickard announced that there was a public demand for a rematch and that he intended to retain Mike's services, the boxing writers scoffed. 'Tex Rickard has raised the ante. He now believes the public will stand for anything not once but twice,' wrote Harry Newman in the *New York Daily*

News. 'Mr Rickard has requested bids for several thousand cots for those customers who wish to sleep through the main event.'

Mike was also down on his luck outside the ropes. He lost five hundred dollars on Tom Gibbons after backing him to beat Gene Tunney. Just before Gibbons entered the ring Mike had gone to his dressing room and after shaking hands asked:

'How are you feeling Tom?'

'Fine,' declared Gibbons.

'Do you think that you will win tonight?'

'Sure I do', replied Tom, 'and I think that I'm going to knock him out.'

Mike shook hands with Tom again and wished him luck as he went out into the hot evening air. He went looking for odds and found someone prepared to take the money at evens that Gibbons would win. Tunney knocked Gibbons out in the twelfth. Mike was furious and was seen patrolling the arena, shouting and swearing. 'What do you think of that fellow Gibbons, knowing he was going to lay down, let me go out and bet on him.'

The *Boxing Blade* commented: 'wonder how Mike would feel if he heard fans saying that he sold his title to Berlenbach and that he didn't try to win? He wouldn't like it, would he? He should be the last one in the world to insinuate that a fighter didn't win fairly.'

Mike's trainer, Frank 'Doc' Bagley, wasn't faring much better. He was directed by Supreme Justice McGoldrick to pay $50 a week alimony and a $200 counsel fee in a suit by Mrs Edna T. Bagley for separation on the grounds of cruelty. Mrs Bagley told the court that 'Doc' hit her with his fists, kicked her and threatened to shoot her. She told the court that her husband had a contract with his fighters by which he got 25 to 30 per cent of their earnings and she believed that Mike McTigue got $50,000 for his recent fight with

Berlenbach. She thought that Doc must have made at least $12,000 a year and some years as much as $55,000. She said that he once bragged of losing $30,000 gambling in less than twelve months. Bagley confessed to making a lot of money when he managed Tunney and Willie Jackson but said that Jackson had retired and Tunney had a new manager. He insisted that his earnings were very small by now and that he'd only made $500 from Mike in the past year. Doc had earned more than that but it was an indication of Mike's standing that the court was prepared to accept such a conservative estimate.

With Doc gone Jimmy took over Mike's training, making corrections in his stance and adjustments to his technique and then he took his fighter out of town for a few fights to restore his confidence. Jimmy's influence was immediate. Mike knocked out Frank Carpenter in Albany, New York in seven rounds and then looked fast and impressive in a six-round exhibition with Art Weigand in Buffalo.

Jimmy believed his fighter ready for a return to New York and Mike was matched with Young Marullo of New Orleans as the feature bout at the Coney Island stadium on 21 August. Mike went to Saratoga Springs to prepare for the match. Gene Tunney was already in Saratoga and Jimmy seized on a great opportunity to generate some publicity. Tunney had chased Mike for a fight for nearly two years while Mike always countered that not only was Tunney not a credible challenger, he didn't even have the right to call himself the American light heavyweight champion. 'How can he be?' Mike once asked. 'As an American citizen and holder of the world's title, I am also automatically American champion. How can a fighter be a world's champion, yet not a champion of his own country? Tunney holds no title at all, but he can have a crack at mine whenever he says the word.'

While in Saratoga in the summer of 1925 Jimmy told the press that the old feud had been rekindled and that the fighters had come to blows. It made for a good story and it got Mike back on the sports pages for the first time since he'd lost his title. Paul Gallico wrote a dramatisation of the affair entitled 'Lessee If You Like Butter':

NEWS ITEM: Saratoga Springs – Mike McTigue denied vehemently today that he had come to blows with Gene Tunney and had injured his hand. Mike said he was in great shape for his scrap with Tony Marullo at Coney Island on Friday. He admitted that he and Tunney had had an argument as to who was American light heavyweight champion, but that it had gone 'no further than the talking stage'.

We will now render a little impression of what that famous argument must have been like, if one is to believe the newspaper stories pertinent to the two famous ring stars and their manners:

SCENE: The porch of a spacious, rambling building, overlooking Saratoga Lake. Uncle Tom Luther's place. To the left a canvas screen, originally erected by Jack Kearns, hides the ring where the fighters work out. The sun shines dazzlingly from the bright, blue lake. The heat waves dance.

CHARACTERS: Eugene Tunney and Michael Mc-Tigue. Two noted pugilists.

TIME: The present.

The curtain rises disclosing Tunney and McTigue lo'ling on the porch of Uncle Tom Luther's place, sipping iced tea. Tunney is deep in copies of *Webster's Unabridged*, *Dream Psychoses of the Chronically Insane*, and *Romeo and Juliet*, which he reads alternately. McTigue is idly caressing the strings of a harp.

TUNNEY: *(looking up from dictionary)*: Unique, those heat waves over the lake. The principle, I am led to believe, is the same as that responsible for mirages seen in the desert, an atmospheric condition conductive to image transference.

McTIGUE: *(sounds the opening bars of 'Killarney')*: Whist!

TUNNEY: Do you know, Mike, I was just thinking what an essentially silly profession we follow. Here am I, for instance, light heavyweight champion of America, while -

McTIGUE (interrupting): Wurra! Wurra! Begorry! Who is the American light heavyweight champion? Bedad, and it's none other than Moike McTigue that holds the selfsame toitle.

TUNNEY: Why, Mike, how utterly ridiculous. Surely you must be cognisant of the fact that I won it from Harry Greb, who took it from Tommy Gibbons.

McTIGUE: *(in a towering wrath, strikes a chord from the 'Gogheen-na-Fardhu', the famous Black March which for centuries has called the McTigues to wars)*: Wurra on you for a shameless spalpeen. 'Tis meself that won the American light heavyweight champeenship from Paul Berlenbach, bad cess to him.

TUNNEY: *(laughs a cultured and carefully modulated laugh)*: Ho, ho, ha, ha, what an amusing fellow you are, Mike, honestly, you tickle my risibilities almost beyond control. Why, every one is aware of the fact that you were thoroughly lambasted by Mr Berlenbach, and lost your world's title to him.

McTIGUE: *(breaks suddenly into the sunny smile for which his race is noted)*: Arrah, bedad, and that proves it. Th' snakes take Paulie and his pounding. Ain't he a Dootchman? An' how can a Dootchman by American light heavyweight champeen. Sure, he won me world's title. Sure, then, subtract the Dootch toitle from the wurld's title and ye get the American light heavyweight champeen. That's me.

TUNNEY: *(deftly paraphrasing Weber and Fields)*: Ooooo, Mike, I luf you so I could Kill you!

McTIGUE: *(juggles some Irish potatoes)*: Whist, Gene, kape your hands down. There's no gat.

(They call for more ice tea.)

Jimmy's ballyhoo lured 12,500 spectators to the Coney Island stadium to watch Mike fulfil his promise to knock Marullo 'stiffer'n a mackerel'. Marullo had recently knocked out Mike's old foe, Jeff Smith, for the first time in his career and it was generally regarded as the Irishman's best performance to date in New York. Shorn of the title, Mike showed himself a better fighter as ex-champion than he was as champion. He discarded the timid, defensive boxing that characterised his work as titleholder and he took up an aggressive approach that was much more to the taste of the customers. The 'hypnotic influence of Mr James J. Johnston' that Runyon wrote of had taken effect. Indeed there seemed to be no limit to Jimmy's magical powers when a bizarre sequence of events led to Mike getting a return match with Berlenbach for the title in a matter of weeks. Firstly the champion sustained a hand injury and was forced to postpone his defence against Jack Delaney from 28 August to 11 September. Then as Berlenbach's hand healed, Delaney was taken to St Vincent's hospital in Bridgeport suffering from septic poisoning following an operation for an abscess on his throat. Tex Rickard needed a replacement challenger and chose Mike.

Mike returned to Saratoga and many of the boxing writers made him favourite to regain his title. They sensed a newborn look of ferocity in Mike, who had developed a deep dislike of Berlenbach. A fight of fast and furious proportions was liable to ensue and Tex Rickard was a very happy promoter as the punters swamped the box-office. But then Mike succumbed to the curse plaguing this fight. On the morning of 2 September he was rushed to Saratoga Hospital suffering from blood poisoning following an infection in his right arm. He was confined to bed for a week as the swelling receded and doctors forbade him to box for a month.

While Mike was recuperating, Jimmy was involved in an unsuccessful bid to take over the sport. A syndicate was formed to buy the contracts of champion boxers and leading contenders with the idea of introducing more business-like methods into the old boxing game. It proposed to handle boxers in the same fashion that moving picture studios handled their star performers. Jimmy Johnston was announced as managing director of the enterprise with a remit to negotiate with champion boxers in all parts of the world. The first fighter to sign was Mike McTigue. But his attempt at global boxing domination never looked likely to happen so Jimmy returned to his day job – getting Mike his light heavyweight title back. One of Jimmy's friends in the press, Sam Hall, the sports editor of the *New York American*, was planning a charity event for the city's poor at Christmas. Jimmy suggested a fight between Mike and a leading black middleweight, Tiger Flowers. Hall doubted the attraction of such a bout but Jimmy persisted. Finally and largely because he could get the former world champion on a low percentage, Hall agreed to the match.

All concerned had to settle for less money because the Commission had ruled that all charity shows had to donate half the gate to the good cause. 'When the revered boxing Commission made a ruling that in all charity shows fifty per cent of the receipts must be turned over to them for the beneficiary, a fearful squawl went up from everyone, and now, b'gosh, it looks as though Mister Jim Farley were right,' wrote Paul Gallico. 'It simply meant a little harder work for the matchworkers, but look at the swell card that will be presented tomorrow night at the New Garden for the Christmas fund. As a colourful, bound-to-get-your-money's-worth card, it won't be beaten all year. And yet it was made under what most everybody considered an impossible ruling by the Commission. But best of all, this will be the first charity show in years in which the charity will get more than the boxers.'

A great deal was written about Mike's willingness to fight black boxers. 'Boxing coloured fighters has been McTigue's pet dish for many years but he probably never met up with so stubborn an opponent as the old Tiger,' predicted Harry Newman. Flowers was a rough, aggressive fighter who'd licked nearly all the boys in his division before he stumbled into Jack Delaney, who'd knocked him out. The winner of the fight had been promised a tilt at Paul Berlenbach who'd given an assurance that he would not draw the colour line in the event of a Flowers victory.

By the morning of the fight Mike was the 6-5 favourite over the Southerner.

'You'll win easily,' Jimmy told Mike on his way into the ring.

'You're telling me?' replied the Irishman.

He didn't. Flowers swarmed all over Mike from the first bell and his southpaw stance was something the Irishman just couldn't solve. Mike reverted to his old defensive style and Flowers slapped, cuffed, pushed and mauled him around the ring. The fifth was the best round of the contest and Mike staggered Tiger as he pumped rights into his body but this tired the Irishman and Flowers opened a cut over Mike's eye with a barrage of lefts just before the bell.

Mike drew blood in the next round when he drove home a right that cut Flowers over the left eye and the claret flowed freely for the remainder of the round. But despite this handicap Flowers was still the aggressor. At the final bell everybody thought that Mike's brief ring renaissance had come to an end. Jimmy went down the steps from the ring, admitting to himself that Mike was even worse than he had thought, joked Paul Gallico. But then came the decision.

'The winner, McTigue!' cried Joe Humphries and according to the *New York Times* it sparked 'one of the wildest outbursts of condemnation ever experienced in local boxing'. For ten minutes after the announcement the crowd stood and yelled. Special officers were called in to clear the building, but the demonstration continued. Even after the crowd had left the arena small groups of spectators, ignoring the commands of the specials, stood about ridiculing the decision.

Gallico wrote that the story of the fight was utterly insignificant compared to the 'most outrageous decision ever rendered in a town where poor decisions are nothing extraordinary. The crowd let out a roar that could have been heard to the East River. If ever an inefficient, blind, idiotic verdict was turned in at the end of a bout, this was it.'

Jimmy walked past the pressmen with one hand over his face. 'Our Michael won all the way,' he said. Flowers took the decision with good grace and resignation and made no attempt to protest. A few days after the fight Gallico wrote that 'the coloured man always shows himself as probably the most well-behaved person in the ring today. I can still see Flowers' break into a cheerful grin the moment the fromagenous decision was announced, and trot over to shake the hand of the man he had beaten, but who will go down in the books as having beaten him.

'Of course there's always the possibility that the Tigah was laughing at the joke. But I only wish to point out that nine out of ten white fighters in his position would have seized their noses between their digits, would have signalled to the crowd that they had been gypped and would have in every way tried to incite the spectators to a demonstration in their favour, a highly dangerous thing at a prizefight. Mistah Flowers did none of these things, and I am not sure that but for his exemplary behaviour, there might have been a small-sized riot at the ringside.'

The judges involved in the fiasco were men whose integrity wasn't questioned, but whose judgement, and the judgement of the Commission in placing them at the ringside, certainly was. Peter J. Brady, the president of the Federation Bank and Bernard Gimbel of Gimbel Brothers were officiating at their first professional fight and both voted for Mike. Eddie Purdy, the trained referee, cast his vote for Flowers. The *New York Daily News* interviewed the two judges:

'McTigue landed the cleaner and harder punches,' said Brady. 'My point score at the end of the contest showed that McTigue had hit Flowers more often than the Tiger had hit the Irishman. I think the crowd's ire was raised more by the fact that it was an inferior fight than by the decision. It was a poor exhibition of boxing and both boys should have been fired from the ring. But McTigue clearly won, according to the methods of adjudging victors.'

'Judges,' said Gimbel, 'must score five points in each round. My sheet showed at the end of the fight that McTigue had registered more points, earning as many as four in many of the rounds. McTigue looked weaker at the final bell than did Flowers but by that time Mike had amassed many more points than Flowers.'

'I believe the crowd permitted its ugly temper to view our decision blindly. They had expected a much better fight and would have yelled murder at any kind of verdict. No doubt the mob thinks today that I should stick to merchandising, but Mr William Muldoon had asked us to officiate and we were glad to oblige him. Of course I shall stick to that decision.'

The total receipts came to $49,972 and a cheque for $24,986 was sent to the *New York American* Christmas Fund so at least some of the needy of New York had a slightly better Yuletide. It was bad news for Rickard; the show cost $36,000 to stage and he lost close to $11,000.

A few days later Jimmy strolled into the Hotel Commodore where a testimonial dinner for Commissioner James A. Farley was being staged. Jimmy was the prime mover in organising the event. In the office Dan Skilling and James Parnell Dawson were counting up the day's ticket sales. Jimmy sat at the table and pulled out a white gold watch, richly set with diamonds.

'This is the first present I ever received from a fighter. I have handled three world's champions, Driscoll, Lewis and Dundee, but McTigue is the only one to show his appreciation by giving me more than a manager's cut of the purse. He gave me this last Monday for Christmas,' said Jimmy.

'Tis simply wonderful,' said Skilling to Dawson. 'This proves Mike isn't in business for himself. This watch Johnston has here proves he's not.'

'If McTigue gets any more decisions like the one against Flowers, he should never stop buying watches for this bandit,' answered Dawson.

'Say, did you notice McTigue went into the ring the short end of the betting and won the decision? Maybe you don't think little Jimmy cleaned up there too,' replied Johnston. Shoving his Derby hat down over one eye Johnston winked at Skilling, tipped Dawson's chair from under him as he was about to sit down, and strode out.

The Broadway gambling fraternity had been 'taken for a sleigh ride' and Jimmy began yelling for a rematch with his Irish protégé with Berlenbach. The charge was frequently made that Jimmy, who was proud of being known as the 'Boy Bandit of Broadway', 'owned' the Commission. He certainly got almost anything he wanted. Jimmy was a close friend of James A. Farley, Chairman of the Commission, and was often seen in his company around town. He was also a close friend of Mayor James J. Walker, the author of the boxing law. It was Walker who had introduced Johnston to Farley. It was no surprise to anyone therefore that when the Three Dukes met on 8 January, they ordered Berlenbach to defend his title against Mike who was instated as the official challenger. Mike had taken a terrible leathering from Tiger Flowers yet Berlenbach was ordered to fight him as a logical contender. If Mike hadn't been under the management of the Boy Bandit he'd have been back in the small clubs, but Jimmy had managed to out-manoeuvre the field of light heavyweights and put an aging, unattractive box-office fighter back in the ranks of the leading contenders. A generation of leading light-heavies would have to wait their turn.

Berlenbach was regarded as the most willing fighter of all the champions and it seemed to be an injustice that he'd been ordered to give a return match to the man now commonly described as the 'world's worst prizefighter'. When it was discovered that the manager of the world's worst prizefighter and a friend of the Dukes needed several thousand dollars to square up a case with the United States government, the press cried foul.

Jimmy had quietly got out of a prison sentence for withholding the government's war tax on the tickets of a fight show held in 1921. Federal Judge Atwell ordered him to report to the warden of the jail in Essex County, New Jersey, to serve his time. But during the Berlenbach controversy it emerged that the Supreme Court of the United States had overruled the embezzlement charge in the indictment and thus had erased the jail sentence. All Jimmy had to do was pay the government the taxes he owed. The scribes believed that Jimmy was using his friends in the Cauliflower Cabinet to pay his way out of jail by dropping in the world's worst fighter against the world's best champion. The Dukes' newfound enthusiasm for the Irishman was certainly surprising considering how unfriendly they were to Mike and his title before he came under Jimmy's ample wing. When Mike had no manager he was suspended and tossed about by the boxing bosses because he refused to defend his light heavyweight championship. The Commission was often righteous and rough with lawbreakers – it had once suspended a bantamweight fighter because he was alleged to be delinquent in his alimony – but this was Jimmy and he was allowed to operate while on parole for chiselling the government's money. 'It is very depressing,' commented one Broadway writer. 'One turns to the crime news for a spiritual draught.'

But if Mike was to get another shot at the title, as decreed by the Commission, it would have to happen elsewhere than the Garden because Tex Rickard didn't want the match. Mike's poor showing against Tiger Flowers removed what little love the Garden impresario had for the Irishman and as one writer explained, 'when Mr Rickard's love turns to hate, it's just that and no more'.

The boxing fathers had picked Mike in preference to a formidable list of contenders. The likes of Young Stribling, Jack Delaney, Eddie Huffman, Tommy Loughran and Ad Stone were all anxiously awaiting a chance to step in with the Astoria Assassin and Rickard didn't see what Mike had done to be at the head of that queue.

Neither did the boxing writers:

Mike McTigue, who recently won recognition as the world's worst prizefighter, has been nominated for another championship match and there are mutinous mumblings among the customers, who say they can sleep better at home. As a compromise, to avert a nasty situation, it has been suggested the fight be held in the dark, but McTigue refuses to fight in the dark for two reasons.

The first is that McTigue can't fight.

The other one does not matter, but it is believed Mike is afraid of the dark.

The New York State Athletic Commission was the author of the order sentencing the customers to watch McTigue in another demonstration. The sentence of the commission read that the customers must spend not less than forty-five minutes watching McTigue with his arms around Paul Berlenbach and listening to his familiar, plaintive cry: 'Me hand is hurted.'

As soon as the official mandate was posted in the saloons the customers began to cry: 'We want Al McCoy! We want Jack Bernstein! We want Tom Cowler! We will stand for anybody but Mike McTigue!'

A large number are reported to have left town and it may require a general extradition to get a quorum for the ordeal even if someone can be found to promote the affair, which is by no means certain. Tex Rickard has refused to do it because, he says, he has no hotel licence for his new Garden and consequently is unable to offer beds for his customers.

Berlenbach made his attitude clear when he issued a statement saying, 'Vas iss los?'

McTigue insists, however, that the customers have never

really seen him at his worst and he is pleading for a chance to perform the masterpiece of his career.

'I can fight much worse than I did in my bouts with Mickey Walker, Willie Stribling and Tiger Flowers,' Mc-Tigue said. 'In fact, I am afraid I was pretty good in those exhibitions. I am ever so much worse at my worst.'

Just why the boxing commission has become so cruel to the customers has not been explained. However, the commission of late has been acting in a manner considered peculiar even for the commission ... The commission recently enjoyed a public banquet at which several laudatory speeches were made concerning its sagacity. It is believed the commissioners took these speeches seriously.

Westbrook Pegler, *Chicago Tribune*, 7 January 1926

Mike offered Berlenbach $25,000 for a championship bout, with a bet of $25,000 on the side. 'Sure, he must be afraid of me,' said Mike, 'or is it really that he's dissatisfied with what money he could get from fighting me? I'll fix it so that he can get fifty thousand dollars if he can beat me.' Berlenbach and his manager, Dan Hickey tried to persuade the commissioners to let the champion fight opponents they believed to be a more lucrative proposition than the aging Irishman. But Jimmy had cast his spell and the Flatiron mob issued an edict that Berlenbach had to fight Mike if he was to fight at all in New York. James A. Farley said that Berlenbach promised Mike a return match when he had beaten the Irishman for the championship several months previously; the champion had to go through with his promise before he was permitted to fight any other challenger in the state. For Farley was an honourable man; so were they all; all honourable men. Hickey denied making Mike any promise but Paul

Gallico urged Berlenbach to take the fight in an open letter in the *New York Daily News*:

Mr Paul Berlenbach, Astoria LI

Dear Paul: You know I've always stood up for you, in print as well as in conversation. I've held you up as an ideal champion. Now a little favour I'd like to ask of you. Please, when you fight McTigue, will you knock him into Officer Muldoon's lap, provided he is at ringside, and not snooping around the New Garden, egging Willie Stillman's ushers on to annoy the customers. Thanking you in advance, your friend, PAUL GALLICO

Well, that makes me feel better. Der Paulie is one of the few fighters who know what gratitude means. I am sure that he will belt Mike right into Muldoon's shirt-front.

Berlenbach was entitled to decline any challenge until some time in June when six months would have expired since his last championship bout. So Berlenbach and Hickey came up with an alternative plan. Hickey said his fighter was thinking of deserting the light heavyweight division and proposed to tour the country in search of some of those heavy guys. Berlenbach was going into the sticks to grab himself plenty of dough by knocking over the big mugs and Mike would have to wait.

Jimmy's propaganda machine went to work. Sports editors around the country were bombarded with stories that Berlenbach was scared of an ancient, but capable, battler. Johnston heckled Hickey whenever he appeared in gymnasiums and he goaded the world champion. He resorted to every artifice at his command to get the match: he even told sports writers that Berlenbach had been a slacker during the War, refusing to join the American forces because of pro-German sympathies. The story was printed in many of the biggest newspapers in the States and it prompted vehement denials from the champion's camp, which enlisted staunch patriot and Great War hero Frank 'Buck' O'Neill to counter the charges. Berlenbach was only fifteen years old when war was declared and therefore was too young to serve.

'Some of Paul Berlenbach's maligners are saying that the great light heavyweight fighter ran out of the party when he had the argument with ole Kaiser Bill some years ago,' wrote Harry Newman. 'Well, Paul was a schoolboy when that jam was on and it is a dollar to a busted nickel that Paul would have been in the thick of the scrimmage if he had been old enough. Play fair, boys.'

Fistic Alley was witnessing the strange sight of a champion on the defensive, declaring, 'he could and would whip McTigue', but refusing to sign for the fight. Berlenbach was seen walking around Broadway hunting Jimmy, threatening to punch him for his insults. Stories appeared in the New York newspapers that Berlenbach was 'gunning' for the Boy Bandit so Jimmy sat at his typewriter and wrote to Ed Sullivan:

Dear Ed:

I bequeath the punch on the nose that Paul Berlenbach is going to give me to Mike McTigue, my hero.

Every afternoon at 3 pm we serve tea at my office, an old English custom. Paulie is cordially invited and after tea is served, McTigue will substitute for me, if agreeable.

We hope fear won't keep Berlenbach away.

James J. Johnston

But Jimmy wasn't the only formidable operator stalking Berlenbach. Pete Reilly, manager of Jack Delaney, had friends in the Garden but knew he had to get past Mike before getting his fighter a shot at the title. Reilly fostered the idea of an elimination bout as the best way to settle the problem and offered to match Jack and Mike, with the winner to get a championship bout in the summer with Berlenbach.

'McTigue has been challenging Berlenbach and talking about promises Berlenbach is said to have made him for a return fight,' said Reilly. 'The commission has ordered Berlenbach to fight McTigue and has denied the champion the privilege of fighting anybody else here until he does fight McTigue, and the situation is deadlocked. My solution to the problem would be to have McTigue fight Jack Delaney and the winner of that bout fight Berlenbach. I am not interested in whether Berlenbach made any promises to McTigue or not. But, if McTigue is convinced he is a genuine challenger for the title and deserving of a title match, he certainly would have no objections to fighting Delaney. I think personally McTigue would get just as much money out of a fight with Delaney as he would out of one with Berlenbach. I'm ready to sign now for Delaney.' Reilly persuaded Berlenbach's manager Dan Hickey of the wisdom of his plan. By signing to fight the winner Berlenbach would be freed to fight in New York again.

The boys on Broadway believed the industry was suffering from too much regulation. The attempt to control the nation's drinking resulted in worse and more expensive liquor, similarly, the fever of regulation in the 'cauliflower industry' resulted in worse and more expensive cauliflowers. On 9 February 1926 Governor Al Smith reappointed James Farley, popularly known as Jimmy Johnston's friend, and William Muldoon, known as the 'Secretary of State for Minding other People's Business' as boxing commissioners. George Brower, whose attitude on various matters was never understood very clearly and who was popularly known as the 'other fellow', was a holdover appointee.

Westbrook Pegler described its reappointment as a 'gubernatorial kick in the flask' for the critics:

Inasmuch as the three ministers of the Cauliflower Cabinet are intelligent and successful men and altruists serving for nothing, it is hard to understand why they take such pains to inject a trace of the ridiculous into so many of their rulings. On stepping into the office to find a floral horseshoe of entwined cauliflowers standing on his desk, the newcomer to the cabinet realises that he will have to take a certain amount of abuse, no matter how wisely he may execute his duties.

It is expected that the hilarious Mickey McTigue decree, by which the world's worst prizefighter is named as the first challenger for the light heavyweight championship, will be retained in the cabinet's repertoire, or routine, as the comedians of Vaudeville describe their sure-fire material.

The boys were quietly confident that Jack Delaney would knock out Mike for the first time in the Irishman's career. Nobody was really sure about Mike though. He was a somewhat unfathomable ring performer who turned in performances in which he looked like a real champion only to follow it up with an exhibition that could only be described as awful. 'Mike cannot deal them out as rough as the handsome Connecticut kid, but suffering mackerel, he won't let the other fellow hit him, and what in thunder are you going to do when you can't find a place to deposit your punches?' asked Harry

Newman. 'But if he nails you, Michael, ole pal, they'll roll you out on a stretcher.'

Mike's hostess at his training camp, Madame Bey, was predicting victory. As well as running a camp for prizefighters in Summit, New Jersey, she was an expert in palmistry and according to Jimmy, she took one look at Mike and exclaimed: 'You win, Michael. I read it in your hand. See these lines. They are a perfect outline of Delaney, and he is horizontal.' But Broadway was nervous; while the experts all predicted a Delaney victory, there wasn't much money being staked on the result. Under ordinary circumstances Delaney would have been a hot favourite for the fight but there was an unexpected amount of smart money on the Irishman. These were not ordinary circumstances however. The evening before the fight, Jimmy took a telephone call at his home from a well-known gambler.

'Jimmy, I'd like to have you meet me somewhere tonight and talk a few things over.'

'About what?' asked Jimmy.

'Oh, there are some things we should straighten out for our own good.'

'I don't know what we have to straighten out that hasn't been attended to already, but I'm going to a dinner with Jimmy Walker and will meet you about two-thirty in the morning at Child's Restaurant on 46th, and we can talk there,' replied Jimmy.

He found his gambling friend in a friendly mood. After Jimmy ordered his tea and lemon the 'sure thing' guy said: 'You know, Jimmy, if we're smart, we can make a nice piece of change on this fight.'

'Yeah, how?'

'Let Delaney win by a close decision and later they will fight in a return match. We can clean up on the bets too, placing a heavy wad on Delaney to cop the decision, cleaning up again on a return match.'

'Nope, I can't do it,' answered Jimmy. 'I've made a good living from boxing and, besides, McTigue feels certain he'll knock out Delaney. The fight will have to be on the up-and-up, with the best man winning.'

Jimmy refused to make a deal despite increasingly attractive terms being offered. The mood changed.

'The fight must go to Delaney and you got to see to it.'

He took an automatic revolver out of an arm holster and laid it on the table, under cover of a handkerchief.

'Delaney has to win,' he said, looking directly at Jimmy.

'Listen, you,' said Jimmy, pointing his finger at his dining companion, 'I don't care if you have all the guns in the world, this fight is going to be on the level, and if Delaney wins, it will be on his merits. McTigue is going to knock him out. Who the hell do you think you're going to scare with that gun?'

'You listen to me, Johnston …'

'Listen to you, nothing. Put your gun in your pocket and don't try any of your tough-guy stuff on me. And go back and say that this is one fight that can't be fixed.'

He got up. Jimmy threw a fifty-cent tip on the table for the waiter and walked out of the restaurant.

Word quickly spread that Mike couldn't be bought and within a few hours a flood of McTigue cash appeared on Broadway. The sums being bet on the Irishman were so startling that Gene Fowler, the boxing writer with the *Daily Mirror*, refused to call a winner for his paper and warned that the fight might have been fixed for the Irishman. By fight day Mike was the favourite in the betting. The Delaney backers insisted on betting only on a knockout, asking for 4-1, but the McTigue backers only gave them 2½-1. There was very little money for Delaney to win by decision.

Mike and Jimmy's hounding of Paul Berlenbach had stoked a feud that kept Broadway amused for many boxing seasons. Paul Gallico was one of the sportswriters who along with the likes of Ring Lardner, Gartland Rice, Damon Runyon and Bill McGeehan illuminated American newspapers in the 1920s. Gallico was particularly friendly with Paul Berlenbach and particularly hostile to Mike and Jimmy. On the morning of the Delaney fight Gallico wrote that the boxing game had left him discouraged:

'When I consider how little truth compared to the enormous number of lies is fed to the public on all things concerning the prizefight game, I am seized with an acute case of the willies. It seems that almost anything can be put over on the newspapers and the public. Handouts, handouts, handouts everywhere and the easiest thing to do is accept 'em and print 'em. To hell with investigations and the like. The public wants to be bunked. That of course is nonsense. The public for the most part is too busy or too tired to examine its alleged entertainment.

'We believe too much of the stuff we read in the newspapers. Take this McTigue-Delaney fight being perpetrated tonight. That thing has been built up and inflated for a week on hot air. Reams have been written on crafty old McTigue, the boxing genius of the ring, and the difficulty of connecting with his elusive chin. Crafty old McTigue, my eye. He can be guaranteed to spoil any fight.

'The lowdown is that Jimmy Johnston and his pull with the New York State Athletic Commission has talked his way into this fight allegedly for the right to meet Berlenbach for his title and I look for a most tiresome evening, with Delaney chasing Mike around and around and around.

'The main bout is a phooey. Let us be honest once in a while.'

Almost eighteen thousand people disagreed and paid $79,599.50 to watch the fight.

Paul Berlenbach was introduced to the crowd from the ring. The world champion wore a red striped tie that stood for a lot of kidding from both Mike and Delaney. Rumours were still rife at ringside that the fight had been fixed for Mike but the wiseacres were fooled as was Delaney's manager Pete Reilly who told his man to go for a knockout. From the opening bell Delaney tore across the ring and threw furious punches. Mike was immediately into his immaculate defensive routine and stayed out of harm's way throughout the first session and just as the bell rang he countered and caught Delaney with a right that staggered the Bridgeport man, so much so that he headed for Mike's corner instead of his own. The Irishman let Delaney walk all the way to the wrong corner and smiled at the crowd. When Delaney realised what he'd done Mike saluted him and drew roars of laughter.

Early in the second Delaney pressed Mike against the ropes and pounded him with both hands to head and body, though the Irishman managed to take most of the blows on his hands and arms. The difference in strength and speed between the two men was marked. After taking a hard right hook on the chin, Mike responded in the third with a right of his own on Delaney's left ear followed by a left to the stomach and another left to the ear.

It looked as though the Irishman was getting back into the fight and the round was even until a few seconds from the end. Delaney sunk a left hook deep into the pit of Mike's stomach. It was a vicious drive and it took the best use of the Irishman's poker face to disguise his pain. The blow shot in wrist deep and as the bell sounded Mike wobbled back to his corner. He had survived three rounds, his defensive skills just about good enough to withstand the onslaught from Delaney.

In the opening seconds of the fourth Delaney missed with a

vicious right uppercut, lost his balance, and floundered past the Irishman.

''Tis over here I am, Jack,' Mike was heard to say and Delaney grinned.

But then Delaney hooked a left to the jaw, Mike stepped in to try and clinch but Jack whipped through a right uppercut that thudded into the Irishman's chin and sent him flat on his back. Mike rolled over on one knee and took a count of eight. As he got up Delaney followed in with a careful, pressing attack, pecking and feinting with long lefts to probe an opening for another smashing right. The opportunity soon came. Mike tried to hold on but was punched back to the ropes. He took a barrage of punches and was gradually slipping down the ropes and his knees were almost touching the canvas as Delaney rained in blows.

Mike was crumpled helplessly over the middle rope when the referee pulled Delaney back and began to count. The Irishman hung there, his knees on the floor, left arm thrown over the middle rope until the count reached seven. Then somehow, at eight, he tried to get to his feet and by nine he was virtually upright. Delaney stepped forward, right hand cocked, as Mike turned his face towards his foe. But referee Patsy Haley, a survivor of many hard-fought ring battles, leaped to Mike's rescue. He had beaten the count as his hands and knees were off the canvas, but really he was out. It wasn't the final punch or even the last series of punches that prompted the referee to intervene. Delaney had hit the Irishman with a barrage of lightening fast punches for a full minute and Mike was not going to recover. He was technically 'knocked out' for the first time in his career.

The customers had waited a while to see it happen. Mike had made them suffer boredom on many a dreary night and they wanted to see him with his nose covered in resin powder just once. Jack Delaney did it. But the Garden crowd was in an unusually charitable and amiable mood and very few cared to see the game old champion beaten up. Mike had put up an extraordinary show of bravery and smiled when he was hit hardest. He was led to his corner, tottering under the terrific beating he had taken and according to the *New York Times*, 'beaten but not disgraced at the end of his pugilistic rope'.

In the fighters' dressing rooms the usual crowd of newspapermen, handlers, cops, politicians and hangers-on all offered an opinion.

Jimmy's was the loudest. 'Why didn't he give Mike a chance?' he asked.

'Your man might have been killed if he had been hit again,' replied Davis J. Walsh of the International News Service.

'But Delaney had time for only one more punch and might have missed.'

'But what if he hadn't missed, Jimmy?' cried someone else.

'Then the bell would have saved him and the one-minute rest would have restored him.'

Jimmy's gripe was that the referee stopped the fight just a second before the end of the round. Even his friends thought he was wrong on this one. Commissioner Farley said Haley had done the right thing, in the right way, in a tough and ticklish situation. 'His action in the interest of boxing should be generally approved,' said Farley. Haley didn't even know that the round was nearly over and couldn't see the two time clocks on either side of the ring.

Jimmy, like many fight managers, thought that any stopping of a bout was premature if it was done before his fighter's death notice had been published in a newspaper for the required three days. It was the point of view of the manager in the safety zone, 'let him hit you. He can't hurt us.' The most poignant analysis of the night's proceedings was written by Mike and Jimmy's arch-enemy:

People, I suppose, go to boxing matches because it is drama in the raw. They go in the hope of living one of those moments when tragedy stalks the blood-flecked canvas. Reputation, a million dollars, a man's life, hang in the balance. Time and his actors beneath the floodlights hesitate for an instant, forming in the minds of the spectators an ineradicable picture, a white arm poised on a hair-trigger, a shattered, broken figure clawing limply at the ropes. Safe in your seat, you can enjoy that terrifying sensation of impending destruction, if that is what you like.

Patsy Haley deserves a bonus. I think that James Jay Johnston and Michael McTigue ought to pay it, but if they can't see it that way, why then the boxing Commission or the public ought to chip in. Patsy in all probability prevented a man being killed in the ring before 20,000 when he stepped between Delaney and McTigue last Monday night before the end of the round.

A good deal of fuss is being made because Haley stopped it one second before the bell that ended the round on the supposition that the gong would have saved bold Michael. As a matter of fact, Haley stepped between Delaney and his helpless victim three or four seconds before the bell rang, plenty of time for Jack to have broken McTigue's neck with a right-hand punch.

McTigue was on the ropes, helpless, with his hands down and his head limp and relaxed as Delaney prepared to throw a straight right could have snapped his spine or broke his jaw. It was Haley's job to stop that punch. He did.

McTigue was as badly broken a fighter as I have ever seen. The last time Delaney battered him to the floor he was a sight to make you weep, bewildered, shaking like the ague, semi-conscious, his shattered co-ordination desperately trying to consummate the magnificent human gesture of getting up off the floor.

Paul Gallico, *New York Daily News*

Mike got $17,083 for his beating and the following day he was written about as a man whose career was over. 'McTigue is an old man as fighters go,' wrote Harry Newman. 'Fighters go and nature demanded its toll.'

When he arrived at the Garden to collect Delaney's cheque Pete Reilly, Delaney's manager, told reporters that his desire was to relieve the unsatisfactory situation that existed in the light heavyweight class. 'Delaney accomplished what I expected he would accomplish last night,' said Reilly. 'He knocked out McTigue without even getting warmed up, and he loosened up the light heavyweight class. McTigue was picked as the outstanding contender to fight Berlenbach, and Berlenbach for his own good reasons, refused to fight McTigue. The class, as a consequence, was at a standstill. The thing to do was remove McTigue and stimulate interest again, and that is just what Jack did.'

Just as Mike had cleared up the Siki problem two years previously, he had become the problem and now had been removed.

FIFTEEN

A negro minister will commend him to the mercy of the Christian God and negroes will shoulder the casket from the tail-board of the motor hearse at the brink of the hole, but even so there will be nobody there who understood Siki, because the difference was no mere matter of complexion.

Westbrook Pegler, *New York Daily News*, 18 December 1925

He never had a chance. Louis Fall died with his boots on, as the majority of those who knew him predicted he would. Battling Siki was killed without a fighting chance by an assassin who shot him in the back at the gateway to Hell's Kitchen.

At about midnight Siki went into a restaurant, the Comet, on West 41st Street just around the corner from his home. A few hours later, Oscar Bilbern, a watchman in a garage on 346 West 41st Street saw Siki come lurching down the sidewalk. It was a clear winter's night and patrolman John Meehan was standing in the shadow of a doorway on West 42nd Street when he saw the man run towards him.

'Hi, boy,' called Meehan.

'I'm on my way home,' came the reply.

'Keep on your way, and don't forget where you're going.'

As the figure passed directly below a streetlight the officer saw that he was a large black man in a dirty shirt and dented plug-hat. Siki looked back at the officer, smiled and gambolled on down the street.

Two hours later patrolman Meehan stopped by a puddle of blood darkening the flagstones outside 346 West 41st. He followed the trail to the front of 348 West 42nd, where the body of the man he'd seen earlier lay. He was face down in the gutter with two bullet holes in his back and three cents in his pocket.

Meehan called the station to inform his captain that the man, who was later identified as Battling Siki, was dead. Later, Siki's wife told the police her husband had been killed because he didn't have the twenty dollars to pay for the liquor he'd bought and that a thin, scrawny youth had threatened him for the money. Police were hunting for a man known only as Jimmy but they never found him. 'As Siki stumbled over the curb and his dented plug hat bounced away, he may have giggled at the irony of the matter, for he had come all the way from the jungle to the haunts of civilization and chivalry to be shot in the back,' wrote Westbrook Pegler. 'He couldn't have received a worse deal back home, where they make no great boast of their civilisation.'

One scribe claimed that Siki had tried hard to understand civilisation but never quite got the idea. The fighter had heard a lot about its virtues in a dozen years of exposure to its decorous influence, but in the last minute of his life, when he fell in a dirty gutter in Hell's Kitchen, where the lights of Broadway threw deep shadows and the churches faced speakeasies across the street, civilisation must have remained a puzzle and a joke to him.

After his defeat in Dublin on St Patrick's Day 1923, the rest of Siki's career was writ in alcohol. He proclaimed himself to be the only fighter alive who could train on brandy and champagne. He fought Paul Berlenbach with drunken merriment until the German pounded him unconscious. After that he fell to boxing 'ham and eggers' for pick-up stakes, but soon no promoter would hire him and he took to fighting in the grubbier nightclubs of Hell's Kitchen.

He was arrested for trying to kill a policeman with a knife and was the subject of strenuous deportation efforts by the United States government; efforts that were frustrated by the French government's equally strenuous efforts to keep him out of France. He lived the life of a clown, squandering his ring earnings as quickly as he collected them. During his time in New York he developed a penchant for taking taxi rides dolled up in a high silk hat and opera cloak but without the money to pay the fare. His behaviour took him into regular contact with police magistrates and prompted the boxing bosses to revoke his licence.

On 18 December 1925 Siki was trundled out over the roads to Long Island to be buried in the 'civilised' way. The white man has written an elegant finis to Battling Siki with a shot in the back. Possible, by this time, whatever he is, and wherever he is, Siki may know what the score is. He never quite caught up with it on this earth. Still, the Battler has no kick coming. All of his woes he owes to the white man, but at the same time all of his pleasures. One of that noble breed of gun toter plugged him in the back, but not before he had a good deal of the white man's fun.

Paul Gallico, *New York Daily News*, 16 December 1925

SIXTEEN

If Mike McTigue can induce some other opponent to meet him in
Dublin, he still has a chance to win at least one more fight.

Washington Post, 18 March 1926

It was the horror of defeat that made Mike McTigue guarded and
defensive in the ring and the fear of such a public humiliation had
haunted his boxing career. Better to walk out of the ring and brave
the wrath of bloodthirsty customers, than to hear a sympathetic
hand while being carried through the ropes feet first. But having
undergone the ordeal Mike discovered, to his surprise, that it wasn't
as bad as he'd figured it to be. It was to be the end of the old stalling,
overcautious Mike.

Four days after the bout he showed up in his manager's office to
collect his end of the purse.

'When do I fight again, Jimmy?'

'Do you want to go on after what's happened?'

'You promised to make me champion again and until you tell me
to hang 'em up, I'm going to keep punching.'

Mike and Jimmy had a long talk.

'I want to get Delaney and Berlenbach back. I know I'll beat
them.'

'What makes you so sure of Delaney, after what happened?'

'I've had a lot of time to think it over, Jimmy, and I've decided I was too fearful of getting knocked out. I used to imagine how horrible it would be to feel someone had scored even a technical knockout over me. Well, the Delaney experience wasn't so bad, and from now on I'm going in there and box or slug with them, whichever way will win for me. Get me some more fights and I'll show you what I can do with my right from now on.'

Jimmy went for his typewriter to see what he could stir up. 'THE MAN WHO FOUND HIMSELF' read the publicity broadsides sent to every newspaper and fight promoter in New York.

Jimmy met boxing writer George Daley at the Empire racetrack and told him how the knockout had boosted Mike's confidence and taken away the fear. Daley devoted an entire column of the *New York World* to the idea. Other writers used it as a theme for feature articles of how boxers through history had reacted to their first knockouts.

Jimmy took his man out of town for a while and they headed off to Mike's old stomping ground in Canada. They arrived in Toronto on 10 June 1926 for a fight the following night with Lou Scozza at the Maple Leaf Baseball Park. Johnny Brown, the English bantamweight champion who was due to fight on the same card, accompanied Mike and Jimmy on the journey.

'You certainly didn't pick anything soft for me, did you,' Mike told reporters at the station. Scozza was an aggressive fighter out to make a reputation by knocking out a former world's champion. According to the *Toronto Daily Star*, 'Michael will never set the world on fire as a human tiger, nor will he ever earn himself brackets in the hall of fame as a knock-'em-dead cuckoo, but it must be admitted that he is the cleverest big man that displayed his wares in this section of King George's bailiwick. Neither his hands nor his feet stutter and his brain is not ossified, even if he is an old man as fighters go.

'The Dublin-born New Yorker is about as excitable as an auctioneer and trying to land on his Irish map is about as simple as hitting a well-greased performing seal with a toy balloon. He sticks out a left as long as a Toronto Sunday and as flexible as a buggy whip, and, any time his opponent gets by that with a punch, Mike bobs a shoulder into that flying fist, takes it on his chest, or turns his head away and goes with the punch.'

Mike got the decision over Scozza after twelve rounds of fast milling. He hit his opponent with a big right in the fifth and Scozza was groggy as he turned for his corner. Maybe he had found himself after all.

Billy LaHiff's Tavern on 48th Street was a famous Roaring Twenties watering hole that attracted movie stars, writers, prizefighters and all those who followed them around. On this particular night Tex Rickard called Jimmy over to his table. Jimmy always talked 'McTigue' to Rickard and that night at LaHiff's, Tex finally relented.

'Do you want to put Mike in with Johnny Risko for ten rounds?' asked Tex.

'Sure do. When?'

'Next Thursday night'

'Short notice, but I'll take it,' said Jimmy. 'Mike's just back from Canada where he beat Scozza.'

'I heard about that. This fight is a "disappointment date" filler and I thought you'd jump at the chance to get in there with Risko. If McTigue could win he'd be right back in the running.' Rickard needed an opponent for Risko in a hurry. Mike got the fight but everybody knew he was to be the victim in it. The match with Johnny Risko was made for the Garden on 1 July. It marked Mike's return to a New York prize-ring after the humiliation of his knockout against

Delaney and also the resumption of hostilities with Paul Gallico. 'A number of young men interested in the column game of discovering the worst fight card in the world, have inquired as to just how the game is played,' wrote Gallico when the McTigue-Risko fight was announced. 'But surely there must have been worse. Matchmakers must have perpetrated even more fearful lemons on the public. Or maybe they are contemplating them. Who knows? A sneer in time may save something dreadful. It will be worth the admission to hear Johnston telling Mike: "Go on, he wants to quit."' Jimmy telephoned Gallico at his *New York Daily News* office to complain that he hadn't kept his promise to mention the place and the date every time he referred to the Risko-McTigue bout. In his column the following day Gallico wrote:

Read below, James, read below.

Tonight at the New Madison Square Garden, presumably at 10 p.m., or fifteen minutes later, there will be perpetrated what, on the face of it, appears to be one of the dullest and stupidest fights pulled off around here in a long time, when the principals, John Risko and Mike McTigue step into the ring and square off.

The prices will be from $1 to $7, and anybody who pays more than a dollar to see it ought to have his head examined.

Even though Risko had given good fighters a good fight, and even put Jack Delaney on the canvas, the punters just didn't show. Only 3,837 turned up and the receipts totalled just $9,045. It was one of the most poorly attended fights in the Garden's history yet it was one of the best ever staged there. Risko was a full-blown heavyweight who was over a stone bigger than his opponent and he'd recently scored a victory over Paul Berlenbach. He was expected to do likewise against the aging Irishman. The customers thought it would be a bust but it turned out to be a thriller and they were up on their chairs for most of the fight. It turned into a strictly pro-McTigue gathering, and deservedly so as Mike outsmarted and outfought the chunky baker from Cleveland. Mike shook Risko with right crosses to the jaw and played both hands to the body. The Clevelander often appeared dazed but managed to stay on his feet until the final bell. The heavyweight looked far worse for his efforts than his smaller, older opponent.

Mike got $1,500 for the fight, the smallest purse since his journeyman days, but it was one of the best nights of his career and on the strength of this showing he was back in line for important matches. 'Mike McTigue, venerable old gentleman of the prize-ring, who was thought to have been pugilistically embalmed after Jack Delaney KO'd him, scored a remarkable victory over Johnny Risko, the Cleveland Rubber Man, in front of the smallest crowd that ever sat in to watch the doings at Tex Rickard's big amphitheatre since the place was opened last winter,' commented *Boxing* on 21 July 1926.

Jimmy was straight back on the 'ballyhoo drums'. As Paul Gallico wrote:

Gentlemen, let us be calm. There is a crisis in which only cool heads can prevail. I pray you keep command of your nerves, be strong, steel yourself to the expected emergency and we will ride safely through the coming storm. Remember that you are men. Eschew the temptation to join the emotional stampede. Fenians, Hibernians, Sons of Erin, be sane. Men of other nations, be fair. Can you hear the rattle of typewritery from Broadway? Does the shrill sound of the postman's whistle come to you down the corridors? And the blast of horns? And the beating of tom toms? Wurra boys, Michael Francis McTigue has won a victory, and James Joy Johnston is preparing to tell the world about it.

Only a few days ago, this Column exposed the fiendish machinations of this James Joy Johnston, namely, that one fine day, JJJ sat in his high tower with his feet on the desk and schemed. What were brains for if not to scheme? What after all was the fun of the game, to play ace with a confident smirk, or to make an innocent little three-spot take a trick? And what is more to the point, what was a fellow to do with no aces, but nothing but three-spots in his hand, and meal time coming around three times a day? And he schemed and he schemed and he schemed.

And as he sat and schemed and plotted and planned the thing suddenly came to him with amazing clarity ... Old Michael, peace to his fistic ashes, so tenderly interred by Jack Delaney, so gently mourned over by the scribes, might there not yet be fried potatoes and gravy and turkey and caviar and pie a la mode and celery and soup and spaghetti and red ink and soup and whatnot to fill the inner man in old Michael. Whist, Charley, hand me that spade whilst I dig down and see if there isn't a bit of life in him yet.

Clink, clank, scrape, scuff went the shovel into the soil, and almost before it had sunk a foot, there arose the muffled but familiar cry: 'I'll knock him out. Me hand is hurted, but I'll knock him out.' With a satisfied smile JJJ rested on his labours.

Another match between Mike and Paul Berlenbach, that was the thing. Fifty thousand people storming the gate at from five dollars to twenty-fives pesos each, and twelve and one half per cent of it all would be theirs. Um, yum, yum. Roast duck and fried yams, and oyster plant, and roast beef, and Jersey beer, and chicken, and huckleberry pie, and pâté-de-foie-gras, and strawberry shortcake, Yummy! But how to bring that about? 'Nothing risked, nothing gained.' The old adage sang through JJJ's head as he sat now and the thought of the delicate viands, the high powered motorcars and whatnot, that would result. 'Nothing risked, nothing gained … risked … risk … risk … RISKO! Ha! Risko! The very man. A wild swinger. Duck soup, pie, apple sauce for old Mike. Risko, who held a decision over Berlenbach. A fight between Risko and McTigue. But who would perpetrate such a thing? Where? What better spot than the one that housed Napoleon Dorval vs Don Lieber, George Godfrey vs Martin Burke, Jack Renault vs Jack De Mave? And so it came to pass.

And so too, did it come to pass as JJJ schemed and dreamed it. Risko accidentally hit Mike twice during the entire *soirée*. And now, clickety, clackety click go the typewriters, jangle, jangle go the wires as they are pulled and tugged, thumpety thump go the pulses in JJJ's temples as he devises and plans and cooks up and plots, and intrigues, and schemes. Any moment the first blast will arrive – 'Mike McTigue licked the man who licked Berlenbach, etc … etc … etc.' Ochone, men, keep calm. Stand firm.

New York Daily News, 3 July 1926

But there was no stopping Jimmy's typewriter.

Paul Berlenbach had been champion for over a year and had fought almost every challenger put in front of him except Mike

McTigue. The Irishman was denied a return largely because no promoter was prepared to take on the expense of a big production featuring a fighter who was as poor a box office proposition as Mike at that time. The biggest draw in the light heavyweight division was Jack Delaney, not only for his aptitude with the gloves but because he had the looks that attracted women to his fights. A match between Berlenbach and Delaney drew a crowd of 41,000 to Brooklyn's Ebbets Field. 'Delaney's screaming mammies', as his female fans became known cheered their idol to victory. He was the new world champion though Berlenbach had the consolation of a big slice of the $450,000 gate.

Mike watched the fight as a guest in the press stand. He wanted a close-up view of the two men who'd beaten him and was plotting revenge.

'Our Michael fears no man,' said Jimmy as Mike embarked on a remarkable series of fights against the best young fighters his manager could find for him in the summer of 1926. On 31 August he took a match as a late substitute with Panamanian heavyweight Emilio 'King' Solomon at the Queensboro Athletic Club in New York. The spectacle of an older man giving away sixteen pounds and pushing his opponent around the ring roused a huge cheer from the crowd. Solomon let go with a lumbering left swing, Mike ducked out of the way and the referee caught the blow on his cheek. The Irishman stepped back and said: 'Now do you see what you did? You hit a guy half your size.' Solomon turned, and at that moment Mike tagged him with a sharp right.

Solomon was floored with a right to the head as early as the second and his right eye was cut open at the start of the tenth. Mike prepared the end by hammering Solomon about the body at the beginning of the eleventh. The Panamanian's guard dropped and a left to the side of the jaw and a right uppercut put him flat on his back for the full count. 'For a moment a silence of astonishment fell over the ring,' reported the *New York Times*. The timekeeper was so surprised, he didn't start the count for several seconds after Solomon had hit the canvas. He needn't have worried. It was several minutes before Solomon was revived and almost ten minutes before his legs were steady enough to carry him out of the ring. The spectators had long since left the arena by then and Mike was back in his dressing room.

On 22 September the local papers in Halifax, Nova Scotia announced the return of a boxing hero to their town. Mike was matched with Roy Mitchell, the light heavyweight champion of Canada in an event dubbed the 'Battle of the Century in the Maritimes'.

'I almost turned back when I reached Saint Paul,' said Mike. 'Everybody began telling me what a terrible hitter Mitchell was. But get me right, I don't underestimate Mitchell. From what I hear, he is a hard hitter and I believe he is a good boy. My job on Wednesday night is to see that Mitchell doesn't hit with that terrific right hand. And I, of course, believe I am capable of doing that. But no matter how good you are if a hitter like Mitchell reaches the button with a solid smack, you are going down.'

Mike arrived in Halifax several days before the fight and trained at his old haunt in St Mary's gymnasium where hundreds turned up daily to watch him. He spent much of the time receiving old friends at his room at the Queen Hotel. 'I'm glad to be back in Halifax,' Mike told a reporter, 'this is where I got my start and I accepted this bout with Mitchell just to come back here again and see those fine friends who were so good to me in 1920.' D. Leo Dolan, of the *Halifax Herald*, wrote that he was 'the same loveable character who won his way into the hearts of the fight fans of Halifax six years ago.'

The advance sale of tickets broke all records in the town and the arena had to be re-seated to accommodate the demand. The promoters said they planned, 'to put this fight over in a manner that would credit Rickard or any other promoter with a world-wide reputation'. But despite the great excitement in Halifax the fight proved to be a big disappointment. 'There were five thousand fans at the Arena last night,' commented the *Halifax Herald*, 'and every one of them left sorely disappointed with the exhibition between two fighters with reputations which McTigue and Mitchell have gained in the realm of fistina.' Mitchell fought defensively from the opening bell as if over-awed to be in the ring with a man who had been world champion and the auditorium filled with jeers, hisses and boos in the last few rounds. Every clean blow landed in the fight came from Mike's gloves and he won a clear decision over ten rounds.

Billy Vidabeck was next up. He was best known as the man who helped Gene Tunney prepare for his fight with Jack Dempsey. Tunney thought highly of Vidabeck and kept him at the training camp throughout his campaign. About 3,500 customers, including a whole mob of writers from the *New York Daily News*, showed up at the Broadway Arena in Brooklyn to turn their astonished eyes on the most recent of boxing miracles. According to Gallico:

In the middle of the second round [Grant] Powers began to emit woeful screams: 'My eyes! My eyes! O, my eyes!' he shouted. 'What's the matter with my eyes?'

We quieted him as best we could and tried to ascertain his trouble. But he would only shout: 'My eyes! What's the matter with them? I see McTigue stepping around the ring and leading. Look! He's leading! There! He did it again! He threw three left jabs. It ain't true! It's my eyes. It musta been those last ones just before they closed down.'

But it was true. The customers had never seen such a Michael Francis McTigue as they had in Brooklyn, unless they were old enough to remember him as a bold, aggressive youth who stepped out and belted and flayed the enemy. He moved around the young, strong Billy Vidabeck, throwing dozens of left hands at the big punch-faced blond. Mike knocked him out in the third round. He cut loose with a right uppercut followed rapidly by a right to the chin and Billy's knees sagged. Another right to the chin and Vidabeck fell in a heap. He lay motionless while the count swung over him.

Jimmy Johnston had transformed Mike from a drab, colourless, timid, boring liability to one of the most interesting boxers in the game. 'I know this makes it look as though I am on Jimmy's list,' wrote Gallico, 'but I cannot help but be popeyed with admiration at what he has done for McTigue.' Mike's defence had always been thrilling to watch – for one round – after that the customers got tired. But when he combined his magnificent guard of arms, elbows, head and shoulders with an offence and a knockout punch that 'laid 'em out' for a minute or so, he became a valuable piece of fistic property and one of the few fighters worth going any distance to see. Suddenly he was the most popular fighter in New York. Just a few weeks after Vidabeck, 'Soldier' King was laid out in Grand Rapids, Michigan by a right hand in the fourth round. Mike was punching his way through any fighter who dared share a ring with him and was back as an obvious challenger for a world title fight with Jack Delaney. But Jimmy wanted Berlenbach first. Mike and Jimmy shared a genuine dislike for him.

'Just get that Dutchman for me again and I'll knock him right into your lap! On the level; go and get that Paul Berlenbach guy for me once more and I'll knock his brains out,' said Mike to Harry Newman when they met outside Tex Rickard's office. The scribe had just congratulated Mike on his recent victories. 'The trouble with me when I was champion was that I didn't fight often enough,' added the Irishman. 'The old rust is what licks many a fighter. Inactivity will beat any fighter, especially champions who are more or less guilty of ducking challenges. I find that I am fighting better now than at any time in my life and I attribute it to the fact that I am fighting more often.

'If I were to win the championship again, I would fight the following week. No more of that six months' lay-off for me. I lost to Berlenbach because I didn't fight often enough.

'I'll fight any man in the world. Of course I would like to get another shot at Jack Delaney, but I'd like to get first crack at Berlenbach. There is one bird I know I can stiffen!'

As champion, Berlenbach had avoided Mike but with his title gone and the Irishman the hottest ticket in town, the Astoria Assassin was more accommodating. When the proposition of a McTigue fight was put to Berlenbach's manager, Dan Hickey, he agreed immediately. Now it was Paralyzing Paul who needed Iron Mike. Tex Rickard secured the match for 28 January 1927 at Madison Square Garden; Mike went into training and Jimmy resumed hostilities with Paul Gallico. This particular squabble was contrived over a dog. Gallico and Berlenbach were friends and the fighter had given the scribe a Great Dane puppy as a present.

'Y'know that German dog or Dane or whatever it is Der Paulie gave you?' said Jimmy.

'Yeah.'

'Well, give it back and Mike McTigue will give you an Irish terrier. That Irishman is going to hit that Dutchman on the chin so hard, he won't wake up for a week.'

Gallico replied in the *New York Daily News*:

OYEZ, OYEZ, OYEZ. Hear ye! Hear ye! Hear ye!

This Column temporarily terminates its friendly connection with James Joy Johnston for the space of ten days or until the battle with Paul Berlenbach and Mike McTigue shall have passed into history.

For be it known that this Johnston hath shamefully tried to bribe ye scribe with an Irish terrier whereas ye scribe hath already been bribed by the most dog there is, a Dane. This Column hopes that Der Paulie will triumph and thus this Johnston becometh an enemy until the battle shall have come to pass.

It was to be Berlenbach's last fight as a light heavyweight because he planned to join the scramble for a shot at Gene Tunney's heavyweight title. 'Punch 'em Paul' had been assured of a big-money fight with another leading contender, Jack Sharkey, if he beat Mike. He was still a young fighter and the loss of his title to Jack Delaney had not dulled Berlenbach's ambition. Up to that defeat he had been one of the busiest fighters in New York who had made his name for being prepared to box anyone put in front of him. Berlenbach could hit hard, had unlimited courage and was about as easy to hurt as a brick wall, but then he got the idea that he should become a fancy boxer and his career stalled. He promised a back-to-basics approach to dispatch the despised Irishman. Berlenbach headed for the New Jersey hills to train where he received a very public declaration of support.

'Letter for Der Paulie' by Paul Gallico,
New York Daily News, 22 January 1927.

Mr Paul Berlenbach

Mme Bey's training camp

Summit, NJ

When I called up your house the other night and your dad said you were at Summit training for Mike, I was tickled to death to hear it, because I was afraid you might think that the Irisher wasn't much any more and would take it easy, just loafing around some local gym until the day of the fight. I meant to get in touch with you anyway and tell you about this vicious Harp and his manager, a little man by the name of Johnston who, I think, does not like you. Every time I meet him he says, 'And don't forget! What our Michael is going to do to your Dutchman will be a shame. He'll knock him so cold he won't know what hit him.'

Well, Paul, of course that's the way he has to look at it and what a fine manager he'd be if he went around moaning, 'O, I'm worried, I'm blue. My Mike is going to get murdered by Berlenbach when they meet. Ow!' But what I wanted to tell you about was Mike. Paul, that feller is under a spell. He thinks he's Jack Dempsey. The story that is going the rounds these days on your dear Broadway is that the night Jack Delaney knocked poor Mike unconscious in the New Garden he never came to, nor the next night either. Sure, he revived enough to climb down out of the ring – you know how you can do these things instinctively – but he wandered around sort of loose-like, kind of in a trance. Jack had hit him an awful belt. You saw that fight, didn't you? Well, the smart Johnston realised that Mike was a magnificent subject for mental suggestion and took him down to a 6th Ave hypnotist, who told him he was Jack Dempsey and ever since Mike has been knocking 'em dead with a punch. Jimmy couldn't take him down to the Sesqui fight because he would have wanted to climb in the ring with Tunney.

Paul, that Mike isn't the same man you won your title from. He's a bad egg. Work hard. Forget that boxing stuff. When the bell rings, sail in and get him. If you don't, he'll get you. I tell you, the Celt's blood lust is nothing short of shocking.

I didn't see Mike go against Johnny Risko, Paul, because I advertised that fight as a phooey and naturally stayed away only to have it turn out to be one of the best fights ever held at the Garden. But I did see Moike take on Billy Vidabeck over at the New Broadway while you were in California, and Paulie, he molded him pretty.

For two rounds, Mike let poor Billy belt him around the ring and it looked like a bad evening for the cautious Celt. Billy was roughing him to the ropes and batting him about the body and generally giving the old man what-for. In the second round Mike hit Billy one hit on the chin with a right hand to try out the range and the leverage and the amount of power to be applied. In the third round he stepped right inside William's two arms and hit him three punches – a short left hook, a short right hook and a short right uppercut. The last one was really a bonus, because Billy was fast asleep before it landed. Paul, honest, he never wiggled while they said the numbers over him.

Now don't get sore, Paulie, and think that I am comparing

you with Billy Vidabeck, although nobody was going around town knocking him off until the Hypnotised Harp got busy, but all chins look alike when they are hit right, and dinged if that murderous Mick hasn't mastered the art.

That's why I want you to work and hard and get yourself into condition. Your long layoff in California may have affected your judgement of distance and, Paulie, we've just got to win this fight.

Listen, Paul, this is under cover and I don't want it to get out. This feller Johnston has been throwing around slurs at our Great Danes, Shorty and Champion Paul Berlenbach, saying that one Irish terrier could lick the whole lot of them and Mike will prove it. Now, you know that Jimmy oughtn't to go around saying things like that about our dogs, Paul, and it's up to you to do something for the breed next Friday night in the Garden ring. You just tie one onto Mike's chin and it will be a victory for the Dane family and will teach Jimmy Johnston not to get so fresh about dogs.

Well, Paul, I'd better close. We're coming out to see you work next week, Grant Powers, Champion Paul Berlenbach, the Dane pooch, and I and get a line on you. Grant says he would like to put the gloves on with you for a round or so, but do me a favour and don't, because good kartooners are hard to find. Remember that you're working for a feller who thinks that he's Jack Dempsey. Knock him loose from the notion, willya, Paul?

One of the strangest things in connection with the jam was that the Broadway gamblers installed Mike favourite to win. Reports from Berlenbach's training camp were not positive. He was particularly poor in a sparring session with journeyman Harold Mays who stuck left-hand pokes onto Berlenbach's face until he grew tired. It was all right to take swipes in a training camp, but it didn't look good. 'If what we saw Paul do against his sparring mate, Harold Mays, a coloured guy with collapsible legs and paper mâché chin, is any direct line on Der Paulie we wouldn't give a plugged dime for his chances against the veteran Irishman,' commented one scribe. When Mays got through with his rough work they gave Berlenbach a guy named Raymond Cabrera to work on. Some said he came from Cuba, others said he looked like an old Seventh Avenue waiter. Paralysing Paul hit him cold in a round so they called Mays back for more.

Mike was working at Billy Grupp's in Harlem. A few days before the fight he hit one of his sparring partners, Al Settle, so hard he broke two of his ribs. Settle was a black light heavyweight from Jersey City who'd been part of the McTigue sparring staff for a few months. 'McTigue is a revelation,' wrote Harry Newman. 'Only the other day it looked as though he was through, yet right now he seems to be the best fighter in the game.'

The Irishman had the reputation of being a good gym performer who hated to be hit by a sparring partner. He did his stuff carefully as though he was in a real fight. The sparring mate who tried to take liberties with Mike usually took a pasting. He trained hard until the day before the fight and after a stiff workout he jumped on the scales and tipped the beam at 172lbs. He then told trainer Dai Dollings that he would don the big gloves once more before the fight.

Jimmy overheard the conversation and told his fighter that only 'saps' boxed on the day before a fight. Mike had been in 'high glee' for a week and was very psyched up for the fight. He exploded a torrent of abuse at Jimmy that shocked even the most hardened journalists present.

'If he won't do as I tell him to do, I won't handle him. Let him get someone else,' muttered Jimmy, crimson faced. 'He has been working for ten weeks for this Berlenbach match. It's all right for Mike to be so anxious. He'll knock the Dutchman into Dan Hickey's lap, if Mike will only do as I tell him. I am responsible for bringing him back,' said Jimmy as he sent orders to Dollings that his charge had done his last boxing before answering the bell the following night.

'I never felt better in my life, and I am hitting better than ever,' Mike told the scribes. 'I was an overcautious fighter when I held the championship and was always fearful to cut loose, fearful that I would blow my title. I know that Paul is tough and all that sort of stuff, but I'll get him. If I can hit him – and I believe I can – I'll stop him.' Mike had a boastful confidence that he would knock out Berlenbach while the Astoria man threatened to knock Mike 'stiffer than a dead mackerel'. Gallico believed the event had re-introduced the art of the pre-fight threat:

This is a fine art that ought not to be neglected. It has been of late. We have so many gentlemanly fighters who are unwilling to state beforehand the dire things they will do to their opponents when they get them into the ring, that some of the necessary venom is liable to be missing.

This is good red-blooded stuff and it helps the fans believe that when the two men come together in the ring nothing short of manslaughter will result and the referee will have difficulty in keeping the two men apart until they can get the gloves on. Frequently, the best part of big fights have been the mouthfilling, awe-inspiring pronunciamentos that the two uglies hurled at one another before the battle. Just as frequently, the fight turned out to be a terrible lemon, but at least you have had the insults and frequently they were most picturesque.

True, Jimmy Johnston has been doing most of the talking for McTigue, but it has been a step in the right direction. I have Der Paulie's word that he will pummel Michael something awful and this Column guarantees that both men will be in earnest.

If Berlenbach will be the slugger he promised me he would in his future fights, his layoff won't hurt him any. He cannot possibly be a worse boxer than he was six months ago. And if he is the old slugger I'd hate to have Mike's arms tomorrow night. Mike is just a little too frail for Der Paulie. Unless Michael clips Paulie early the way Risko did and befuddles him, Paul will take every bit of sting out of Mike's punches. That looks like sense, doesn't it?

There was no title at stake yet the fight stirred up a huge amount of emotion among the city's boxing aficionados. The morning newspapers predicted a gate of fifteen thousand, but 17,747 showed up, one of the largest the venue had ever held, and they paid $93,235 in total for the privilege of seeing one of the great comebacks in boxing. The odds in no way reflected the fact that Berlenbach had already beaten Mike once, that he was younger by at least fifteen years and he was a much bigger man who was building himself up for a tilt at the heavyweight title.

As Mike entered the ring, Paul Gallico, sitting directly under the Irishman's corner, yelled: 'I'm right here to catch you, Mike, when the German knocks you in my lap.'

Mike smiled, it was old stuff, the business of 'razzing' a fighter. 'Listen, Mug, when I hit this German, I'm going to try and make it right in this corner. Don't forget.'

The weights were announced; McTigue 169, Berlenbach 177. As the fighters came from their corners for the referee's instructions, Mike slapped Berlenbach's manager, Dan Hickey, on the back.

'Sixteen years ago tonight I had my first fight. Do you remember who my manager and second was then, Dan?'

Hickey growled a reply.

'Time changes everything, doesn't it, Dan?'

Hickey turned to the referee, Kid McPartland, and ignored Mike's baiting.

'Go and get him,' said Jimmy as the bell rang for the first round.

'Mike hated Paul Berlenbach with all the deep passion of an Irishman who knew how to hate,' recalled Jimmy. 'I could sense it before the fight, but I didn't realise it completely until the two of them were in the ring for final instructions from the referee. As they shook hands Mike leaned over and said, "I've got you now." I'll say he got him. In all the years I've been in this racket I never saw a fighter better than Mike McTigue was that night.'

The mutual dislike was obvious. Mike had his right hand poised threateningly, but for the first two minutes he was content to parry Berlenbach's leads and counter with snappy left jabs. Then, in the last minute of the first round, after he'd seen what he wanted, Mike drove Berlenbach back to the ropes where he sent three consecutive fearless, accurate right hooks onto his jaw and face. The final punch opened up a small cut on Berlenbach's nose.

The second round resembled a boxing match in the early exchanges but then Berlenbach drew first blood with a slashing hook that cut a slit over Mike's right eye. The Irishman responded with a volley of spiteful right hooks. One shot landed over Berlenbach's heart and rebounded under his chin. The Astoria Assassin went down for a count of four, got up and fell again without being hit. He remained on one knee until the referee reached two and then the bell sounded. The spectacle of the aged fighter smashing a bigger, more youthful man to the floor sent the packed Garden into a blaze of excitement. From ringside to attic, the spectators were on their toes, hands waving in the air, screaming. 'Even in the prize-ring Berlenbach was never regarded as an intellectual,' wrote Bill McGeehan, 'but the first right to the chin jarred up what little intellect he had and the Assassin spent most of his time in the ring that night in being knocked down and getting up again.'

Berlenbach hadn't shaken the effects of his second-round battering as the bell rang for the third. The customers were in a frenzy of excitement. The Irishman drew on all the tricks he'd gathered from half a lifetime in the ring and battered the spirit out of Berlenbach. Mike fended off a left swing by raising his right arm and as the blow slipped off he dropped his right onto Berlenbach's face. He was patient and peppered his man with countless left jabs that brought the claret from Berlenbach's lips. The jabs were punctuated with the occasional, shattering right hook and Paul fell to his hands and knees under a barrage of punches. He got up quickly, too quickly, and Mike was standing over him raining in blows from all angles.

All thought of boxing had gone; Mike was battering a man he didn't like. The final shot in this flurry, a long right, put Berlenbach on the canvas again. He was back up before the referee could begin counting only to drop without being hit as Mike charged from a neutral corner ready with another right. The fans were screaming that he'd automatically disqualified himself by going down without being hit but referee McPartland ignored them. As the timekeeper tolled the seconds he was almost drowned out by Jimmy shouting, 'He's out, he's out, disqualify him.' The crowd roared its disapproval as the bell rang to save Berlenbach from being counted out. His seconds rushed to his aid. The Garden was in uproar.

Berlenbach eventually made his way, open jawed to his corner where Dan Hickey and Ben Stern worked frantically to try and revive their man. He was groggy on his feet but made it to the centre of the ring for the fourth. But unlike the third round when Mike looked calm and collected, as the bell rang for the fourth he unleashed a furious volley of blows onto the man who'd taken his precious title. 'It was a strange sight, this elderly, cranky old fellow, with his little button nose and his little watery blue eyes set in a face puckered with wrinkles like the last apple in a barrel, banging Paul Berlenbach on the chin so hard that Berlenbach's head spun round and his big, hairy legs collapsed, letting him down,' wrote Westbrook Pegler.

Mike ripped into Berlenbach, never once allowing him the chance of a respite. The round wasn't a minute old when a huge right sent Paul down for a count of nine. When there was nothing more in front of him to punch Mike leaned from a neutral corner and leered at the body on the canvas as the referee's arm rose and fell. Berlenbach got to his feet only to be battered back to from where he came with another sickening right. The referee reached eight before Berlenbach got up, staggering around helplessly as he reeled into Mike's corner and within a yard of Gallico's lap. He grasped the ropes to stay upright, his nose and mouth were bleeding, his eyes were glassy and he was rocking hopelessly. Mike glanced down at the writer and took a pace forwards, his right hand cocked. McPartland, seeing that Berlenbach was virtually unconscious and within seconds of being hit into the press tables, pulled Mike back and called for Hickey to rescue his man.

The end to Berlenbach's suffering came after two minutes and forty-three seconds of the fourth round by which time Paralysing

Paul was oblivious to his fate. One scribe counted as forty-five, the number of times Mike bounced his right hand off Berlenbach's jaw in the four rounds. Five in the first, eight in the second, sixteen in the third and sixteen times again in the fourth. Harry Cross, writing in the *New York Herald Tribune* commented that 'both Berlenbach's jawbone and McTigue's right hand contain a hard species of bone'.

Mike danced with glee and then stood under the glare of the arc lights acknowledging the plaudits of the crowd. 'Not since the sheep killed the butcher has there been such consternation,' commented one reporter at ringside. Mike scrambled down the cast-iron steps from his corner to shoulder his way through a crowd of customers in evening dress surging up to have a closer look at him. Mike stopped by Gallico and motioned towards the other corner where Hickey and Ben Stern were trying to revive a semi-conscious Berlenbach. 'That's your little playmate over there, Boy Scout,' he said. Mike was nearly mobbed on his way back to the dressing room.

'In victory Johnston's boxer met with one of the biggest demonstrations ever accorded an exponent of the manly art,' commented the *New York Evening Post*.

Mike had knocked out Berlenbach just as he said he would; but many claimed that Jimmy Johnston did it. Nobody knew how. Accept our congratulations and tell us your system wrote the scribes. One of Broadway's finest noted that an Indian mystic had recently been buried alive for a few hours and was then brought back to life. Yet Mike McTigue was buried for years.

The last word on an extraordinary sporting occasion, however, has to go to Paul Gallico:

Ring History Was Made

I was pretty glum watching Michael, the miraculous Mick, destroy Paul Berlenbach at the New Garden.

I think that every man in our press row was sorry to see Paul go, but at the same time we were popeyed with admiration for McTigue, a curious mingling of feelings. When all was said and done it was one of those intensely dramatic and human fights that sometimes reach out beyond the ring ropes and touch our hearts.

You might think it strange that this could be and it only happens once in a while. Intrinsically, a prizefight is utterly debasing. Nine-tenths of them have nothing to offer as an honest sports spectacle. Prizefighting has no appeal of which one can be proud.

There, for instance, was Harry Newman, who has seen more fights than he can remember, shouting, 'Stop it! Stop it! Stop that slaughter! McPartland! Stop it! Or there was Jimmy Johnston carrying his marvellous old Mike around the ring as though he were a child when it was all over. Or there was Paul in his corner at the end, not knowing what had happened, thinking that the round was over, or, perhaps, the saddest sight of all, there was Paul again, at the call of the bell, getting wearily up from his seat, advancing three slow, hesitating steps, and then standing stock still, waiting for old Michael to COME TO HIM. Nobody ever saw Berlenbach do that before. Actually it makes me furious when I find myself growing sentimental over a thing like that, but there it is. Who can help himself?

It was a fight that went to the heart because Mike was

marvellous. No-one who has not followed his career or seen him in his worst fights can appreciate how thrilling the old man is. If someone told you he had read a story of a timid old Irish boxer, who never in his life had given his public a thrill and who suddenly at an age where most men have nothing but yellowing clippings to remind them of former glory, began to fight like an 18-year-old and developed a knockout punch that rivalled that of Jack Dempsey, you would put it down as far fetched fiction. But here it is happening beneath our eyes, and it is one of the miracles of the prize ring. Fifty years from now it will be a standout in ring history along with the prowess and strength of John L Sullivan, the skill of Corbett, the punching power of Fitzsimmons and the defensive skill of Jack Johnson. The mild Irishman, who turned knockout king, will be one of the great stories of the ring. Mark that down.

SEVENTEEN

Michael McTigue, the Methuselah of the prize-ring, has changed the entire complexion of the cauliflower market.

Bill McGeehan, *New York Herald Tribune*

Jack Dempsey had been the heavyweight champion throughout the Roaring Twenties and the customers went to his fights in numbers unimaginable today; 90,000 to Jersey City for the 'Battle of the Century' with Carpentier; 80,000 at the Polo Grounds for the match with Luis Firpo. Dempsey's reign ended on 23 September 1926 in Philadelphia. The official attendance figure was 120,757 although the *New York Times* put the figure, including gate-crashers, at closer to 135,000. His conqueror was Gene Tunney.

Tex Rickard then sponsored an elimination tournament to find a worthy challenger for the new champ. Such a bout would be worth between two and three hundred thousand dollars to a challenger and five or six pretty good men were in line for a shot. Mike was one them. He had beaten one of the fighters Rickard had picked for the tournament and was entitled to Berlenbach's place in the shake-up. Finding an opponent for Tunney wasn't Rickard's main priority: the tournament ran on and on as contenders emerged and challengers were eliminated, but the whole affair was always more about the bankroll than boxing. Four big heavyweight contests were to be staged in as many weeks. The four winners would then pair off and meet in two big outdoor shows in the summer to eventually determine Tunney's challenger in a September bout at the Yankee Stadium. Altogether the elimination bouts would run up a cash register count almost as great as the tally for a championship fight.

The leading contender was Jack Sharkey from Boston. Born in Binghamton, New York to Lithuanian immigrant parents, Joseph Paul Zukauskas got his new name by combining those of his favourite fighters, Jack Dempsey and Tom Sharkey. Mike accused him of assuming an Irish name to make people believe he was a real fighter. Sharkey put himself at the head of the pack by beating Harry Wills convincingly in thirteen rounds at Ebbets Field just a few weeks after Tunney defeated Dempsey. The long-suffering Wills, who was well past his prime, was disqualified for a backhand punch. Sharkey had already signed with Tex Rickard to fight at the Garden on 25 February 1927 against an unnamed opponent. The promoter assumed that Berlenbach would beat Mike and had figured on the Astoria Assassin as a logical opponent. But the Irishman put an end to that plan. According to Westbrook Pegler, 'one peculiar thing about this competition is that the only man in it who has shown any theatrical colour thus far is one who used to be the dreariest man among all the thousands of all sizes, colours and nationalities in the ring, Mike McTigue.'

Rickard's matchmaker, Jess McMahon, called Sharkey's manager, Johnny Buckley, on the telephone to offer him a fight with Mike. Sharkey butted in on the conversation to tell McMahon that the Irishman was much too small for him and it would be 'cruelty to animals' to even consider such a match. The real reason for Sharkey's refusal was that had very little to gain from beating an older, smaller man – but he did have a great deal to lose. Leading contenders didn't fight. An ambitious pug entering an elimination tournament is liable to be eliminated and that was a dreadful prospect. 'Your modern pugilist dreads elimination like a pest,' wrote Gallico. 'He isn't quite sure what the word means except that there is less sugar for eliminated young men.' The Bostonian didn't want to fight Mike because he was a leading contender and the Irishman was a dangerous eliminator.

But Rickard was a powerful man and he 'persuaded' Buckley and Sharkey to take the train to New York the following day and the match was signed within two hours. There was a hitch over Buckley's demand for 30 per cent of the gate but he eventually settled for 25 per cent, the same as Mike. The number of rounds was another sticking point.

Sharkey was a much bigger man and the weight tended to tell towards the end of longer fights.

'I want it over fifteen rounds,' demanded Buckley.

'Ten rounds or nothing,' countered Jimmy.

The argument raged for over an hour. Jimmy left Buckley with Rickard and went to the washroom. He met Mike on his way back in the hallway.

'I want it for ten rounds and Buckley's holding out for fifteen,' said Jimmy.

'Take the fight for thirty or anything he wants, because I'll beat the Polack before ten rounds are over,' came the reply.

Jimmy went back in and signed. The match was scheduled for 3 March 1927 at Madison Square Garden; a week later than originally planned. Sharkey had broken a bone at the base of his right thumb in a previous fight and was a week late starting his training.

Mike was finally earning bigger purses. Jimmy had been so sure that his man would beat Berlenbach he'd accepted just 20 per cent of the net while the Astoria man got 32 for his end. It was good business; the fight had packed out the Garden to the tune of an $89,000 gate and Mike drew down $18,000 for the ten minutes it took him to batter Berlenbach. And it was all about the money for Mike now. 'The title? I'm not anxious to win back the light heavyweight crown,' said Mike. 'It was more bother than it was worth. I can make more money now without it. I'd like to fight Jack Delaney again to settle accounts, but I'm willing to meet any of the heavyweights in Tex Rickard's elimination tournament, starting with Sharkey.'

His win over Berlenbach had made Mike big box office for the first time in his career. The *New York Daily News* reported that some of the offers were attractive enough to prompt Jimmy to tell Sharkey to 'go and jump in the nearest lake in the event that Jack thinks he is too big a boy to pick on the undersized McTigue or else puts in a demand for all the sugar in Rickard's bowl.' But it had taken nearly fifteen years for Mike to win over the customers and it left little time to exploit his popularity. 'Flaming age' said Jimmy after the Berlenbach fight.

Mike's age was still a mystery in boxing circles with reports placing him everywhere from thirty-five to forty-five. Before the Sharkey fight Mike told one reporter, 'I hope I may never see the light of another day if I was more than thirty-three on my birthday last November.'

Bill McGeehan wasn't convinced:

At the current writing the record books, which never are accurate, credit Michael with being thirty-five years old. Michael admits to being thirty-nine. The chances are that Michael is past forty, at which age a pugilist is supposed to be cutting out paper dolls or following the similar sports indulged in by ex-pugilists.

As the light heavyweight champion Michael was looked upon as being strictly fromagenous. It was felt that he had earned the title by a knowledge of geography, rather than any power he had behind his fists.

When the McTigue-Berlenbach bout was arranged it was generally agreed that it was a crime to permit a husky young man like Berlenbach to pound the ribs of an old gentleman like McTigue. While Michael was a more-or-less fromagenous champion, the customers declared that some respect should be shown for age even in the manly art of modified murder.

But the Methuselah of the ring performed the miracle … If Michael the Methuselah continues to progress he might be heavyweight champion when he is fifty and by the time he reaches sixty who can tell?

There are many theories as to how Michael developed so late in life the punch that jarred the durable lower maxillary of Berlenbach. One is that Michael possessed the punch all the time, but never would let it go while he was in his thirties. He was saving it for a rainy day in the forties.

Another notion is that Michael started thinking about letting the right go ten years ago, but, being of a cautious nature, he decided to hold it in reserve while he thought the matter over. Too many fighters were impetuous with their rights. Finally Michael in a fit of recklessness decided to let it go and, when he did, the Astoria Assassin was retired from the manly art of modified murder.

He is the first of the gladiators who showed signs of facing a bright future at forty.

In the matter of testimonials alone, Michael should be able to collect no small sums by attributing his sudden combativeness and sock to some potent medicine.

It was a match to pack the Garden to its doors. At first glance a bout between Jack Sharkey, the 190-lb conqueror of Harry Wills, and Mike McTigue at 170lbs didn't sound reasonable but there were two customers for every ticket. Much of the credit went to Jimmy Johnston. He took a fighter who was considered by the scribes as a candidate for the old man's home, made him as good as new and managed him into the big money. 'Mr Johnston poured red-hot metal into Michael's heart until it weighed as much as the biggest of them,' wrote Walter Turnbull. Mike, meanwhile, had helped patch up one of the great hatreds in boxing as Westbrook Pegler explained:

> Tex was a pretty fair journeyman-hater, but every now and again you would find him tearing a page out of his hate-book and starting a new account with some one who had been a sworn enemy. Human forgiveness had something to do with this, but he was no man to forego a pleasant profit merely to honour a grudge.
>
> His hatred for James J. Johnston, manager of a weird succession of physical prodigies, many of them with child minds, was a thing of awesome beauty when it erupted. For a long time he couldn't speak of Johnston in any tone below a berserk scream. A man had told him he couldn't tell a viper from a humming bird; that Johnston had the run of his office and, at the same time, was holding conversations with the federal prosecutor who was troubling Tex about the interstate transportation of the Dempsey-Carpentier fight films, contrary to law.
>
> I am loathe to believe that Mr Johnston ever blew the whistle on a trusting friend, but Tex believed it, and he carried Johnston on the book for years. He carried him until

James, one day, discovered little coal in his cellar and Michael McTigue, an unemployed drawing card, soaking up heat in his office.

Mr Johnston was willing to let the dead past bury its dead, and he trotted right over to Rickard's office to ask for a match. He was a gifted ballyhoo man himself, and his fighter had a way with the customers. They did not exactly cry or kiss in the reconciliation, but the hate was declared off to their mutual profit, for Michael jammed the Garden three or four times in the second childhood of his career.

Sharkey arrived in New York on 22 February to train in Stillman's gym. 'That Mick can start his alleged rejuvenated right hand at my chin, but he will find my right on his kisser before he gets very far,' said Sharkey. 'As a rule I don't go in for knocking them out, but it won't be my fault if McTigue is in there for half of the fifteen scheduled rounds.'

Sharkey boxed six rounds with sparring partners on the day before the fight and did little to impress the boxing writers present. 'Sharkey shaped up as a fighter who has been inoculated with the germ of overconfidence,' wrote Jack Farrell, 'one who figures he doesn't have to train in the usually accepted fashion for a fight of such major importance.' His timing of punches and judgement of distance appeared all awry and his sparring partners were hitting him with relative ease, though Sharkey did rough them up in the clinches. 'If he resorts to such foolhardy tactics in actual combat "this old guy McTigue," as Jack refers to Michael, is just as likely to knock his chin down to his waistline with a right hand punch as not,' commented Farrell.

Mike returned to work at Billy Grupp's place in Harlem and

indulged in six rough rounds of sparring with a few local heavy-weights for the benefit of the boxing writers. 'What a fine time Mike had cuffing those big eggs around,' wrote Harry Newman. Mike was an old hand at sparring sessions and never failed to give the writers plenty of action and plenty of comment. First in the ring with the Irishman was a 228-lb young fighter called Pat Lester. He lasted two rounds before being relieved by another 200-lb fighter, Tom Roper, followed by Tom Sawyer of Detroit. Abie Bain, an Irish middleweight gave Mike his fastest session in the last round. Mike then got annoyed when one journalist reported Sharkey's intention of killing him.

'Well, that bird won't have to wait long to kill me. He'll kill me will he? Why, I'll hit that egg on the kisser about the eighth round and he won't know what the devil fell on him. Remember now, I said eight rounds. That guy will be easier than Berlenbach. I'll take care of him plenty. When I get him down there, he will stay there.'

The betting was none too brisk in the week leading up to the fight but those who were letting their bankrolls see the Broadway sunlight were laying 9-5 on Sharkey to get the decision. There was virtually no money on a knockout. Kemp & Co, betting commissioners of 515 Seventh Avenue, placed a wager of $2,200 against $1,000 that Sharkey would defeat Mike. The firm claimed there'd been a flood of money, principally from Boston on Sharkey at those odds. Odds of 2-1 were taken that Mike would not go the distance. 'Why, these fellows who have been betting against my Michael on the assumption that Sharkey will have between twenty and twenty-five pounds, the best of the weights, are daffy,' said Jimmy. 'Remember, Mike was trained down fine for Berlenbach. This time we are building him up. He will weigh about 171, two pounds more than he did for the Berlenbach fight. Sharkey will come in around 188, which will give him not more than seventeen pounds to carry to the canvas when he takes his nose dives.'

The morning newspapers were in general agreement that Mike's only chance was to 'wing Jack with his TNT right and make him stay put'. If Mike failed to land that right early on then Sharkey was expected to win with plenty to spare. 'If McTigue can win tonight he should be added to the usual wonders of the world,' wrote Walter Turnbull in the *New York Post*. 'He would outclass any of the others.' Nobody was predicting a great fight because both men were rated as 'clever' boxers, a pejorative term in 1920s boxing. The only cleverness in the ring that meant anything to the customers was the brand that led to a crack on the chin. Expectations had also been muted by the succession of disappointing bouts in this 'heavyweight epidemic' that had hit New York in the winter of 1926-27.

But this turned out to be by far the best battle of the heavyweight tournament.

The crowd was 14,181 and they paid $120,099 in total to see the scrap. The audience included the elite of Harlem and the Bronx and the famous 'Six Hundred Millionaires' that promoter Tex Rickard claimed flanked the Garden ring on fight nights. Master of ceremonies, Joe Humphries, introduced Joe Walcott, a small grey-haired man with a bristling moustache who was one of the greatest welterweights to have donned a glove. Tommy Loughran and Tom Heeney also took a bow, and then the fighters were introduced. Mike was welcomed like a king, Sharkey's reception was less vigorous. Mike smiled while Sharkey scowled, a deep ridge appearing between his brows and a sneer on his lips. The weights were announced as Sharkey 189½lbs, McTigue 170½lbs.

Mike went after Sharkey from the first bell and he shocked the crowd by making the much bigger man hold on and give ground.

The heavyweight came rushing in, flailing away and according to one scribe, 'he looked bad'. Sharkey did all the forcing, hooking continually with his left but they all bounced off Mike's impregnable defence. There was nothing to choose between them in the first but in the second Mike countered with two slashing right hooks that roused a fury in his opponent. The Irishman won the third round easily. He made Sharkey miss continually and lured him on to several straight lefts that bloodied his lips. It was first blood to the Irishman and he returned to his corner at the end of the third with a triumphant smile.

There was very little to separate the fighters in the fourth but the fifth went clearly to Mike. He grinned over his opponent's shoulder in the clinches and made what one reporter at ringside described as 'cutting remarks'. Mike fought as well as he ever had in the sixth. 'No-one ever boxed more superbly than the scion of the ancient kings,' wrote one ringside scribe. 'He kept the young giant missing, he rolled with the punch, ducked inside, wove about, picked blows out of the air. Sharkey launched a thousand blows, but they were wasted on the Garden air. It was a foil against a knife, a teacher against a pupil.'

Mike smiled at Sharkey who was bitter with anger by the seventh round. But the right hook with which Mike had scored five knockouts in a row was unable to bring Sharkey down. It frequently shook him, cut and dazed him. But Sharkey was still on his feet.

The Irishman won five straight rounds and as the bell sounded at the end of each period he glanced with contempt at his opponent. Then, at the end of the seventh round, it was Sharkey's turn to smile. Mike appeared to tire and the sheer size of his opponent became the dominant factor in the fight. He could no longer stave off the bigger man, he couldn't duck as low and his legs were no longer fast enough to get him away. Now Mike was forced to trade blows. In one vicious exchange Mike's left eye was cut and he was jolted backwards. He couldn't pick off the Sharkey lefts anymore and he lost the eighth, ninth and tenth by increasing margins. But he was still clearly in the lead and had the fight finished in the tenth as Jimmy had wanted, he would have won.

When he felt himself weakening, Mike tried craft. He claimed a foul but when Kid McPartland shook his head he came back to make a gallant last stand.

Sharkey's left eye was swollen as they came out for the twelfth. The sound of the bell was still reverberating around the arena when the younger fighter shot his left fist to Mike's jaw with horrifying results. The Irishman had been forced against the ropes on the Eighth Avenue side of the Garden. Sharkey threw the left hook and Mike turned his head away from it. He thought he was out of danger and was slow to put his right glove up to block the punch. But he hadn't turned his head far enough and Mike knew he'd been hit hard when he saw Sharkey's left glove go back bloody. The force of the punch tore a false tooth from Mike's bridgework and drove it through the upper gum and ruptured a small blood vessel. A cascade of blood spurted out covering both fighters. Sharkey continued to jab away at Mike's mouth until the Irishman's face was crimson. Mike hung on to the other blood-wet body, his head bowed over Sharkey's shoulder.

It was obvious that an artery had burst and Mike would bleed to death in the ring unless the fight was stopped. Shouts of 'Stop it' came from all sides. Referee McPartland ignored the cries and Sharkey continued to rein blows at Mike's mouth. The press and ringsiders were splattered with blood. McPartland looked down at the doctor who motioned the fight to go on.

'He'll bleed to death if he lasts the round out. I'm going to climb in there, bets or not,' said Jimmy. But because of fight-fixing, the Commission had banned seconds from throwing in the towel. Jimmy could only join with the crowd in baying for the referee to stop the bout. McPartland lost his footing in one of the pools of blood that covered the white canvas at the Garden but still managed to push Sharkey away. Mike was getting visibly weaker as the blood gushed out of his mouth but he still had his guard up when the referee finally heeded the crowd's pleas to stop the fight. 'Both fighters were smeared from head-to-heel with Celtic gore. Spectators, bloodthirsty of nature, were visibly relieved when referee McPartland stopped the fight,' reported *Time* magazine.

The calls to stop the fight were not unanimous. Many in the crowd jeered, much of it coming from the 'short-end betters' because the wise money had made Mike the outsider at 13-5. According to Bill McGeehan who was sitting ringside, 'it was also quite evident that there were some of the customers who would have been just as pleased to see Michael bleed to death in the ring. In fact, they were bellowing because they were baulked of this spectacle.'

The passing of Mike as a heavyweight contender was a gory sight. He embraced Sharkey and patted him on the back, smiling though bruised and battered lips. After Mike's blood had been wiped off both fighters, Sharkey was more marked-up than the Irishman. His left eye was cut and partially closed and his mouth showed a jagged gash thanks to a glancing blow from a McTigue right. The old man was led from his corner and stepped down in glorious defeat; he got the cheers and Sharkey was jeered. Mike also got $28,000 for his pains.

The following day at his apartment in Harlem, Mike, through a puffed upper lip, surrounded by his wife and children said:

'Why should I quit now, when I have most of the boys on the

run? Sharkey got a great break, that's all. Jack Sharkey up until then reminded me very much of a little boy walking through a graveyard and whistling to keep his courage up.'

Paul Gallico admitted in his column that Mike would have won the fight had it been over ten rounds. He wrote that it was the performance of 'an old man who, bit by bit, is paying off a debt that he owes the public.'

It was Michael Francis McTigue, my favourite Irishman, who was the hero of the evening's doings at the Garden. He provided the thrills and he was an honour to his clan. He didn't have to stand toe to toe and slug with a man twenty pounds heavier. He didn't have to take the punches he did. He could have mounted his bicycle or he could have held. But he gambled like a youngster. He took three, four and five punches to the head to sucker Sharkey in so that he could lay in his own right hand. He made it a far more interesting encounter than the one between Maloney and Delaney. I'll be sorry when Mike hangs up his gloves. Right now he and Delaney are our most colourful ringmen. Imagine that – old Mike, who, when he was champion, was the worst lemon who ever drew on a boxing glove in public.

Though he was eliminated as a heavyweight contender Michael 'Methuselah' McTigue had become the grand old man of the blood splattered canvas. 'It is a strange commentary on the manly art of modified murder that Michael did not start to fight until he was in the sere and yellow leaf of the cauliflower,' wrote Bill McGeehan. The scribe was also concerned about Mike's health and called on the Commission's doctors to examine the Irishman. 'Michael has reached the age when hardening of the arteries and other symptoms that come with maturity start to set in, wrote McGeehan. 'If anything happens to the venerable Michael in the next bout, the Boxing Commission, now that it has accepted the responsibility of guaranteeing the health of the athletes, will be responsible.'

Mike's response to McGeehan's concerns was published in the *New York Herald Tribune* entitled, 'A Note from Methuselah'.

MICHAEL METHUSELAH McTIGUE waxes ironical in his correspondence. He writes: 'Thanks so much for the splendid manner in which you have given me publicity. My name is now fast becoming a household word throughout this great nation of ours. Thanks to you and once again I ask you to keep up the good work. I hope and trust that your health is the best.

'I have bought a home for my wife and kiddies here in Jackson Heights, Long Island, with plenty of trees about the place. We all extend to you an invitation to come out and take some tea some afternoon.'

The mention of the trees sounds sinister. Where there are trees, there may be rope, as Mr McTigue discovered when he was touring through Georgia on the invitation of Mr Young William Stribling, his ma and his pa and some impulsively hospitable Cracker friends in the vicinity of Macon, Georgia. I do not wish to be entertained in any home that is surrounded by trees. Michael's invitation is null and void until deforestation sets in on Long Island.

Mike's letterhead bore the legend, 'Ex-champion,' which led McGeehan to conclude that the Irishman believed that 'it is better to have champed and lost than never to have champed at all'.

The smart boys thought Mike was finished – again, but Jimmy thought differently. Sharkey was a heavyweight and Jimmy believed his man was still the leading contender for Jack Delaney's light heavyweight title. He managed to 'persuade' his friends at the Commission to rule that Delaney would have to meet the Irishman before he did any more fighting.

But Jack Delaney had his eyes set firmly on the riches on offer in the heavyweight ranks and a title defence against Mike was a dangerous fight. Even with Jimmy's connections it was a difficult match to make. Mike wanted to keep fighting while he waited for Delaney so he signed for a charity show at the Garden. His bout with Pat McCarthy was the feature on a card arranged by Sheriff Charlie Culkin for the Kiddie Camp Fund. Whatever cash was left over after Mike and the 'Boston Bust' had been paid was given to sending poor children away to the country for a summer vacation. McCarthy had won a decision over highly regarded Harry Persson several months previously and was shouting from the housetops that Jack Sharkey ran out on him. It was a risky fight for Mike to take and a defeat would certainly cost him the chance of getting his old title back. McCarthy was considered dangerous enough by Rickard to postpone signing up Delaney until the result of the McTigue-McCarthy clash was known.

There was bad feeling between the boxers after Mike had written for the *New York Evening Post* that McCarthy had bored him stiff in a recent contest. Most hurtful of all was the suggestion that McCarthy didn't have the heart to become a leading fighter.

The Garden had hosted the circus for five weeks and there'd been no boxing, so a big gate was ensured. Sheriff Culkin was predicting a sell-out after he'd sold $10,000-worth of tickets himself.

Mike was only a marginal 7-5 favourite in the betting. He entered the ring with an elastic band covering a boil on his right elbow. The fight was late in starting and the dreary affair dragged on until 11.15 pm by which time many of the fans had gone home. Mike hit McCarthy with a hard right in the second and the Boston Bust spent the remainder of the fight making sure he didn't buy another one. The elastic bandage had three crimson splotches staining it from the fourth round onwards. Referee Crowley beseeched the pair to fight as the crowd bayed for blood, but McCarthy couldn't and Mike wouldn't so the customers went home unhappy. They started leaving as early as the sixth and by the end those who remained wished they gone home as well.

Paul Gallico wrote, 'to see this burly youngster simply scared to death of an old gent who in his day had himself run more distance in the ring than many a marathoner, was something of a sight, even if the fight was terrible as an exhibition'. Speaking strictly from a fighting standpoint, the affair was a 'fliv', but the 11,403 cash customers who paid $41,324, enabling the fund to show a profit, had the satisfaction of seeing an old-timer chalking up another clean cut win in his declining days. Jimmy claimed Mike's poor showing was due to an elbow dislocation in training the previous week.

Mike wrote about the contest in the *Evening Post*:

I don't know whether to tell you first about my tennis arm or apologise for the kind of fight another Irishman, with the fighting name of Pat McCarthy, put up.

When I saw that Pat wouldn't fight, I was ashamed to be in the same ring.

I know quite a few of the boys will be throwing bricks instead of bouquets at me today, but they will not be fooling the customers who saw the match and who will not deny that one man was fighting, and that man's name was Mike McTigue.

My grandfather always preached to me never to beat an Irishman that was afraid, but to apologise for him. Last night I was reminded of what my father's dad told me when I was a little fellow back in the Old Country.

I always was of the opinion that when two Irishmen go into the same ring there was bound to be a fight. I am willing to admit now I was mistaken. When Pat butted me I asked him if he thought I was a foreigner.

A few days after the McCarthy fight came the shock announcement that Jimmy was no longer Mike's manager. But the news wasn't as dramatic as it first appeared. Jimmy became the matchmaker for the Coney Island stadium and matchmakers were not allowed to manage fighters. It was just a technicality and Jimmy got around it by designating his brother, Charlie, as Mike's manager. Charlie's first act was to book Mike to fight New Zealander Tom Heeney at Jimmy's Coney Island venue. Heeney withdrew from what was to be the opening night contest at Coney Island just a few days before the fight after straining a muscle in training.

Jimmy had managed to persuade his friends at the Commission to rule that Jack Delaney would have to defend his title against Mike before he did any more fighting, either as a light heavyweight or heavyweight. Delaney wanted to defend his title in the lower weight division and also join the rush for Tunney's heavyweight crown. Tex Rickard appreciated the appeal of a Delaney-McTigue bout and signed the boxers for a fifteen-round championship fight at Yankee Stadium on 7 July 1927.

Mike set up a training camp at Andover, New Jersey while Delaney worked at his New Hampshire mountain camp. Mike was so confident of victory that he instructed Charlie Johnston to bet ten thousand dollars on the outcome. He wanted 2½-1 for his money but the best on offer was 8-5. Tickets for the fight went on sale on 15 June at the Garden box office. But nobody was particularly interested. There was only one boxing story in the summer of 1927 – Jack Dempsey was making a comeback.

The expected announcement that the Delaney-McTigue fight was off was made on the afternoon of 29 June. The postponement was necessary because of the overwhelming publicity generated by Jack Dempsey's return to the ring to fight Jack Sharkey while Mike and Jack's argument seemed to be a deep, dark secret in the press. The State Athletic Commission announced its approval for the postponement, stipulating that neither man could engage in another contest in the meantime. But the world light heavyweight champion had another good reason to ask for a delay. He scaled 178lbs after several weeks training and was finding it hard to shed the extra weight. Delaney also wanted to join Rickard's heavyweight elimination tournament and had been offered a fight with the 'Basque woodchopper' Paulino Uzcudun, with a match against Jack Sharkey promised in the autumn if he was victorious. Delaney was left with little choice but to tell the Commission he was no longer able to make the 175-lb limit and abdicate his light heavyweight title.

Long before boxing commissions were dreamed of and when the barbaric rules of English bare-knuckle fighting dominated, forfeiture of titles was by no means an infrequent occurrence. Back then there were no rules or laws bearing on the subject but as the result of unwritten agreement between the fighters, a champion who failed to cover a forfeit posted by a qualified challenger automatically lost his title, which went to the challenger. The fighters under the London rules rigidly lived up to this custom. Jimmy Johnston thought it a fine tradition.

'After hearing of Peter Reilly's plan to declare Delaney's title vacant, Jimmy Johnston, Michael's bashful and unassuming manager, took McTigue into his private office and in the presence of little brother Charlie and Toots Sullivan, secretary of the Johnston Publicity bureau, spread both hands over Michael's noble dome, and after making a few mystic passes James informed the puzzled Michael that he was again the world's light heavyweight champion,' wrote Jack Farrell, writing in the *New York Daily News*.

It was as easy as that. With a little persuasion from Jimmy, the New York State Athletic Commission transferred the light heavyweight title from Jack Delaney to Mike McTigue. The only string attached to Mike's title was that he had thirty days to agree to a match with long standing challenger, Tommy Loughran. Jimmy agreed readily as he'd already signed a contract with Tex Rickard for Mike to fight Loughran whenever the promoter wanted to stage it.

Just over two years since Jimmy had spotted Mike wandering aimlessly along Broadway he'd made good on his promise to get the Irishman's world title back for him. 'Faith is the torch that guided Colonel Charles Lindbergh across the Atlantic in a plane and Mike McTigue, veteran Irish boxer, back to the world's light heavyweight title,' commented the *New York Evening Post*. 'Jimmy Johnston told Mike he would get the 175-lb title back for him if he had patience. Mike not only persevered, but he had faith in Mr Johnston. There is quite a story with a moral to it in this for those who like their boxing unmixed with politics.'

In his column Paul Gallico wrote:

You, Jimmy Johnston, get away from that mimeograph machine, do you hear? I can see you preparing that statement to the press that Mike McTigue drove Jack Delaney out of the light heavyweight division. Don't you dare say anything like that. You put that nasty typewriter right away.

The Commission's action in awarding the title outside the ring was unprecedented, despite the assertion of the board that it was the established custom of ancient and modern times to award the title to the man the champion was signed to meet, if the champion steps aside and waives his right to the throne without a contest. Mike had signed and sealed papers for a crack at the title against Delaney at the Yankee Stadium on 11 August. If a championship fight was arranged and the titleholder failed to go though with the contest because he was unable to make weight he automatically lost his crown through forfeiture. Mike could make the weight, was ready to fight Delaney and was recognised by the New York State Commission as the leading contender. Hence if Mike was the leading contender before Delaney retired from the division, and was capable of making the weight, he was entitled to be recognised as world's champion. But there was much consternation over the Commission's decision. In the event of a resignation of a champion, the usual action was to order the two next-best fighters to box for the title. Occasionally the Three Dukes had ordered an entire tournament before anointing a champion. It triggered a resumption of hostilities in the McTigue-McGeehan battle:

Back To Methuselah

Mr McTigue gracefully accepted the title, and the responsibilities it will incur. Mr McTigue made it plain that he was making considerable personal sacrifice in accepting the post, which he once held for a number of years without marring his record by fighting anybody. It seems that every time he was forced to defend the title Michael had to buy new teeth afterwards. In fact, Michael's teeth, according to Mr Johnston, have been eating up all of the profits he has earned in the prizefight business.

'But what of his defective dentistry?' demanded Mr Johnston. 'He'll fight them. He will not bite them.' In spite of the impressive manner in which Michael Methuselah McToothless was made light heavyweight champion, a number of those present at the commission said, 'What of it?'

On the whole, the Boxing Commission acted wisely in appointing Michael Methuselah McTigue to the post of light heavyweight champion without putting itself in the position of encouraging brawling or ill feeling among the other prizefighters of the division. Only the presence of mind and firmness of the Boxing Commission prevented a fight for the light heavyweight championship.

Friends of Tommy Loughran even hinted that Mr Loughran would be willing to fight McTigue for the title. Naturally this shocked the members of the commission and they frowned down such truculent tendencies. They were shocked particularly by the intimation that a nice looking young man like Mr Loughran would strike a gentleman of Michael Methuselah's years. An investigation may follow and if it can be shown that Mr Loughran was really ready to commit such an offence against the peace and dignity of the Boxing Commission he will be dealt with severely.

There have been too many fights over matters of this sort of late. The commission is contemplating having all champions appointed by the New York State Boxing Commission, or it may have the ring titles decided by a popular vote. It stands to reason that if this policy is enforced with the firmness for which the commission is noted that all fighting may be eliminated or at least reduced to a minimum.

A week after the Commission gave Mike the world title, Jimmy got a call from his apartment-block doorman:

'There's a man down here with a new car, says he has orders to deliver it to you.'

'What kind of car is it?'

'Buick.'

'I don't own a Buick; ask him if he has the name correctly.'

There was a pause, and then the doorman came back to the telephone: 'It's for you Mr Johnston. He says a Mr McTigue bought it and ordered it over to your apartment.'

The next time Jimmy met Mike he asked him why he'd bought the car.

'When we first got together, you told me you'd make me light heavyweight champion, and I promised you a car if you did. Well, the Buick is a discharge of my pledge.'

When he persuaded the Flatiron mob to anoint Mike champion, Jimmy wasn't only figuring on the principle of the thing but also his own interest. As challenger for the title Mike would have been entitled to 12.5 per cent of the net receipts. As champion he got 37.5 per cent. When Jimmy met up with Tommy Loughran's manager Joe Smith to discuss terms at the Garden everything was amicable, for a short while. When it was over Smith came out waving his arms and spluttering threats over Jimmy's insistence on the champion's percentage of 37.5 per cent. Jimmy held firm and Joe eventually relented. The match was made for 7 October 1927 at the Garden.

On 20 August, Mike was one of a cluster of boxing champions to entertain members of the Grand Street Boys' Association at the organisation's first outing at Duer's Place, Whitestone Landing, Queens. A cavalcade of cars and buses took over 1200 boys from the Association's clubhouse on 106 West 55th Street early in the morning. Mike fought an exhibition bout with middleweight contender Johnny Kreiger and then had a 'mighty battle royal' with Sheriff Charles Culkin of New York County. After some shadow boxing Joe Humphries, the master of ceremonies from the Garden, announced the Sheriff had won by knockout in the second round. Humphries asserted emphatically that the winning blow was not a foul, thereupon the Sheriff was hailed as the new light heavyweight champion of the world. Mike returned to Grupp's in Harlem to prepare for the Loughran fight.

'If McTigue gets his Oolong he'll knock Loughran out,' Jimmy told one boxing writer at the gym.

'What d'ya mean?' asked the scribe.

'This will be their fourth meeting. The first was about even. The second battle, it was pretty generally accepted that Mike lost. The third time, in West New York Ball Park, Mike got the Oolong and won.'

'What d'ya mean, "got the Oolong and won?"' Jimmy had an audience by now.

'It happen betwixt and between the eighth and ninth round of the West New York fight. Up to that time, the Philadelphia lad, whom the darlin's find so easy to look at, had been having a bit the better of the milling.

'My Bowld Michael seemed to be having a bit of carburettor

trouble. As he slumped down in his chair at the end of the eighth, one of his seconds handed him a bottle. Mike tilted his head back and took a man-sized swig. A beatific look suffused his genial Celtic countenance.

"Slieve na Mon, or Bushmills!" yelled a Mayo man in the first row. "He's havin' a drop of the craychure."

The Grupp's regulars who'd heard the well-rehearsed yarn before began to giggle.

'Me Bowld Michael smacked his lips and tilted the bottle again. He gave a shiver and glared across the ring, as if Loughran, bad cess to him, had stolen his colleen bawn.

"It's potheen from the ould sod itself," gurgled a Tipperary man. "T'w'd warm the cockles o' your heart!"'

Jimmy stopped his story for a moment to watch Mike sparring in the ring, then went on:

'Again, Bowld Michael crooked his elbow. After the third swig they had to hold him in his chair, so crazy was he to be up and at Tommy.'

"Hooch," yelled some Jerseyites from the dollar seats and the smacking of lips sounded like a heard of Texas Longhorns lifting their feet out of the mud.

'Would you believe it, the effect on Mike was magical. When the bell sounded for the ninth, he tore at Tommy with all the fury in him, bashing, crashing, and dashing at him like Myles the Slasher at the Bridge of Finca. There was no holding Mike back, no stopping him. He bate Tommy like Paddy "bate the drum", and if the fight had gone another round, he would have kilt him entirely.'

"What was that they gave you at the end of the eighth round?" Liam O'Shea asked him in the dressing room after the fight.

"Oolong. Just a bit of cold tay," answered Mike.

"Bedad," commented O'Shea, "if a Chinaman got three swigs of your tay he'd step out and lick a whole army."

'So,' concluded Johnston, 'If the codgemohons don't steal Bowld Michael's Oolong bottle from him, what a bating Tommy Loughran is in for next Friday night.'

Mike was the favourite in the betting in the week leading up to the fight at 7-5. A crowd of 13,472 paid $72,562 to see the contest, which exceeded even the most optimistic predictions. New York Mayor Jimmy Walker took his seat at ringside next to James Farley, Chairman of the Commission. Mike entered the ring second and was greeted with a salvo that drowned out the strains of jazz sent through the arena by the band of St Monica's naval battalion.

It was a fast, spectacular, dirty fight. 'Fifteen more vicious rounds are seldom seen in the prize ring,' reported *Time*. Mike, his ringcraft gone, his puncture-proof defence swept aside, was always pressing forward, never taking a backwards step, even when Loughran's blows sent him off balance and rocking on his heels. But for much of the contest, Loughran looked younger, fitter and stronger. He cuffed, slapped and smacked Mike around the ring.

There were frequent claims of foul in the early rounds but there was also a great deal of heavy punching. Loughran threw the first low blow in the third and Mike complained bitterly to the referee. He muttered to his cornermen, 'I want to get goin', but I can't.' Loughran kept a stinging, pecking left hand constantly on the well-worn face of the old champion. He used it, said the radio announcer, 'like a paint brush: daubing, tapping, slapping.'

The champion, his lips drawn in a savage snarl for most of the fight, kept trying to throw the one punch that could finish matters. His corner yelled 'bloody murder' at the body blows that were wearing their man down. Mike was hit very low at the end of the thirteenth round and he stumbled back to his corner doubled up in pain. He sank, without looking, onto the small stool he knew Jimmy had swung into place.

Amazingly, he came out stronger than his opponent in the fourteenth and drove him around the ring with a furious barrage of lefts and rights. The fifteenth was Mike's best round and it looked as if he would knock out Loughran. According to one ringside scribe, Mike went berserk. He smacked a right hook onto Loughran's chin, followed by ripping lefts to the body and another right hook to the jaw. Loughran tried to ward off the assault with left jabs but Mike walked through them, snarling and swinging.

But it was just too late and Loughran survived. At the final bell Mike walked to his corner with his left eye swollen almost closed with a lump above it and a cut below. His nose was trickling blood from both nostrils. As referee Lou Magnolia and Judges Charles F. Mathison and Harold Barnes had totted up their ballots, Mike turned to Jimmy and said: 'It's too bad I didn't have my Oolong, Jimmy.'

'You won, Mike.'

'No, I didn't. The kid will get the decision. I couldn't get started.'

Joe Humphries walked over to Loughran and announced: 'Winnah and new champion.'

Philadelphians noisily celebrated Loughran's victory and the city had its first world champion since Jack O'Brien held the same title back in 1905. It was generally written up as one of the best performances seen in a Garden ring – an exhibition that hinted at what a great champion Loughran was set to become. Loughran won because he was too fast and agile, too light on his feet and quick with his hands. He won because he was over fifteen years younger.

Mike congratulated the new champion then took a slow walk

around the ring, listening to the cheers of the gallery. Age was taking its toll and Mike knew it. Before leaving the ring, Loughran said in Mike's ear: 'Anybody but you, Mike. I'm sorry you had to lose.' The Irishman left the ring an idol, more popular than he had ever been in New York, because he fought a greater fight than anybody expected. 'Mike is one of the most thorough sportsmen and greatest fighters that ever lived,' Loughran told the scribes. 'Before I had a chance to realise that I had reached the goal of my ambition the other night he came to me into the dressing room and while extending his hand in congratulation said:

'Well, Tommy, I told you five years ago that you would be on top. I couldn't have lost to a better man or a cleaner fighter. I wish you all the luck in the world and that you will hold the title for many years to come.'

'I felt a lump in my throat when I tried to respond. It was the first time in my life that I ever regretted winning a fight. After groping around for something decent to say in return, I finally managed to tell Mike that I was sorry he had to lose but that I was glad I won. What I wanted to say was: Mike, if I ever lose my title, I hope you win it back. I'm sincere about that too.'

Then they led the old champion away into the shadows as the boys of Broadway used to say.

EIGHTEEN

Silent heresies of reason should have told him to pack it in, but
not yet ready to store his career away in lavender and mothballs,
he stayed on ... and on ... and on.

For Whom The Bell Tolls: Fighters Who Have Failed To Punch Out Time

Bert Randolph Sugar

The Toy Bulldog suddenly lashed out with a right hook to the jaw,
following it up with a left that sent Mike to the ropes. Mickey
Walker charged in driving spiteful punches and Mike, looking a very
old man, slid towards the canvas before getting caught on the second
rope from where he hung for a count of nine. He just beat ten but
was too far-gone to fight back.

Instinctively, Mike fell into a clinch and made a weak, hopeless
effort to sew Walker up. There was a swinging of gloves and the Irishman was thrown onto posts, ropes and then the canvas. He held his
hands high but Walker threw punches from all angles to head and
body and Mike finally lowered a glove to get his bearings. As he did
so, Walker shot across a left hook. The Irishman crumpled down
in Walker's corner and grovelled in the resin as the crowd shouted
for a knockout. He got up and stood with expressionless eyes while
Walker beat him around the head unmercifully. The barrage sent
Mike down again. He rolled over and got on one knee, shaking his

head a little, and listened to the count until it got to nine. Then he got up, the referee wiped resin from his gloves and stepped aside. Walker charged in and cracked the Irishman with rights and lefts. Mike fell across the middle rope, his hands by his side, eyes closed, helpless. The referee reached eight when Jimmy jumped into the ring, which automatically disqualified his fighter. The referee stopped counting. Mike was kept in Walker's corner, where he'd received all the punishment and where he'd made his last stand. He was out cold with grotesquely swollen eyes and bleeding lips. The seconds worked on him for five minutes before he regained consciousness. The six thousand fans paid $50,000 and they were still shouting long after the fight was over.

Chicago promoter Jim Mullen had matched Mike with world middleweight champion Mickey Walker at the city's Coliseum on 1 November 1927, just over three weeks after his brutal fight with Loughran. Mike had been the favourite in the betting at 6-5 because the boys were sticking to the belief that a good big man will always beat a good little man.

'McTigue is through,' wrote Walter Turnbull. 'The drink to which Jimmy Johnston staked him at the bar of the fountain of youth seems to have been synthetic. It had a great kick while it lasted, but the after-effects were not so good. Had Walker caught McTigue as Berlenbach and Sharkey did while that draft was still stirring in him, we doubt whether Mickey could have knocked him out in a week, much less a round. Mike's recent bout with Tommy Loughran must have softened him up more than at first appeared.'

Another chapter in the glorious annals of the prize-ring had ended. A strong young fighter had battered an old man insensible in two minutes and fifteen seconds of ferocious slugging. Bold Michael had reached the crossroads at last thought the boys. The veteran had sprung one surprise after another in recent years and then came another upset, with Mike himself as the victim. He took it with a smile. It was inevitable. Youth must go on. Age must bow.

But Mike's adversaries knew him better than that.

The passing of Michael Francis McTigue in Chicago calls for something damp and teary, to be typed with a lump in the throat. Somewhere in it there will be references to the weak and pitiful old man falling before the merciless and cruel attack of Mickey Walker, and there will be a little picture of Mickey's soggy gloves nailed to the wall forever.

This story, however, I will leave to others if they care for it. I can't see it that way. To me the sighs of the prize-ring are confined to the preliminary boys. I can't shed tears for the headliners. It was not a year ago that McTigue stood in the Garden ring with a strong young fellow and battered him insensible with the same cruelty that Walker showed to him. McTigue snarled over Berlenbach's broken body as Walker snarled over McTigue's wrecked form. Dog eat dog! Old Mike owed the boxing public a great debt of fighting. Mike is about square now.

What will you bet he doesn't hang up his gloves? They don't hang them up now as long as there's a penny to be squeezed out of the customers. The name of Michael Francis McTigue is too big an asset still to be thrown away. It will turn out after a week or so that Mike wasn't feeling right, that he was not himself, that he couldn't get started and that he is going away to the woods for a long rest, after which he will start from the bottom again to regain his light heavyweight laurels.

Some say that Jimmy Johnston waited too long before

scrambling in the ring to save Mike from punishment, but I don't believe that. Jimmy, whatever his faults may be, is a humane man and he loved his Moike. A second is torn between two duties at a fight. He must protect the life of his fighter and at the same time he must not jeopardise his chances of winning by stopping a fight while his man still has a chance to come through. Two minutes of the fight had passed. Johnston may have thought that McTigue could bull through the final minute and recuperate in the rest period.

It would be nice if Michael stopped fighting now, but they never do, because they haven't any sense. If they had they wouldn't be fighters in the first place. Perhaps James Joy Johnston will be able to persuade him to sit back and cut coupons for the rest of his life or take up boxing instruction for youngsters at some gymnasium. Michael endeared himself so much with me in the last year or so that I'd hate to see him walking on his heels. But he WILL go on.

'A Sad Story'

Paul Gallico

Mike and Jimmy left Chicago for New York the following morning. The fighter's face was marked up and swollen but he vowed to fight on. Red Smith once wrote of aging fighters, 'young men have vision; old men have dreams. But the place for old men to dream is beside the fireplace.'

Within days Jimmy filed Mike's challenge for a return match with Loughran for the title. 'McTigue? What does McTigue mean now?' asked the boys along the Fast and Furious Forties of Broadway. 'Give some other fighter a chance.' But it wasn't time to give up yet. The sticks hadn't seen a 'rejuvenated' McTigue, so Jimmy took him on a tour. 'We'll be able to make some money and you can lick the kind of guys they'll ask you to face.'

Mike arrived in Toronto just eight days after his battering by Walker in Chicago. Reporters were told how he had 'stepped into one' coming out of a clinch and remembered nothing else. He offered a reward to anyone who could get Mickey Walker back into the same ring as him. Mike claimed to have made $394,000 in seventeen years in the ring and was longing for the time when he could give up the game and retire to spend time with his family. He hinted that the time would be soon.

His opponent in Toronto was Larry Gains, the Canadian heavy-weight champion. It was the largest crowd to watch a fight in the city since Jimmy Wilde beat Patsy Wallace back in 1920. Gains was eighteen pounds heavier than Mike and he had the Irishman in trouble in the second and again in the seventh round, when he landed eight or nine punches without reply. But Mike stayed on his feet. In the third, Gains opened a cut over his opponent's left eye with a sharp right hook and it bled for the rest of the fight. Mike fought back in the fifth and the sixth when Gains had to hold on and was warned for kidney-punching in the clinches. Mike won both the eight and ninth rounds and nearly knocked out Gains with a vicious left hook followed up by two straight rights onto the mouth. During these two rounds Gains was cautioned for butting as was Mike for use of the elbow. The tenth was three minutes of toe-to-toe slugging and the 6,000 fans in the arena screamed with excitement. Gains tried to make his extra weight count by rushing Mike back to the ropes but the Irishman not only held his own in the exchanges but he threw punches as fast as his hands would allow.

The referee scored the fight a draw.

Mike returned home to spend the festive season with his family.

It had been a brutal year during which he'd been hit harder and more often than in the rest of his career put together.

'Mr McTigue showed a generous and forgiving spirit in sending me a Christmas card at all, unless it could be that he is showing a contemptuous spirit in a subtle way, because I have written quite severely about him in the last year,' wrote Westbrook Pegler.

The rest gave Mike time to convince himself that the Walker fight had been an accident and he just forgot to duck a right hook. The truth was that age had dulled his co-ordination, rhythm and reflexes and that his dimming eyes saw the punch start but it landed before he could shift his snowy-stubbled chin to a point of safety. And while Mike was busy convincing himself, Jimmy was convincing the boxing powers to give his man one more shot. Unfortunately, both men succeeded in their respective tasks.

Leo Lomski was a young fighter who had made an unsuccessful attempt to win the title against Tommy Loughran. But he'd put up a good show and even floored the champion. Lomski was being prepared for another shot at the title, so he was matched with Mike with the winner promised a fight with Jimmy Slattery as a final eliminator to challenge Loughran. Somehow, Jimmy got his man back in the picture once more. Jack Koford asked in the *New York Evening Post*: 'Just why the Old Man of the Mountains is there is hard to figure. He made one of the most astonishing comebacks ever seen in the ring, but he seems to be at the end of the trail now.'

The match was what was known in the cauliflower industry as a 'good money' shot for Mike, with everything to gain and very little to lose. The advance ticket sale had been unusually large and several ringside seats were reserved for William T. Cosgrave and his party. New York Mayor Jimmy Walker was also at ringside.

Mike seemed tired from the early rounds and was bereft of almost everything but a fighting instinct. Lomski came close to scoring a knockout several times and Mike could be heard wincing when an especially hard right caught him in the ribs at the close of round one. The old champion's face was a crimson smear from the fifth round onwards when he was cut twice on the forehead and over the left eye. Lomski raked Mike's left eyebrow with a glancing swing and opened it up, bringing the blood in a rivulet.

In the next flurry Lomski grazed Mike with a right and split the skin in the middle of his forehead. According to Westbrook Pegler, 'as they broke away Mike looked as though someone had spanked him in the face with a brush dipped in red lead and magnolia.' The referee made a motion as if he was going to stop the fight but Mike protested and he was allowed to continue. Then later on in the round Lomski showed up with his right cheekbone laid open after a few jabs had painted his face as badly as Mike's. Pegler wrote that 'from a sentimental point of view it was quite a show, with an elderly, chalky white man using the skill of twenty years in the ring to minimise or completely thwart the rushes of a pugnacious kid, who had only muscle, stamina and eagerness on his side.

'As they clinched, old Michael's pale-china-blue eyes would peer out from his tangled sorrel eyebrows, sometimes through a veil of blood from cuts on his forehead, into the impudent green of the youngster and his lips would move in panting phrases.'

The crowd roared encouragement to the veteran Irishman and he responded by fighting furiously. But the blood was flowing freely once more in the sixth and in the next round he was staggered and stunned under the pitiless attack of Lomski's punches. 'Mike's shoe-button nose was smashed into the appearance of a cranberry,' wrote one ringside scribe. Lomski smashed over a stunning right that landed between Mike's eyes. He was dazed. He blinked and tried to wipe away the blood with gloves.

For ten rounds the youthful Leo Lomski threw everything he had at Mike who wobbled, skidded, danced and parried, and although blood gushed from deep gashes above both eyes, the Irishman was still on his feet, fighting gamely, at the bell. Everybody in the crowd of 12,000 spectators knew that Lomski had won. Mike congratulated the victor.

'If he is wise he will hang up his gloves and avoid such beatings as that to which he was subjected last night,' commented the *New York Times*. 'It was pitiful to see McTigue trying with only what is left of his once-wonderful fighting head to offset the youth of Lomski and all that goes with this overwhelming advantage.'

'The crowd permitted the veteran Irishman to leave the ring without a salvo of applause,' wrote William Morris in the *Evening Post*, 'wherein it must be recorded that the loser was a better sport than the fans.'

Even his staunchest critics took no pleasure in reading of how Mike was being punched around by second-raters. He had money enough to retire comfortably and he was considered a 'smart son of Erin', but it took a smarter man than most to know when he was through and Mike signed to box Tony Marullo at the St Nicholas Arena in New York. The New Orleans fighter was a good draw who pleased the fans, win, lose or draw.

Most of the newspapers thought Mike won easily. He hit Marullo with straight lefts to the face and right hooks to the body. Marullo was cautioned five times for a variety of illegal punches. At the final bell he chopped a short right onto Mike's jaw as they came together for the handshake. Marullo won the judges' decision, however, and the verdict was met with an outburst of jeering from the customers. This was a reaction to Mike being the heavily backed

5-1-on favourite rather than a collective sense of injustice. 'These guys wouldn't have been able to lay a glove on me a few months ago,' he told Charlie Johnston. The defeats were mounting up, and against fighters he considered bums. Still Mike kept plodding along hoping that the magical elixir that had worked once could work again. He set off for a tour of California to see if he could find it out there.

Mike was cleaning up what money he could before retiring and one of the most lucrative fights he could get was against the Basque 'woodchopper', Paulino Uzcudun. He had been scheduled to fight Paulino on the East Coast but the match had fallen through. Mike blamed Paulino for ducking out. Paulino had a strong following in the Spanish community and Mike knew that the Basque had pulled a gate of $125,000 for a recent fight with George Godfrey, so he felt the scrap would 'be well worth while all round'. He could have picked much softer opposition in California had he chosen to do so, but he prided himself on not being a sucker-picker. 'Fight a good man and if you lose, it doesn't hurt the social standing,' said Mike. 'But if an unknown blows you over, you have to start all over again and I'm too old for that now.'

Boxing had only recently returned to the State after many years of prohibition and Armand Emanuel, an attorney-at-law, was rated the best heavyweight the Pacific Coast had developed since the game had been tolerated there once more. He was undefeated in twenty-six starts and when the fight was announced with Mike he was a 2-1 favourite to beat the Irishman.

The two men packed the Armoury in San Francisco. Mike came close to stopping his opponent in the first round but he tired as the fight went on. His eye had been cut in the first and it bothered him throughout the bout. He had a particularly torrid fourth session after Emanuel landed with a hard right hook that spun the Irishman around. But Mike had done enough to earn a draw against an un-beaten fighter half his age and half a stone heavier.

Following this impressive showing he was signed by matchmaker Wad Wadhams for a ten-rounder against Cowboy Jack Willis at the Olympic in Los Angeles on 8 May 1928. Mike moved into the Barbara Hotel, Los Angeles and trained in searing heat at Barney Dempsey's Manhattan Gymnasium where the crowds flocked to watch him work. He told Paul Lowry of the *Los Angeles Times* that his intention was to round out 1928 by giving 'boxing lessons to five or six of the younger element, win back his light heavyweight title from Tommy Loughran and then retire for keeps.

"'It's a grand game, this boxing. It has kept my mind clear and my body in wonderful condition for many years. I'm thirty-six and I don't feel it by a long shot.'"

Probably because he was forty-six! Before the fight Jack Willis was trying to lay a thousand dollars on himself to stop the former champion. He didn't come close and the referee called the fight at the Olympic Auditorium, Los Angeles, a draw. The first eight rounds were scored even, Willis took the ninth and Mike the tenth.

But as the Irishman dislocated his shoulder in the fourth round, he had to cancel a fight in Phoenix, Arizona and return to New York with Charlie Johnston. The shoulder injury kept him out of the ring for a month and then he was back to give Armand Emanuel his New York debut. 'Old Michael Francis will check his wheelchair and ear-trumpet in the dressing room, shave off his long snowy beard and attempt to turn back the youthful Hebrew hope through a veteran's ringcraft,' reported the *New York Herald Tribune*.

One subway car could have taken the entire crowd to the Garden that night. Emanuel entered the ring a 4-1 favourite but Mike put up quite a show for an old guy who was supposed to have 'one foot in the bucket'. He let fly early with his right hand. It only travelled twelve inches and put Emanuel down on his knees for nine.

It startled the San Franciscan, the crowd and Bill McGeehan at ringside.

> Michael Methuselah long since has quite been through with the prize-ring, and if there had been a Society for the Prevention of Cruelty to Old Gentlemen he never would have been permitted to be wheeled into that ring. Yet, with his venerable joints creaking and his ancient dogs barking defiance, Michael Methuselah walked over to the rising generation of heavyweight and popped him on the chin.
>
> Armand Emanuel dropped to the mat, sat a few seconds and meditated. Then he waited on one knee apparently in the hope that the referee might order that peevish old gentleman out of the ring. But the referee seemed to think that it served Armand right for slapping a grandfatherly person like Michael in the face. Armand rose at the count of nine and took courage in the knowledge that Michael was in the ring without his crutches.

Mike didn't manage to land the right again for the remainder of the contest. He did fight desperately and savagely to the end, but Emanuel's youth and stamina prevailed. In almost every round Mike piled up an early lead but weariness took its toll in the final minutes and he was forced to retreat to the ropes and cover his head. Emanuel got the verdict but the cheers were for the Irishman.

A slim crowd of 5,860 contributed just $17,230 to see the contest. The small gathering paid tribute to Mike but ignored Emanuel and the more vociferous partisans hurled abuse in disapproval of the decision. 'The "Old Man of the Wicklow Mountains", looking more than ever as though he had swung from every tree in those hills in the days of his youth, lost the decision as the corporal's guard of customers lost interest in the proceedings,' wrote McGeehan. 'It was in reality one of those trials to see if Armand had anything. He hadn't, but it cost the curious customers in the ringside seats $11 each to find out. Experiments of this sort in the very near future will have to be conducted in the seclusion of a cauliflower laboratory. The prices are killing off the curious.'

It was typical of bouts in the declining days of an industry that had once been booming. Mike was many years past his best and the young pretender, Armand Emanuel, was a terrible disappointment. What was coming into the cauliflower industry was little better than what was going out or what had already gone out. Tex Rickard was reported to be a lone and melancholy figure, standing in the shadows of the Garden at this particular show, brooding over his lost customers. It was a matter of supply and demand. In the summer of 1928 the supply was awful and that there was very little or no demand.

The critics blamed the Commission that had held full sway over the business since it was re-established in the State through the celebrated Walker Law. The Three Dukes of the Flatiron Building had caused the 'blight that is on the cauliflower' by allowing exorbitant prices and terrible bouts. 'The boxing commission might save the industry if it could arrange to chloroform the McTigues, the Levinskys, the Brittons, the Ted Kid Lewises and a few of the others, or dispose of them in any human fashion,' wrote Bill McGeehan. 'They come around making the current generation look very bad indeed and create the impression that the industry is going from very bad to very much worse.'

Mike continued with his policy of picking up a little money on the strength of the fact that he once held the title of light heavyweight champion of the world. He travelled to Philadelphia for a match with Matt Adgie. It looked like easy money for three rounds and Mike was leading on points. Then all of a sudden, as he was coming out of a clinch, Mike hit Adgie low with a left uppercut. Adgie was doubled up on the canvas and examined by Dr Abe Baron. The bout was stopped and referee Hindin awarded the fight to Adgie on a disqualification. The Pennsylvania State Athletic Commission suspended Mike indefinitely.

'Why don't you go into some business, Mike?' a well-meaning friend wanted to know, before advising Mike to retire.

'Show me a better business than this one I am in, and I will. I have been fighting seventeen years and fighting is a pleasure to me. I am not afraid of going goofy. I was going to quit, but when I see fellows like Risko and Sharkey claiming titles, how can I quit and not be ashamed to look a looking-glass in the face?'

Back in 1924, Mike had told a reporter: 'One of my very good friends is a former champion. He gathered a big following by stepping in and socking. He wasn't clever and didn't try to be. He stopped them with his chin and he won most of his fights by lasting out the other fellow. He did well. He is well fixed now. He has no family and no dependents. But he is 'dizzy'. He's still young and he has a lot of future because he's rugged and in good health, but he can't enjoy it.' Five years on and Mike was becoming like his very good friend. In the fall of 1928, every fight seemed to cost him just that little bit more.

Jimmy signed Mike for two fights: with promoter Mique Malloy in Chicago on 24 September against Tuffy Griffith and against Benny Ross in Buffalo on 4 October. The Griffith fight was postponed for three days because of the cold weather but Malloy announced the fight would take place on 27 September whatever the temperature. Mike resumed training on hearing the news and the extra work helped get him into better condition.

It was a bleak, cold fall in Chicago and there was a sense of foreboding in the air.

Despite the cold weather there was a crowd of 3,500 at Midway Gardens on the corner of 60th street and Cottage Grove Avenue when they rang the bell for round one. To a man they were there to see Griffith, the new 'kayo' sensation, stiffen anybody, and the fact that Mike McTigue was in there made it just that much more certain. Griffith, at twenty-one, was less than half Mike's age and he had scored a long list of knockout victories that made him a leading contender for a shot at Tommy Loughran's title.

Mike sat in the dressing room watching the steam swimming about the pipes directly overhead as the announcer bellowed out the names of the preliminary fighters, pointing to the respective corners as he briefly described trumped up reputations. Mike was never nervous before a fight anymore. What was there to be nervous about? He had caught every kind of punch already.

Shortly after the opening bell Griffith threw a vicious overhand right and then caught Mike with several unanswered shots to the stomach. The veteran lowered his arms to protect his midriff so Tuffy crossed a hard right to the jaw that staggered the old champion. When he realised he had hurt Mike, Griffith displayed a streak of viciousness in finishing the aging fighter. He tried to herd the veteran into a corner where he could club his brains out. A hard left swing to the jaw put Mike down for a count of five. He got up but was unable to defend himself and Griffith tore in and showered rights and lefts on Mike's head until referee Davis Miller stopped the fight just before the bell.

Reporters found Mike lying completely still on the rubbing table under the light bulb that dangled from the ceiling at the end of a long cord until, finally, some expression came back into his eyes. It took him nearly eight months to feel well enough to return to the ring – but return he did.

On 13 May 1929 Mike beat Paul Hoffman in front of a small but appreciative New York fight crowd. The fight was held at St Nicholas arena, a smoky little low-ceilinged club, and Mike was back in the ranks of the semi-final fighters. He played with the younger, heavier man. Hoffman's nose was streaming blood from the sixth round and he was floored in the seventh. Mike had the customers at the St Nick laughing throughout and got a standing ovation after taking an easy decision over ten rounds. 'Father time has taken his toll,' commented William Morris in the *New York Evening Post*, 'but the customers like to see the Irishman manoeuvre his man around for a straight right on the jaw.'

A fortnight later it was another fight and another Hoffman. George was no relation to Paul and was a much better fighter. He was the amateur heavyweight champion in 1928 and the former ironworker was looking to establish himself in the professional ranks by beating a former world champion. It was obvious from the start that Mike was in for a painful evening. Hoffman pounded his body in the first round and jarred his head back several times. Coming out of his corner for the second, Mike was caught with a glancing blow to the chin that swung him clean off his feet. He landed on his back near the ropes. He got up before the count started and tried to clinch but was driven off. Mike would have gone down under another right but he held on to Hoffman to avoid falling. The referee separated them and Mike was forced to step back. As he did so Hoffman drove home a single right hook to the jaw that sent the Irishman to the canvas. He made it onto one knee for the count of nine, tried to straighten out but fell unconscious. He had to be carried to his corner where Dr Alexander Schiff, the State Athletic Commission doctor examined him before he was allowed to leave the ring.

The morning after the fight Mike sent a letter to the newspapers in New York announcing his retirement from the ring 'for evermore'. He also settled the mystery of his age. In a postscript to his letter he said that on 26 November next he would be forty-five. In an interview with Frank Getty of the United Press, Mike looked at his broken and twisted knuckles and said:

> You weren't a bad old fist in your day, but your day is done. Praise be, I can still put you in my pocket and find something there.
>
> I made a small fortune in the past twenty-five years, and I saved some of it. After careful investments, I find my family and myself in comfortable circumstances for the rest of our lives. I owe it all to boxing.
>
> In September I am going back to the old country. I am going to scour Ulster, Munster, Leinster and Connaught, for surely there must be one Irish heavyweight in some secluded spot, whom I can find and bring over to this country, where fame and fortune can be found.

On 12 June 1929 Mike became a licensed boxing manager in New York State but he found the lure of the prize-ring irresistible and his 'for evermore' retirement lasted barely ten weeks. Mike set off on a whistle-stop tour fighting on an almost weekly basis for Depression-era purses. He knocked out Steve Thompson in three rounds in Manchester, New Hampshire, beat Jimmy DeCapua in Miami, Battling Bozo in Birmingham, Alabama and knocked out

Jeff Richards in three in Hopewell, Virginia. He followed that up with a five-round knockout victory over Bobby Lyons. He took a terrible beating at the hands of Jack Gagnon in Boston and his seconds had to save him in the first round.

But still Mike wasn't finished. He went to Grand Rapids, Michigan, to knockout Emmett Curtis in five before losing two ten-rounders in Florida to 'Big' Jeff Carroll at West Palm Beach and Bob Godwin at Daytona Beach. Godwin was a stone lighter than Mike who now weighed 179. But still he wouldn't give up. Mike stayed in Florida and knocked out Ralph Schneider in Fort Pierce. He sailed to Havana, Cuba to be knocked out in the first round by Isadore Gastanaga. Back to Florida and another defeat; Bob Godwin over ten rounds in Miami. That fight ended his winter in the sunny climes and he returned to New York to embark on another frenetic series of fights. Mike got the decision over George Neron, a 200-lb New York Greek, after ten rounds in Schenectady then drew with Tiger Armand and lost to Patsy Perroni.

Then on 22 September 1930 Mike was on the canvas once more, watching the resin dust rise towards the swaying lights overhead. He got up as he nearly always did, but the referee had seen enough. Mike had lost to Garfield Johnson in Utica, New York, having failed to land a single blow and the fight was stopped to save him taking any more needless punishment from the man from Buffalo. Mike was nearly fifty years old. The following day, Jimmy called him into his office in the Longacre Building.

'How much have you saved since I've been managing you?'

'About two hundred and fifty thousand dollars and I had a little money before we got together.'

'Own your own home?'

'Yes.'

'Got a nice wife and family, too.'

'You should know, you've been out there to dinner enough.'

'Then take my advice and quit the ring. You can't fight any longer.'

'I was thinking of the same thing myself, but I wanted to hear some real friend say it. From now on, I'm through with fighting.'

Leaving Johnston's office, Mike ran into Eddie Zeltner.

'When's your next fight?' asked Eddie.

'From now on, any decisions I win will be from my wife.'

NINETEEN

It was borrowed time anyhow – the whole upper tenth of a nation living with the insouciance of grand dukes and the casualness of chorus girls.

F. Scott Fitzgerald, *Tales Of The Jazz Age*

Mike was standing in the lobby of the Putnam building on Broadway and saw in the corner an old fighter who had been held up as one of the greatest fighters that ever lived. They said he was so fast he could stand on a dollar bill, drop his hands at his sides and still no one could hit him. While he was standing there in a corner some pals were going around trying to 'touch' his friends for a few bucks. They were trying to get him out of town and set him up where he would have a chance to get something to eat. Mike noticed when the boys were going around with the hat that the fellows who had been shouting a few minutes previously about what a great fighter the old guy was were the first to slip out of the door.

'Well, I said to myself, Mike, you ought to be glad you're a poor fighter. You wouldn't want to be the greatest boxer that ever lived and end up like that. You get out and be on the level, get the money where it is fair getting and, even if you get old and they still say you are a ham fighter, you will not have to see any cheer-leaders sneak out on you.'

Since the advent of the Walker Law in 1920 legalising boxing in New York State and similar legislation that followed in several other big states, many fighters had earned and generally squandered fortunes. Francis Albertanti wrote an article entitled 'What Price Cauliflowers!' in *The Ring* in March 1929, in which he considered the varying ways in which boxers and their bankrolls had been separated. Many of the champion fighters of the Roaring Twenties were broke or in asylums. 'They were not incarcerated from beatings in the ring but from worry over loss of money that could never be retrieved,' claimed Albertanti.

It is sad, mates, but nevertheless true. Many boys, a great majority still in their teens, earned thousands of dollars. Wine, women and song dissipated not only their bankrolls but health as well. Some are walking around with battered countenances and doing the best they can, which isn't much. Others have taken menial jobs and are happy to get a crust of bread, whereas perhaps a few weeks before, they were the toasts of the nightclubs.

Twenty-five years earlier boxers didn't save a quarter. The boys that Mike fought in the 'blood-bucket' clubs squandered everything they owned, usually at the racetracks and various other unbeatable gaming enterprises. Mike learned the lesson. He held on to his ring earnings and didn't squander them on the delights of Broadway. 'His parents are living the life of ease back on the auld sod,' commented one scribe, 'thanks to the thoughtfulness of this dutiful son who never neglects sending home part of his earnings.'

After hanging up his padded gloves Mike bought a café near Madison Square Garden on Eighth Avenue, a bar on Woodhaven

Boulevard in Queens County and invested in mortgage bonds and 'Wall Street stuff'.

'There is no telling how much Mike McTigue is worth,' wrote Albertanti. 'Some claim he can write a check for $350,000. Mike is a shrewd investor. He makes his money talk. McTigue wouldn't spend a nickel to see the Statue of Liberty do a dance, which may or may not be against him. He lives in a palatial home on Long Island and is a real daddy to his fine family ... There is nothing too good for the McTigues. Mike is a tough one to put the arm on. He'll not listen to the shop-worn tales of woe.'

'I had to fight hard to get mine,' Mike told Albertanti, 'and I'm not going to throw it away.' The palatial home referred to was at 33-46, 86th Street, Jackson Heights, Queens. Mike had bought the house in 1927 when he was at the height of his box-office popularity following the victory over Berlenbach. The construction of private homes in the area started in 1924 and in the next four years fifteen streets were built with what the Queensboro Corporation called 'English Garden Homes'. They were relatively expensive, $20,000 to $38,500, with large front and rear gardens.

The idea was to fill Jackson Heights with an affluent professional class and the prices were prohibitive for the vast majority of New Yorkers. The community was 'restricted'; it wasn't explicit in the advertising, but it was well known that only white Anglo-Saxon Protestants were welcome. Being an affluent world champion boxer was obviously a way around the religious qualification. The land appreciated, demand was high and the prices rose. Some more than doubled their money in just a few years.

Mike put a big slice of his money in second mortgages on apartment houses being erected on Riverside Drive. These investments paid high interest and the properties were considered safe and desirable. Between May 1928 and September 1929, the average price of stocks in the United States rose by forty per cent. Mike had invested well and became a wealthy man.

Then, on 24 October 1929, the stock market crash began, reaching its nadir five days later on 'Black Tuesday'. Losses for the month totalled $16 billion. Just about everyone was 'minced'. Jack Dempsey dropped three million dollars in the crash and the ensuing Great Depression. Mike also suffered. His mortgage investments became virtually worthless but he managed to ride out the worst of the financial crisis and even more remarkably escaped the ring with his faculties intact. He took a job in real estate in New York. The city was still reaching for the sky at the lowest point of the Great Depression and Mike's office at 45 West 34th Street was in the shadow of the construction site that was the Empire State Building. But these were desperately hard times and the building was jumped off so many times in the early years that he quickened his step when walking past Fifth Avenue and 34th Street.

Life was still good. Mike was introduced from the stage of the Strand at the opening of *Bring 'Em Back Alive*, Frank Buck's animal adventure film, with fellow champion fighters including Benny Leonard, Johnny Dundee and Jack Britton. A few nights later Mike joined Paul Berlenbach, Jack Johnson, Georges Carpentier, Tommy Loughran, Jack Dempsey and Gene Tunney at the Max Schmelling-Jack Sharkey title-fight.

Thanks to Jimmy, Mike kept company with some of the most powerful men in town, including one of the most adroit and charming campaigners in American political history, James Joseph Walker. Mayor Walker exuded great charm and always had a wisecrack at the ready. A reformer, he once said, is 'a guy who rides through a sewer in a glass-bottomed boat.' He had penned a hit song, 'Will You Love Me in December as You Do in May?', loved the company of sportsmen, especially prizefighters, and the city's glamorous nightlife.

Dressed in tailored double-breasted jackets and derbies, he earned the nicknames of 'Beau James' and 'Gentleman Jim'. With his showgirl mistress, Betty Compton, at his side, it was said that he spent more time quaffing champagne at the Central Park Casino than he spent in City Hall. Jimmy Johnston and, very often, Mike McTigue enjoyed Gentleman Jim's company and hospitality. Mike even retained the services of Mayor Walker's personal business agent, Russell T. Sherwood, to look after some of his money. Big mistake.

Walker learned early that publicity was the essential component in the creation of a political hero. So he treated newspaper reporters like family. Walker was kind to them, lent them money and always gave them something to write about. But the good publicity cloaked a bloated and corrupt administration. Walker had raised his salary to $40,000, almost three times the salary of members of the cabinet of the President of the United States, and appointed his friends as district leaders; the real political rulers of New York.

When New York, along with the rest of the United States, was booming, Walker's excesses and wrongdoings were forgotten in the national exuberance. But when the bad times came along, a series of investigations slowly unveiled the sleaze and Walker was called to account. On 1 September 1932 Walker resigned and not long afterward he sailed to join his mistress in Europe.

It was the unexplained millions in the accounts of his personal business agent, Russell T. Sherwood, that did more than anything else to put Walker out of office. Sherwood had been a $3,000-a-year assistant in Walker's former law office. When Walker became mayor, Sherwood's bank balance jumped to $98,000 in the first year. Deposits totalled $961,000 during the first five years and eight months of the administration's rule. Almost $750,000 was banked in cash. Sherwood paid many of the Mayor's and Mrs Walker's bills out of his bank account and then, when asked to explain where it had all come from, fled to Mexico.

In the hearings that followed it emerged that Sherwood's celebrity clients included the dancing 'Dolly Sisters', the actress Beatrice Lillie and prizefighters Johnny Dundee and Mike McTigue. They had availed of Sherwood's expert advice on 'sound investments', but the financial advisor was on the run and his assets had been seized. Quite how much of Mike's money was lost with the collapse of the Walker regime will probably never be known. But Sherwood's disappearance started a sequence of events that unravelled the Irishman's dream life with his dream family in his dream home in Jackson Heights.

On 1 May 1933 a man telephoned Mike to demand $5,000 or he'd kidnap one of the children. The McTigue telephone number was unlisted, a fact that caused Cecilia to believe at first that one of her husband's pals was playing a practical joke. But when Mike was told of the threats he left his office in the city and hurried home. He was in Jackson Heights when the second call was received. Grabbing the telephone from his wife, he listened while a voice in a thick Italian accent instructed him to leave $5,000 in a tin can in a nearby lot that night.

'Say,' yelled Mike, 'you come here and meet me face to face and I'll knock you cold.'

The caller laughed and hung up. Mike called the police at Elmhurst Station and detectives were posted to maintain a twenty-four hour guard over his home. The girls, Rosaleen, thirteen, Cecilia eleven and Margaret, ten, were escorted to and from the Joan of Arc Parochial School. 'I'm not afraid for myself,' Mike told reporters, 'I can lick any man in the world with my bare fists, but I can't let anything happen to my children.' He threatened to 'punch the devil' out of the terrorist if he ever found him. The police placed a dummy package in the specified lot, but no-one claimed it.

About a year previously the infant son of Paul Berlenbach had been threatened by kidnappers who demanded a large sum of money. The threat was never carried out. However, Mike was still reputed to have saved more of his ring earnings than most fighters and the police believed this may have 'aroused the envy of hangers on in the sports world'. Five subsequent calls were made following the original message, and though all were traced to stores in the neighbourhood, police were unable to trap the perpetrator.

Mike and his wife were reluctant to answer the door and there was 'an ominous quiet' in the neighbourhood. 'I'd call it an annoying call,' said Inspector John J. Gallacher, in charge of Queens detectives. 'Somebody, in my opinion, is trying to worry these people. Of course, we'll keep a strict watch, however, until the matter is settled.' But no further word was heard from the caller.

Mike was still keeping dangerous company however. On 29 September 1933 he and Jimmy Johnston attended a dinner at the Madison Square Garden Club in honour of Primo Carnera, the new world heavyweight champion. Carnera had what was known as 'colour'; he was a freakishly big man and many people paid to see him fight, much like they would pay to see a freak-show in a circus. He was cleverly publicised and the newspapers were only too happy to play along. Carnera packed them in from New York to Hollywood. But Carnera's boxing career was a fraud; a succession of fixed fights, farcical knockouts and artless dives. The masterminds behind Carnera were members of a syndicate made up of hard-core criminals. Two had served over twenty years in prison.

Mike's run of bad luck had eroded away much of what it had

taken him nearly two decades to earn in the ring. The stock market crash and Russell T. Sherwood's disappearance had taken most of it away and he 'sold' the Jackson Heights property to his wife Cecilia for one dollar, to keep the home as far away from creditors as possible.

When he had finally quit the ring one scribe wrote, 'the boxing game owes McTigue nothing. He has plenty of money salted away in gilt-edged stocks and bonds and is reputed to be worth approximately $250,000. If Mike were to quit tomorrow there would never be any need of holding benefits for him.' He was wrong. The Jackson Heights lifestyle was over, the house was eventually sold to Umberto Buldrini, first bass violinist of the Metropolitan Opera Orchestra and the McTigues moved to an apartment in the Bronx. But the family's woes were only just beginning.

At 3 am on the morning of 5 January 1935 a middle-aged man, accompanied by a young girl, walked into the Golf Grill, 855 Amsterdam Avenue, near 100th Street, drew a revolver from his pocket and ordered ten customers to raise their hands and line up against a wall. The girl ran behind the bar, took $45 out of the cash register then searched the customers, taking jewellery, watches and a total of $10 in cash. As she and her accomplice neared the door on their way out one of the customers threw a beer glass at them. It crashed against the door close to the gunman's head. Enraged, he turned and fired, killing Michael Cuniff of 598 West 177th Street. Cuniff was Cecilia McTigue's brother. He was hit in the eye and the bullet came out of the top of his skull. The robbers escaped in a car.

In November 1935 Mike testified that he had lent $3,000 to Bernard Livingston, a Washington jeweller and had taken a valuable unset diamond as security. Mike claimed to have met Livingston in New York on 22 April 1935 and was persuaded to allow the jeweller to have the stone so that it could be sold at 'an attractive figure' thus repaying the loan. The complaint alleged that neither the stone nor the repayment of the loan was forthcoming. Charged with grand larceny of a $2,800 ring from Mike McTigue on a bench warrant from New York, he was placed on a $1,500-bond and an extradition hearing set for November 16 by Police Court Judge Walter J. Casey. However the District Court of Columbia heard witnesses testify that Livingston was in Washington on 22 April and not in New York as Mike had alleged. The hearing was adjourned for a week to permit government witnesses from New York to contradict Livingston's alibi. No witnesses could be found.

Mike got back to the only business he really knew, boxing. He managed a young heavyweight, Bob Pastor, who according to the *Washington Times* was 'a cinch to be a top fighter in a year'. Mike was a great boxer but a poor manager and Pastor never made it. From a fight manager Mike became a floor manager, at the Tuxedo Ballroom on 59th Street and Madison Avenue. It was a magnet for Irish immigrants and Irish-Americans in New York City.

After one particular shift at the Tuxedo, Mike took the worst lacing of his long career. He was returning home to 338 East 142nd Street at 4.30 am on a northbound Third Avenue elevated train. The car was crowded and Mike was standing. Next to him stood a group of six or seven young Irishmen who began hurling insults at him. He ignored them and as the train approached the 129th Street station he started for the door. One of the young men stopped him. 'You called me a Nazi,' he said. 'I'll be after knowing why you called me a Nazi.'

'I called no one a Nazi,' Mike replied and continued his walk to the door. Suddenly he felt a blow on the back of his neck. Some of the men stamped on him and kicked him in the face. Passengers shouted for the conductor who jerked the whistle rope as the train approached the station. The shrill blasts caught the ear of Patrolman

John Kenny who ran to the platform. Jack Weinhiger, an insurance agent, witnessed the assault and identified two men as the chief assailants. James Carr, twenty-seven, of 340 East 142nd the Bronx and Frank McElhatton, thirty-four, of 429 East 147th the Bronx were arraigned before Magistrate Michael Ford on the charge of felonious assault.

Mike was confined to his home for several days, painfully injured and under the care of his family physician. He had suffered severe lacerations to the head and mouth although fears that he had a fractured skull were dismissed. Cecilia said he 'never looked like that' after any of his fights.

At first Mike believed the attack had some connection with the larceny proceedings he had taken against the Washington jeweller but changed his mind after talking with the wife of James Carr, one of the men arrested in connection with the attack. It emerged that Carr lived across the street and his wife convinced Mike that he was normally 'meek as a lamb', but would fight when he had a few drinks. He agreed to accompany Mrs Carr to the jail the following day. Because all involved were Irishmen 'and I wasn't hurt much' Mike withdrew the charges. Carr and McElhatton were released on suspended sentences on a disorderly conduct charge. 'I lost a couple of teeth, and got a couple of black eyes, but I don't want to press any charge against them,' Mike told the magistrate. He and the two men left the court seemingly friends.

Mike became a labourer and got a job shovelling snow off the Pennsylvania railway. But by now he was drinking heavily and on Sunday 28 February 1937 he walked into a police station in the Bronx, shaking and sick, and told the officers: 'I've got the DTs. Do something for me.'

They sent him to Fordham Hospital from where he was transferred to the psychopathic ward at Bellevue, 'suffering from alcoholism'. His condition was said not to be serious. Three weeks later he appeared before State Supreme Court Justice Charles B. McLaughlin for committal to an institution for the mentally ill. Mike balked at the idea but was finally persuaded by Justice McLaughlin. Doctors said he had hallucinations. The court heard how Mike's $500,000 fortune had gone 'in the way of bad investments'.

Mike, who gave his occupation as that of foreman, admitted to drinking heavily for some time. 'You certainly don't look like the man I saw fight Berlenbach in '25,' said the judge. 'Probably it would be best for you to go away for six months for rest and cure.' Mike was sent to Rockland County Hospital.

Jimmy Johnston told reporters: 'Say, that Michael isn't crazy. He's just been telling lies again. He always was a great liar. But he's a harmless liar.

'The doctors think he's crazy because he got cute when they asked him questions,' said Jimmy. 'One of them says, "Do you ever hear voices when you're alone in your room?"

"Sure," says Mike.

"What kind?" says the doctors.

"Why, the voices over my telephone. I'm all alone then, ain't I?" yells Mike, thinking he's being very smart. It's best for him, I guess, but he's not crazy. He's just cute.'

On 26 March 1937, under the headline – Fame, Fortune Gone, McTigue Takes "Rest"' – the *Washington Post* reported:

> They sent 'Bowld Michael' McTigue, once the greatest 175-pound man in the world with his fists, off to Rockland County Hospital today to rest his battered head and test his sanity.

It was mostly Michael's own doing.

Forty-five years old now, flabby, the $500,000 fortune he won in the ring gone by the way of bad investments, and lonely with fame and attention gone, Michael, by his own admission, has been drinking heavily for a long time.

He had gotten down to jobs that paid a dollar or two a day. When in his cups the boxing urge rode high in him again, and he has taken several bad beatings lately. The most recent of these was in a subway, when five thugs beset him and creased his head with fists and blackjacks.

Conditions in state mental institutions had deteriorated as a result of Depression-era financial hardships and Rockland County Hospital was not a good place to be. It housed 4,700 troubled souls and used electroconvulsive therapy. But just like he had done so many times in the ring, Mike fought back. He was allowed to return home and was invited to appear in a play, *Taken From Life*, written by Arthur Chalmers, about a police officer awaiting trial for murder. Mike appeared in a scene as one of a number of old fighters in Madison Square Garden.

Then, just as in the ring, misfortune struck again. On 5 July 1938 Mike was a passenger in a car that collided with an Intercity bus on West 36th Street, between Ninth and Tenth Avenues. Twenty passengers in the bus were badly shaken and Mike was taken to French Hospital with an injured spine and cuts to his knee and elbow.

Once again, Mike recovered and became a physical instructor at a naval base on Staten Island during the early part of the Second World War. Then on 23 February 1941 he was 'painfully injured' after being struck by a closing subway door that knocked him down as he was leaving a Seventh Avenue IRT train at Times Square station. He was taken to Roosevelt Hospital with injuries to his head and back. Patrolman Thomas Hackett of the West 30th Street station, a fan who had attended many of Mike's fights, treated him at the scene.

Mike became more accident-prone as his drinking increased. It also cost him his family. The police were called to a scuffle at Mike's home after which the old fighter became estranged from Cecilia and his daughters. After the separation he went through a very bad time during which he drank heavily, and one day he was found wedged into his bathroom, unconscious; he had been hit by a car and dragged himself into his tiny rental and passed out.

Mike's brother-in-law arranged for him to be put into Welfare Island public hospital to recover. 'After some time Mike was released into the care of a brother,' recalled Mike's nephew, Joe Breen. 'Actually it was some real bastard who pretended to be Mike's brother and perhaps Mike went along with it because he hadn't had a drink in a long while and he had a pile of pension cheques. These were cashed and Mike was found in the basement of a Willis Avenue tenement, barely alive. My father and Gene Casey, a New York City detective married to my sister, arranged for Mike to be hospitalised again and he was adjudicated incompetent to handle his own affairs and a Mr Lee, a Democratic party man was appointed to be his Committee [the person to whom the charge of a committed person is given].'

Since there was no one to take care of him and since his back and leg required medical attention Mike was sent to Creedmoor State Hospital. Joe Breen was serving with the United States Marines in Korea at the time but when he got out he visited Mike and was appalled by his neglected state so he took over as Mike's Committee. 'I really loved the guy,' said Joe. 'When I was a kid he'd come out to Queens and he'd teach me how to box. I took care of his affairs when nobody was going out to visit him. He got a disability pension, which I collected. It almost paid enough and I paid the rest and helped him out when he needed teeth and glasses and stuff like that. He was so brave.

'My boys and myself visited him often and we'd get dressed up in fine tweeds and go out to fine restaurants. A fellow who was a runner on the Olympic team, John Devaney, was the floorwalker in John Wannamaker's store and I would go there and get Mike some good clothes. The first time I did it and left the clothes there [in Creedmore], by the time I came back they were destroyed. So when I would take him out I would bring clothes and then when I would take him back in I would take the sports coat or the nice sweater off him. He'd shrug his shoulders and with his hand that was closed in almost like a claw he'd shake my hand and he'd say best to your mother and father and he'd take a great sort of sigh and he'd turn his back and he'd walk right in to this ugly building, but he'd square his shoulders and you could see how his feet would sort of flop as he would take a step. I guess we used to call it walking on eggs.'

Joe remembers his uncle as being in 'a state similar to [Muhammad] Ali except Mike had no speech impediment and needed to wear a brace for his lower back and knee. He was confined to the institution for over a decade until on a summer's day in 1966, the eighty-two-year-old prizefighter took one final blow. 'The story I got was that somebody hit him with a chair,' said Joe. 'I was away up in Cape Cod with my family on vacation when I got word of that. I couldn't really find out a lot about what had happened but that he had a bad hit on his head and he was in hospital and they were saying he'll be dead in a day or so because he'll get pneumonia and die. But he just lasted for weeks and weeks because I guess he had strong lungs. He just wouldn't catch pneumonia and die.

'It wasn't a good end. It wasn't a good end for a long time.'

Mike died in Queens General Hospital on 12 August 1966. He was survived by his widow Cecilia, two daughters, three brothers, Thomas, Patrick and James and two sisters, Ellen Smith and Catherine Breen. A requiem Mass was held at the Roman Catholic Church of the Good Shepherd on Broadway and 211th Street. Among those who attended were Gene Tunney, Tommy Loughran, Jack Dempsey and Mike's old adversary, Paul Berlenbach; fighters from boxing's golden age reunited to say good-bye to one of their own.

BIBLIOGRAPHY

Blake, Frances M, *The Irish Civil War, 1922-1923 and what it still means for the Irish people* (Information on Ireland, 1986)

Coogan, Tim Pat, *De Valera, Long Fellow, Long Shadow* (Hutchinson, 1993)

Corri, Eugene, *Gloves and the Man* (Hutchinson, 1927)

Corri, Eugene, *Fifty Years in the Ring* (Hutchinson, 1933)

Dartnell, Fred, *Second's Out* (T. Werner Caurie, 1924)

DeLisa, Michael C, *Cinderella Man* (Milo Books, 2005)

Dempsey, Jack, *Dempsey* (Harper Collins, 1977)

Dempsey, Jack, *Round by Round* (McGraw Hill, 1940)

Fleischer, Nat, *Gene Tunney, the Enigma of the Ring* (F. Hubner & Co Inc, 1931)

Fleischer, Nat, *Jack Dempsey* (Arlington House, 1972)

Goldstein, Ruby, *Third Man in the Ring* (Funk & Wagnalls, 1959)

Green, Benny, *Shaw's Champions, G. B. S. & prizefighting from Cashel Byron to Gene Tunney* (Elm Tree Books, 1978)

Griffin, Marcus, *Wise Guy, James J Johnston, a rhapsody in fistics* (The Vanguard Press, 1933)

Gwynn, Denis, *De Valera* (Jarrolds, 1933)

Hemingway, Ernest, *Men Without Women* (C. Scribner's sons, 1927)

Johnston, Alexander, *Ten-And Out! The story of the prize ring in America* (L. Washburn, 1943)

Kahn, Roger, *A Flame of Pure Fire* (Harcourt Brace International, 1999)

Kisane, Bill, *The Politics of the Irish Civil War* (Oxford University Press, 2005)

Lardner, John, *White Hopes and Other Tigers* (Lippincott, 1951)

Mitgang, Herbert, *Once Upon a Time in New York, Jimmy Walker, Franklin Roosevelt, and the last great battle of the Jazz Age* (Free Press, 2000)

Morrison, George, *The Irish Civil War* (Gill and Macmillan, 1981)

O'Brien, Mark, *Fianna Fáil and the Irish Press* (Irish Academic Press, 2001)

O' Connor, Richard, *Hell's Kitchen; the roaring days of New York's wild West Side* (Lippincott, 1993)

Purdon, Edward, *The Irish Civil War, 1922-1923* (Mercier Press, 2000)

Rice, Harold, *Within The Ropes; champions in action* (Stephen-Paul, 1946)

Ritter, Lawrence S, *East Side, West Side, tales of New York sporting life, 1910-1960* (Total Sports, 1998)

Spivey, Donald, *Sport In America, new historical perspectives* (Greenwood Press, 1985)

Vergani, Orio, *Lo, Povero Negro* (Poor nigger, translated from the Italian by W.W. Hobson) (Hutchinson 1930)

Walsh, George, *Gentleman Jimmy Walker, mayor of the jazz age* (Praeger, 1974)

Wignall, Trevor, *The Sweet Science* (Chapman and Hall, 1926)

Wignall, Trevor, *The Story Of Boxing* (Hutchinson & Co, 1923)

All Sports Weekly, Atlanta Constitution, Atlanta Georgian, Atlanta Journal, Boxing, Boxing and Sporting Gazette, The Boxing Blade, Boxing News, Boxing Record, Boxing World, Chatham Press, Chicago American, Chicago Daily News, Chicago Daily Tribune, Chicago Bulletin, Chicago Evening American, Chicago Evening Post, Chicago Examiner, Chicago Herald, Chicago Journal, Chicago Sunday Record-Herald, Chicago Tribune, Clare Champion, Cork Free Press, Daily Chronicle, Daily Mail, Daily Express, Daily Mirror, Daily News and Leader, Daily Sketch, Daily Star, Daily Telegraph, Dublin Evening Mail, Eiré-The Irish Nation, Evening Express, Evening Herald, Halifax Herald, Irish Times, Irish Independent, Irish World and American Industrial Liberator, Liverpool Express, London Evening News, London Morning Advertiser, London Morning Leader, London Star, London Sun, Los Angeles Evening Journal, Los Angeles Examiner, Los Angeles Herald,

Los Angeles News, Los Angeles Telegraph, Los Angeles Times, Los Angeles Tribune, Louisville Times, Mirror Of Life, Montreal Daily Herald, Montreal Daily Star, Montreal Daily Telegraph, Montreal Evening News, Montreal Gazette, Montreal Standard, Moose Jaw Evening News, Moose Jaw Times, Morning Post, National Police Gazette, New York American, New York Daily News, New York Evening Herald, New York Evening Mail, New York Evening News, New York Evening Post, New York Evening Telegram, New York Evening Telegraph, New York Evening World, New York Globe, New York Herald Tribune, New York Journal, New York Morning Sun, New York Post, New York Times, Newark Evening News, News Of The World, Philadelphia American, Philadelphia Bulletin, Philadelphia Evening Star, Philadelphia Evening Times, Philadelphia Inquirer, Philadelphia Ledger, Philadelphia North American, Philadelphia Press, Philadelphia Public Ledger, Philadelphia Record, Philadelphia Telegraph, The Ring, Sheffield Daily Telegraph, Sports Illustrated, Sporting Budget, Sporting Chronicle, Sporting Life, Sporting World, Sportsman, The Strand Magazine, Summit Herald, Summit Record, Sunday Independent, Sunday Sun, Sunday World, Time, The Times, Times Democrat, Toronto Daily Star, Toronto Evening Telegram, Toronto United Empire, Toronto World, Washington Post, Weekly Dispatch.

INDEX

Flowers, Tiger 238, 243, 244, 246
Foley, Tom 66, 67

G

Gaffney, Gertrude 87, 96, 118, 120, 122,
123, 124, 129, 132, 136
Gallico, Paul 9, 57, 198, 211, 216, 235,
239, 240, 246, 253, 258, 261,
265, 266, 273, 275, 280, 284,
299, 302, 305, 317
Gibbons, Tom 48, 160, 183, 186, 198,
202, 233
Godfrey, George 268, 322
Greb, Harry 39, 62, 65, 160, 161, 162,
183, 186, 193, 236
Grupp, Billy 168, 278, 293
Gyp the Blood 231, 232

H

Haley, Patsy 255, 257
Harris, Jim 45, 84, 123, 145
Heeney, Tom 295, 303
Hemingway, Ernest 80
Hickey, Dan 15, 77, 215, 246, 249, 273,
279, 281, 283
Hogan, Patrick 92, 101
Huffman, Eddie 244
Humphries, Joe 193, 223, 225, 240, 295,
309, 312

I

Ireland, Tom 54, 120

J

Jacobs, Joe 21, 77, 148, 155, 158, 160,
161, 162, 164, 170, 171, 172,
181, 184, 186, 200, 218
James Farley 213, 249, 311
Johnson, Jack 9, 32, 34, 43, 286, 335
Johnston, Charlie 304, 322, 323
Johnston, Jimmy 77, 228, 230, 231, 232,
237, 238, 248, 249, 253, 267,
272, 274, 277, 280, 284, 285,
292, 305, 306, 315, 317, 336,
338, 342
Jones, Major J. Paul 168, 174, 175, 176,
178, 179, 180, 181

K

Kelly, John 59, 77
Kramar, Billy 62, 76

L

Lardner, Ring 57, 253
Lawrence, Jack 218, 223
Leftie Louie 231, 232
Leonard, Benny 168, 203, 335
Levinsky, Battling 73, 146
Lewis, Ted 'Kid' 65, 81, 145
Lewis, Whitey 231, 232
Lomski, Leo 319, 321
Loughran, Tommy 79, 162, 167, 244,
295, 305, 307, 308, 311, 315,
319, 323, 327, 335, 346
Lynch, Liam 23, 157

M

Mack, Billy 55, 86
Madden, Bartley 55, 86, 125, 154
Marullo, Tony 235, 321
Marullo, Young 205, 234
Mathison, Charles F. 225, 312
McAnerney, James 135, 142
McCartan, Patrick 163, 165
McCarthy, Pat 301, 302
McCormack, William J. 186, 188
McCoy, Al 166, 232, 245
McDonald, Roddy 65, 77
McGeehan, Bill 57, 177, 190, 218, 221,
224, 253, 282, 287, 290, 298,
299, 324, 325
McMahon, Jess 58, 60, 169, 288
McPartland, Kid 281, 297
McTigue, Cecilia 15, 22, 339
Minh, Ho Chi 17, 19, 31
Moran, Frank 20, 123, 136
Morris, William 321, 328
Muldoon, William 213, 242, 249
Mullins, Paddy 77, 190, 193, 198, 199,
201, 203, 210, 217, 218
Murphy, Dan 93, 119

N

Newman, Harry 182, 203, 214, 217, 219,
222, 232, 239, 248, 250, 258,
273, 278, 285, 294